Precariousness, Community and Participation

This book attempts to explore the effects of neoliberalism on particular forms of community. Guy Standing (2011) has popularised the notion of precariousness to describe the unpredictable neoliberal conditions faced by radically different people throughout the world. Members of Standing's 'precariat' lack occupational identities, treat work and other money-making activities instrumentally, are focused on the short-term and have no 'shadow of the future' hanging over their actions, leaving little incentive to sustain long-term relationships and productive, but unpaid, social activities. This issue presents an interdisciplinary account of the challenges faced by communities at a time in which neoliberalism seems unchecked and uncheckable by the rise of nationalist populism. At points, responses are presented, but it is perhaps reflective of the general sense of helplessness of those committed to tackling neoliberalism that the final article highlights serious deficits in an approach commonly presented as a practicable response: basic income. In the spirit of participation, each article is accompanied by a reply by a non-academic as well as an academic. This ought not to be seen as tokenism – the experience of the project has been that discussions can be advanced much more effectively through engagement with community members and professionals.

The chapters in this book were originally published as a special issue of *Global Discourse*.

Matthew Johnson is Lecturer in Politics at Lancaster University, UK. His research examines issues such as Englishness and the relationship between culture, policy and wellbeing. He led a participatory project entitled 'A Cross-Cultural Working Group on "Good Culture" and Precariousness', which involved exchanges between people from Ashington and Aboriginal Australian communities.

Precariousness, Community and Participation

Edited by
Matthew Johnson

LONDON AND NEW YORK

First published 2018
by Routledge
2 Park Square, Milton Park, Abingdon, Oxon, OX14 4RN, UK

and by Routledge
711 Third Avenue, New York, NY 10017, USA

Routledge is an imprint of the Taylor & Francis Group, an informa business

© 2018 Taylor & Francis

All rights reserved. No part of this book may be reprinted or reproduced or utilised in any form or by any electronic, mechanical, or other means, now known or hereafter invented, including photocopying and recording, or in any information storage or retrieval system, without permission in writing from the publishers.

Trademark notice: Product or corporate names may be trademarks or registered trademarks, and are used only for identification and explanation without intent to infringe.

British Library Cataloguing in Publication Data
A catalogue record for this book is available from the British Library

ISBN 13: 978-1-138-49931-7

Typeset in Myriad Pro
by RefineCatch Limited, Bungay, Suffolk

Publisher's Note
The publisher accepts responsibility for any inconsistencies that may have arisen during the conversion of this book from journal articles to book chapters, namely the possible inclusion of journal terminology.

Disclaimer
Every effort has been made to contact copyright holders for their permission to reprint material in this book. The publishers would be grateful to hear from any copyright holder who is not here acknowledged and will undertake to rectify any errors or omissions in future editions of this book.

Contents

Citation Information vii
Notes on Contributors ix

Introduction: precariousness, community and participation 1
Matthew Johnson

1. The role of coal-mining towns in social theory: past, present and future 5
   Gibson Burrell

2. The isolated mass and contemporary social theory 23
   Paul Edwards

3. Changing precarities in the Irish housing system: supplier-generated changes in security of tenure for domiciled households 27
   Joe Finnerty and Cathal O'Connell

4. Understanding housing precarity: more than access to a shelter, housing is essential for a decent life 43
   Kelly Greenop

5. Precarious living in liminal spaces: neglect of the Gypsy–Traveller site 50
   Joanna Richardson

6. Gypsy-Traveller sites in the UK: power, history, informality – a response to Richardson 70
   Ryan Powell

7. Traveller precarity, public apathy, public service inaction, a reply to Jo Richardson's article from a community work perspective 75
   Denis Barrett and Siobhan O'Dowd

8. Universities as key responders to education inequality 81
   Siobhán O'Sullivan, Séamus O'Tuama and Lorna Kenny

9. An ongoing challenge and a chance to diversify university outreach to tackle inequality: a response to O'Sullivan, O'Tuama and Kenny 93
   Ann-Marie Houghton

10. A reply to O'Sullivan, O'Tuama and Kenny 97
    Tom Fellows

CONTENTS

11. Affective collaboration in the Westfjords of Iceland 102
    Valdimar J. Halldórsson

12. Protean possibilities: attending to affect in collaborative research – a reply to Valdimar Halldórsson 119
    Elizabeth Campbell

13. Cooperation in adversity: an evolutionary approach 125
    John Lazarus

14. Cooperation in adversity: a political theorist's response 153
    John Baker

    Index 157

Citation Information

The chapters in this book were originally published in *Global Discourse*, volume 7, issue 4 (December 2017). When citing this material, please use the original page numbering for each article, as follows:

Introduction
Introduction: precariousness, community and participation
Matthew Johnson
Global Discourse, volume 7, issue 4 (December 2017), pp. 447–450

Chapter 1
The role of coal-mining towns in social theory: past, present and future
Gibson Burrell
Global Discourse, volume 7, issue 4 (December 2017), pp. 451–468

Chapter 2
The isolated mass and contemporary social theory
Paul Edwards
Global Discourse, volume 7, issue 4 (December 2017), pp. 469–472

Chapter 3
Changing precarities in the Irish housing system: supplier-generated changes in security of tenure for domiciled households
Joe Finnerty and Cathal O'Connell
Global Discourse, volume 7, issue 4 (December 2017), pp. 473–488

Chapter 4
Understanding housing precarity: more than access to a shelter, housing is essential for a decent life
Kelly Greenop
Global Discourse, volume 7, issue 4 (December 2017), pp. 489–495

Chapter 5
Precarious living in liminal spaces: neglect of the Gypsy–Traveller site
Joanna Richardson
Global Discourse, volume 7, issue 4 (December 2017), pp. 496–515

CITATION INFORMATION

Chapter 6
Gypsy-Traveller sites in the UK: power, history, informality – a response to Richardson
Ryan Powell
Global Discourse, volume 7, issue 4 (December 2017), pp. 516–520

Chapter 7
Traveller precarity, public apathy, public service inaction, a reply to Jo Richardson's article from a community work perspective
Denis Barrett and Siobhan O'Dowd
Global Discourse, volume 7, issue 4 (December 2017), pp. 521–526

Chapter 8
Universities as key responders to education inequality
Siobhán O'Sullivan, Séamus O'Tuama and Lorna Kenny
Global Discourse, volume 7, issue 4 (December 2017), pp. 527–538

Chapter 9
An ongoing challenge and a chance to diversify university outreach to tackle inequality: a response to O'Sullivan, O'Tuama and Kenny
Ann-Marie Houghton
Global Discourse, volume 7, issue 4 (December 2017), pp. 539–542

Chapter 10
A reply to O'Sullivan, O'Tuama and Kenny
Tom Fellows
Global Discourse, volume 7, issue 4 (December 2017), pp. 543–547

Chapter 11
Affective collaboration in the Westfjords of Iceland
Valdimar J. Halldórsson
Global Discourse, volume 7, issue 4 (December 2017), pp. 548–564

Chapter 12
Protean possibilities: attending to affect in collaborative research – a reply to Valdimar Halldórsson
Elizabeth Campbell
Global Discourse, volume 7, issue 4 (December 2017), pp. 565–570

Chapter 13
Cooperation in adversity: an evolutionary approach
John Lazarus
Global Discourse, volume 7, issue 4 (December 2017), pp. 571–598

Chapter 14
Cooperation in adversity: a political theorist's response
John Baker
Global Discourse, volume 7, issue 4 (December 2017), pp. 599–601

For any permission-related enquiries please visit:
http://www.tandfonline.com/page/help/permissions

Notes on Contributors

John Baker is Emeritus Professor at the School of Social Policy, Social Work and Social Justice, University College Dublin, Ireland.

Denis Barrett is Cork City Learning Co-ordinator at Cork Education and Training Board, Ireland.

Gibson Burrell is Professor of Organisation Theory at the universities of Leicester and Manchester, UK.

Elizabeth Campbell is Doctor of Education in Curriculum and Instruction, Marshall University, USA.

Paul Edwards is Professor of Employment Relations in the Department of Management, University of Birmingham, UK.

Tom Fellows is an Independent Researcher based in the UK.

Joe Finnerty is based at the School of Applied Social Studies, University College Cork, Ireland.

Kelly Greenop is Lecturer at the School of Architecture, The University of Queensland, Brisbane, Australia.

Valdimar J. Halldórsson is based at the Museum of Jón Sigurðsson, Hrafnseyri, Iceland.

Ann-Marie Houghton is Director of REAP and a Teaching Fellow at the Department of Educational Research, Lancaster University, UK.

Matthew Johnson is Lecturer in Politics at Lancaster University, UK.

Lorna Kenny is based at the Centre for Adult Continuing Education, University College Cork, Ireland.

John Lazarus is based at the Centre for Behaviour and Evolution, Institute of Neuroscience, Henry Wellcome Building, Newcastle University, UK.

Cathal O'Connell is based at the School of Applied Social Studies, University College Cork, Ireland.

Siobhan O'Dowd is based at the Cork Equal and Sustainable Communities Alliance (CESCA) and is a volunteer member of the Board of the Traveller Visibility Group, Cork City, Ireland.

Siobhán O'Sullivan is Lecturer at the School of Applied Social Studies, University College Cork, Ireland.

NOTES ON CONTRIBUTORS

Séamus O'Tuama is Director of the Centre for Adult Continuing Education, University College Cork, Ireland.

Ryan Powell is Director of Research at the Department of Urban Studies and Planning, University of Sheffield, UK.

Joanna Richardson is Associate Dean of Research and Innovation and Professor of Housing and Social Research at the Centre for Comparative Housing Research, De Montfort University, UK.

INTRODUCTION

Introduction: precariousness, community and participation

Matthew Johnson

This issue of *Global Discourse* represents the culmination of a series of collaborations exploring 'precariousness' stemming back to 2013 – the year in which we last published an issue on the topic (see Johnson 2013). Here, we attempt to explore the effects of neoliberalism on particular forms of community through the work of participants in 'A Cross-Cultural Working Group on "Good Culture" and Precariousness', a participatory project involving academics, community co-researchers and community professionals from a range of backgrounds. The notion of precariousness has been popularised by Standing (2011) to describe the unpredictable neoliberal conditions faced by radically different people throughout the world. Members of Standing's 'precariat' lack occupational identities, treat work and other money-making activities instrumentally, are focused on the short-term and have no 'shadow of the future' hanging over their actions, leaving little incentive to sustain long-term relationships and productive, but unpaid, social activities.

The broader project from which this special issue is drawn sought to examine these conditions through participatory engagement with community co-researchers from Ashington, Northumberland and Aboriginal communities around Brisbane, Australia. While the groups are radically different, there are similarities in traditional cultural commitments and the effects of neoliberalism that give the groups grounds for collaboration in examining political responses to their exclusion. The two groups worked, during visits to each other's communities, with academics and others to explore means of advancing policy grounded in traditional cultural commitments that served them well at various points in their histories. That work led into a British Academy Rising Star Engagement Award-funded series of three conferences on participatory research. These conferences (videos of which are available on the project website: http://wp.lancs.ac.uk/good-culture/) advanced a range of related discussions regarding the challenges that an increasing number of people from an increasing number of backgrounds face. The demographics of the participants in those conferences expanded beyond the original cohort, drawing in academics and community professionals from parts of the UK, Ireland, Iceland and Australia.

This issue traces some of the discussions between the participants and presents an interdisciplinary account of the challenges faced at a time in which neoliberalism seems unchecked and uncheckable by the rise of nationalist populism. The first article, by Burrell (2017), explores the past, present and future of coal mining towns at a time in which their productive function is eroded in industrialised societies, but relatively buoyant in societies such as India and China. In response, Edwards (2017) reflects upon his own work on mining communities and the concept of the 'isolated mass'. In the second article, Finnerty and

O'Connell (2017) outline the effects of neoliberalism on housing across both communities and classes. Highlighting the way in which young people are now actively deprived the possibility of certainty and permanence in satisfying this most basic of needs, they present a picture of an Ireland ill-equipped to deal with its recent history of property speculation. Greenop (2017) highlights broader trends in response. Focusing on a particular example of precarity in housing, Richardson (2017) examines the effects of insufficient accommodation on Gypsy and Traveller groups. Richardson shows that even groups traditionally committed to transitory lifestyles are increasingly prevented from securing predictable and appropriate forms of housing. In response, Powell (2017) examines a number of related concepts, while Barrett and O'Dowd (2017) draw on their experience of working with Traveller groups in Ireland in their reply. Ó'Sullivan, Ó'Tuama, and Kenny (2017) then consider the precariousness of education, arguing that universities have a responsibility to deal with exclusion and alienation. Houghton (2017) offers an overarching analysis of that responsibility, while Fellows (2017) examines issues affecting practice in the UK.

The issue then considers the way in which these sorts of conditions affect the capacity for cooperation and collaboration. Halldórsson (2017) works through the examples of community engagement with Local Authorities and the Red Cross in the Westfjords of Iceland to consider the conditions under which collaboration can occur, advancing an 'affect-based' account of participation. In reply, Campbell (2017) considers the role of affect in ethnographic work. Finally, Lazarus (2017) draws upon the evolutionary psychological literature to present an account of co-operation under conditions of adversity. Baker (2017) replies, fostering cross-disciplinary conversation between political theory and natural science.

While not comprehensive, the issue offers insights into the range of quandaries that communities and political bodies must consider as they deal with the challenges of a world full of bleak alternatives. It is my hope that the issue will serve to strengthen and advance the discussions developed over the project's past five years. In that regard, I must thank the following for their help during that time: 98.9FM; Aboriginal and Torres Straight Islander Indigenous Community Health Service; Adam Iqbal; Adam Luke; Al Jazeera; Alexandra and John Copley; Alex Croom; Alison's Apartments; Alastair Stark; Andrew Parkin; Andrew Thomas; Arbeia Roman Fort and Museum; Ashington Community Football Club; Ashington Community Development Trust; Ashington Life Centre; Ashington Men in Sheds; Bar Loco; BBC Look North (North East and Cumbria); BBC Radio Newcastle; Bogaine Spearim; Brightmoon Media; Brisbane Indigenous Media Association; British Academy; Cameron Parsell; Chrissie O'Sullivan; Christopher Macleod; Christopher May; Clare and Steve Flynn; Community Organisers; Connie and Tommy Johnson; Dale Ruska; Deborah Tait; Denis Barrett; Dennis, Wendy and Anthony McCartney; Durham Miners Association; Egle Dubankaite; Frank Dawes; Fulcrum Arts and Research; GDR PR; Ged Henderson; Gibson Burrell; Great North Museum; Ian Lavery MP; Inala Wangarra; ID&D: Indigenous Directions and Development; James at Survivaltraininguk.co.uk; John Baker; John Chalmers; John Lazarus; John McVan; John O'Sullivan; Johnny Handle; Norm Sheehan; Keith Shaw; Kelly Greenop; Kevin Robson at Wild Dog Outdoors; Leslie Condon; Lesley van Moelenbroek; Lilla Watson; Linda O'Keeffe; Linus at Northern Wilds; Louise Bennett; Mark Wood; Michael Thewlis at ERC; Morgan Brigg; Murri Mura Aboriginal Corporation; Neil Taylor; Newcastle Sunday Assembly; News Post Leader; Northumberlandia, which is managed by The Land Trust with the support of the Northumberland Wildlife Trust; Red Text Films; Richard Baguely; Richard Cullen; Roger Appleton; Rosie Mutton; Sarah Howarth; Séamus Ó Tuama; Simon Mabon; Steve Harmison;

Sue Mendus; System Gallery; The Evening Chronicle; The Journal; The Ration Shed Museum, Cherbourg; The Sunday Sun; Tiger Bayles; Tobias Raub; Traveller Visibility Group, Cork; Tynemouth Cricket Club; Tyneside Cinema; University College Cork; Wansbeck Disability Forum; Woodhorn Museum; Yugambeh Museum. Special thanks to: Tom and Kay Johnson; Carolyn Gallagher; Fiona Rowley; Katherine Young, who provided tireless support for organisation of the conferences; Rosie Mutton, who helped to organise and run the conferences and to construct the YouTube archive; Robert Geyer and Patrick Bishop, who accommodated and supported eccentric and complicated work plans with sage-like understanding and compassion; Lancaster University Travel Team, who have dealt with so many requests with such patience, Amran Ghoni, Graham Winwood and Jill Sanctuary; Lancaster Procurement Team: Sarah Metcalfe, Susan Flynn and Suzanne Pritchard; Lancaster University Accounts Payable: Georgia Faloone and Janet Wood; Lancaster University Finance Team: Sharon Jennings and Jonathan Dutton, and Lancaster University Press Office: Beth Broomby, Anne Rothwell, Russell Reader, Vicky Tyrrell, Gillian Whitworth, Ian Broydon and Laura Mitchell.

Disclosure statement

No potential conflict of interest was reported by the author.

Funding

This work was supported by the British Academy [EN140110].

References

Baker, J. 2017. "Cooperation in adversity: a political theorist's response." *Global Discourse* 7 (4): 599–601.
Barrett, D., and S O'Dowd. 2017. "Whether to shine a light or curse the pothole of doom: a reply to Jo Richardson from a community work perspective." *Global Discourse* 7 (4): 521–526. doi: 10.1080/23269995.2017.1408291
Burrell, G. 2017. "The Role of Coal Mining Towns in Social Theory: Past, Present and Future." *Global Discourse* 7 (4): 451–468. doi: 10.1080/23269995.2017.1332473
Campbell, E. 2017. "Protean possibilities: attending to affect in collaborative research – a reply to Valdimar Halldórsson." *Global Discourse* 7(4): 565–570.
Edwards, P. 2017. "The Isolated Mass and Contemporary Social Theory." *Global Discourse* 7 (4): 469–472. doi: 10.1080/23269995.2017.1332472.
Fellows, T. 2017. "A reply to O'Sullivan, O'Tuama and Kenny." *Global Discourse* 7 (4): 543–547.
Finnerty, J., and C. O'Connell. 2017. "Changing precarities in the Irish housing system: supplier-generated changes in security of tenure for domiciled households." *Global Discourse* 7 (4): 473–488. doi: 10.1080/23269995.2017.1399708.
Greenop, K. 2017. "Understanding housing precarity: more than access to a shelter, housing is essential for a decent life." *Global Discourse* 7 (4): 489–495. doi: 10.1080/23269995.2017.1393788
Halldórsson, V. J. 2017. "Affective collaboration in the Westfjords of Iceland" *Global Discourse* 7 (4): 548–564.
Houghton, A.-M. 2017. "An ongoing challenge and a chance to diversify university outreach to tackle inequality: a response to O'Sullivan, O'Tuama and Kenny." *Global Discourse* 7 (4): 539–542.
Johnson, M. T. 2013. "The Precariat." *Global Discourse* 3 (3–4): 385–387. doi:10.1080/23269995.2013.904649.

Lazarus, J. 2017. "Cooperation in Adversity: An Evolutionary Approach." *Global Discourse* 7 (4): 571–598.
O'Sullivan, S., S. O'Tuama, and L. Kenny. 2017. "Universities as key responders to education inequality." *Global Discourse* 7 (4): 527–538.
Powell, R. S. 2017. "Gypsy-Traveller sites in the UK: power, history, informality – a response to Richardson." *Global Discourse* 7 (4): 516–520. doi: 10.1080/23269995.2017.1404335
Richardson, J. 2017. "Precarious living in liminal spaces: neglect of the Gypsy–Traveller site." *Global Discourse* 7 (4): 496–515. doi: 10.1080/23269995.2017.1389232
Standing, G. 2011. *The Precariat*. London: Bloomsbury.

The role of coal-mining towns in social theory: past, present and future

Gibson Burrell

ABSTRACT
Coal mining has ceased in Britain to all intents and purposes. For centuries, it was a source of employment and even economic security for thousands of men, and the women who lived with them. Miners clung on to life in dangerous occupations – second only to fishing in accident and mortality rates – but strong trade unionism and collectivism mean that for some periods they were regarded as relatively well-off within the working class, if one used internal comparisons. And whilst this group may have all but disappeared from the United Kingdom and most parts of Western Europe, today in other regions of the world, coal mining continues to expand. This article discusses a brief comparison of two pit villages in the 1950s when arguably coal mining in Britain was at its height, both in terms of tons produced and recorded manpower at work. It then turns to look to coal-mining villages in China today as sources of sociological insight for our collective futures.

Coal mining has ceased in Britain to all intents and purposes. For centuries, it was a source of employment and even economic security for thousands of men, and the women who lived with them. Miners clung on to life in dangerous occupations – second only to fishing in accident and mortality rates – but strong trade unionism and collectivism mean that for some periods they were regarded as relatively well-off within the working class if one used internal comparisons. And whilst this group may have all but disappeared from the United Kingdom and most parts of Western Europe, today in other regions of the world, coal mining continues to expand. This paper is about the past and present, in the United Kingdom (Cronin 1979) and elsewhere (Shorter and Tilly 1974; Korpi and Shalev 1980; Conell and Cohn 1995), looking to coal-mining villages as sources of sociological insight and even inspiration for our collective futures.

This article begins with a brief comparison of two pit villages in the 1950s when arguably coal mining in Britain was at its height, both in terms of tons produced and recorded manpower at work. And of course it was 'man' power, for women were totally excluded from the coal-mining industry in the nineteenth century (John 1980). The National Coal Board was only 5 years old when our comparison begins and much hope had been grasped by the coal miners that this, long fought for, achievement would improve their living conditions dramatically. As Bulmer (1975, 64) stated,

> Mine-workers constitute a group of workers who are exploited – and experience exploitation – in an extreme form.…. As such, miners are a distinct and important group within the working class as a whole, characterised both by the extreme conditions under which they are required to labour and by the solidarity which they display towards employers and the outside world.

Since the private mine owners had been bought out, those colliers that descended into newly nationalised pits in the Great Northern Coalfield on 'Vesting Day' in January 1947 expected much to have changed for the better. They were to be bitterly disappointed. A character in the play 'Close the Coalhouse Door', by Alan Plater, says acerbically, on looking at the composition of the nationalised management structure, 'Same bloody gaffers'. The Coal Board itself was constituted of 11 members, 7 of whom were Knights of the Realm. Several others were soon to gain this honour. It was here, with the composition of the National Coal Board's directors, that the miners' great expectations began to fall away in disappointment.

Research on these expectations and how they had been met – or not – began in the late 1940s. The first case we shall look at is Ashton, a pseudonym for a village in West Yorkshire studied in the early 1950s by Dennis, Henriques and Slaughter and published as Coal is Our Life in 1956. The other, though it lies some 100 miles to the North, is a real mining community named Ashington in Northumberland where the author was born and lived through the historical period being discussed by Dennis et al. This comparison throws up many points of similarity but also points of difference. The methods used by Dennis et al. are essentially drawn from anthropology and rely upon the case method with interviews, anecdotes, statistics and observation as the main (and eclectic) forms of data collection. Analysis is aided by recourse to anthropological classics like Evans-Pritchard's work on The Nuer (1937) and there is more than a faint whiff in Coal is our Life of the observers' assumed superior understanding of culture, beliefs and habits as compared to those who practice them. Bearing this authorial authority in mind let us read what Dennis, Henriques and Slaughter (1956) have to say.

Ashton

Ashton is a fictitious mining village in West Yorkshire in the United Kingdom which at the time of the study (1953–4) had a population of 14,000. The village is dominated by pit heaps and air pollution, increasingly generated after the first pit was sunk there in 1868. Expansion was rapid between 1891 and 1901 when the number of dwellings doubled and took the form of 'thread' development along existing roads. According to Dennis, Henriques and Slaughter (1956), the skills of a miner are not transferable into other jobs and this has influenced their mobility. There was no work for women in the area and only 6 in every 100 women living in the village had a job outside the home. There was an ageing demographic at work in the community whilst of the two pits in the village, one employed 1755 men and the other employed 653 men. The description of life down the pit is detailed and is based on observation, anecdote and statistics in equal measure woven into a story of life in the community as if this was a village in some far-flung part of what remained of the British Empire. This community study tries then, in true anthropological manner, to look at life beyond the pit and considers the leisure time activities of the pit men and their families.

In a second edition, published in 1969, Henriques, writing alone, complains that criticism of the 1956 book was sometimes based on the 'smug provincialism of the Fabian Society' (Dennis, Henriques, and Slaughter 1969, 10) and that 'the facile assumptions of middle class observers of the life of the working class are questionable at every point' (Dennis, Henriques, and Slaughter 1969, 9). Yet, the original authors, Dennis, Henriques and Slaughter, evince this set of value positioning themselves. For the tone of this 'community study' is surprisingly moralistic and condescending in places. It is judgemental about the values and behaviour of the people of the village so that, for example, we are told that a local dance hall advertised the following

> 'Saturday Night is Riot Night'. When attendance is invited in these terms it is not surprising to find that the local Court of Summary Jurisdiction records show many cases of obscene language, assault, disturbing the peace, and so on which occur at these Saturday night dances. (Dennis, Henriques, and Slaughter 1956, 126)

This is 'normal behaviour' we are told, as if this marked off Ashton as somehow miles away from polite society and such goings-on did not happen up and down the land on a Saturday night! The book begins by describing 'filthy houses' and is very judgemental about the miners' alleged habit of going absent from work if there was 'money in their pocket'. It sees gambling on the 'football pools' and horse racing as worthy of expressing a judgement about and, in the process, makes an interesting point about disabled men acting as bookies' runners in the period. This is productive of a similarity with Ashington to which I will come back to in a later section.

Dennis, Henriques and Slaughter (1956, 173) then address the issue of the family as part of the 'total social system' which is the pit village. They argue that families in a pit village come to know the vast majority of other families by a whole range of cross cutting ties of kinship, school, leisure and work interconnections. Expectations become shared through these deep-seated communal roots. There is no expectation of possessing material goods at the standard of 'the urban middle class ... Nowhere does one find luxury' (Dennis, Henriques, and Slaughter 1956, 179). Cosiness, tidiness and cleanliness are the values espoused and these are to be provided particularly by the wife of the miner. The collier looks to the outside of the family whilst his wife looks inward according to the writers of this case study – written at a time of course before the television set occupied its prominent and seductive place in the family home. Women know little of both what precise work her husband will undertake down the pit, and the contents of his wage packet. She is paid housekeeping money which is a fixed amount per week agreed between them, and the rest of the pay – whatever production bonuses it includes and so on – is his. Knowing his wages in any particular week is likely to be somewhat unusual. Dennis, Henriques and Slaughter (1956, 188) feel able to say 'this financial arrangement has severe disadvantages in that very often a large amount of a man's good wages is frittered away on his amusements and the wife has little say in saving'. They quote, somewhat gleefully, a widow of a miner who reported of her husband that there was not a single day when he did not go the bookies nor had less than a £1 in his pocket to spend on cigarettes and the football pools (Dennis, Henriques, and Slaughter 1956, 193). Women, on the other hand, need the approval of their husbands before spending on their own amusement and before taking up smoking in the period of the early 1950s. They see neighbours and friends during the day and according to Dennis et al. engage in 'callin' which means visiting the homes of others, being visited at home oneself and engaging in either location with gossip about others. Men never swear in front of women or children (Dennis, Henriques, and Slaughter 1956, 218). This rule is followed assiduously and there are penalties for those that transgress. Incidentally, it is worth noting that the movie 'Billy Elliott' set in the 1980s is totally incorrect in this aspect of mining life, for no typical miner would swear in front of his young son and certainly not his mother. The romance of labour is often exaggerated but Dennis, Henriques and Slaughter constantly 'describe' the miner in quite critical terms. It is a case study that is by no means value free.

Ashington

This comparison with Ashton is one rooted in my own personal experience and is based on a village well to the North and, at the time of Dennis et al. writing up their research, the writer was only 8 years old. Yet, in many ways it is very familiar to me. So this section is based on participation for 18 years, and close observation for many years thereafter, of a particular 'real' pit village. It is described by McManners and Wales (2002, 57) as follows,

> Ashington ... is a product of the late Industrial Revolution. Its location is in the south east of Northumberland, the very north of the Great northern coalfield. The town has been described as the world's largest pit village.

At its height, the village contained nearly 40,000 people, within which the Ashington Coal Company employed 80% of the male workforce in the town. The land had originally been leased from the Duke of Portland who owned nearby Bothal Castle and thus the Dukes were able to manipulate what happened in the development of the town. It was in 1849 that the first colliery was established and by 1891 it was a boom town. In the years before the First World War, a huge new area of building was erected called 'the Hirst' which used a grid iron system of architectural arrangement and offered a consistent standardised appearance, as every house was built in yellow segar bricks from the Ashington Coal Company's own brickyard. Even by the standards of the time, this was poor quality housing, despite its appeal to conformity, rationality and modernity in town planning. Earth roads, 2 standpoint water pipes for every 25 houses and an average of 6 people in every house were the norm. This was the maximisation of housing density expressed in one pit village and it was not driven by philanthropic motivations. There were at least six collieries in close proximity and each sported a large pit heap that sometimes gave off fumes. The air was often yellowish brown in appearance and sulphurous in odour as every house was fuelled by 'free coal' delivered once a fortnight by the colliery and stored in a coalhouse in each and every dwelling. Certain atmospheric conditions trapped these fumes above the town and smog was often the consequence. Health implications for all inhabitants followed.

The description in Dennis, Henriques and Slaughter (1956) of face work in Ashton would adequately describe that in the six local pits of Ashington, Woodhorn, Linton, North Seaton, Lynemouth and Newbiggin collieries, assuming this same point in time (Trist and Bamforth 1951). We have the pictorial evidence provided by the 'Ashington Group' of pitmen painters who were active between approximately 1930 and 1980. These pictures have attracted much attention for their portrayal of work down the mine and brought Ashington the special interest of the Mass Observation organisation which started its work in 1937. McManners and Wales (2002, 66) speak of Tom Harrison, a self-trained anthropologist visiting Ashington around this time.

> Harrison saw the Ashington Group as an ideal unit for observation, being highly motivated and, above all, an authentic group for study. He and his group of observers arrived in Ashington with ill-judged, pre-conceived ideas. His background had been in studying primitive societies and he probably saw the Ashington group as primitives, capable of being bought with gifts – in this instance a crate of beer which dumbfounded the group, many of whom were teetotal.

Also realistic in Dennis, Henriques and Slaughter (1956) would be their description of leisure activities in a mining village. But in Ashington, things were on a bigger scale; there were only 3 pubs but 56 working men's clubs. The Duke of Portland was a teetotaller so in his planning had allowed, for 30,000 residents, only 1 public house, named of course the Portland Hotel. The Central Hotel was to be a place for visiting mining engineers and those seeking commercial business whilst, outside of the Hirst, a pub named the North Seaton Hotel was set up to attract custom from the south side of Ashington. It was quickly named 'The White Elephant'. So three pubs existed to slake the thirst of the miners. But in addition, 56 private clubs were set up to cater for the working man. Women were allowed into the premises at weekends but were not, and could not be, members, even as the 1950s progressed. They had to signed in by a club member and convince the Doorman that they were going to be well behaved. Clubland was very big in Ashington and on Fridays, Saturdays and Sundays, people began a peregrination between their favourite clubs, leaving and departing on a tight schedule in order to see and be seen elsewhere. Typically, by the 1960s, Fridays were for men and women to go out in single sex groups and maybe enjoy a dance in the club – but not with their partners. Saturdays were for married couples to leave the children with their grandmother to be babysat, and to go to the club together. Sundays were usually men-only affairs. Spatial segregation on a Friday meant that (childless) married couples moved independently from each other on a different schedule. Gambling on bingo (housey-housey) was a key activity and the practice of betting on horses was overseen by bookies' runners. As was the case in Ashton, the one 'runner' often ensconced at the end of our street (named, as all colliery rows were in this section of the Hirst, after a Shakespearean character, Rosalind) was called 'Bowkey Isaac' and he was very disabled, typical perhaps of runners. His body's stance was noticeable from a long way away as he stood on our street corner. To 'bowk' is a dialect term meaning to belch very loudly indeed, and Bowkey Isaac could be heard, in many yards, from many yards away. This bowk was how he called out his presence. His call to customers in Rosalind, Beatrice and Katherine Streets could hardly be missed, especially if doors were open.

Familial and husband–wife relationships (Bulmer 1975) seem to be well described by Dennis, Henriques and Slaughter (1956) but they adopt the anthropological, middle class lens throughout their study. 'Descriptions' always have to use language and, in the choice of words taken, we create an image that we probably mean to achieve. Anthropology brings with it something of the upper class view of the exotic and in some way less 'successful' tribes when compared to our own. I had not remembered this in my reading of *Coal is Our Life* many years ago but today it seems very patronising indeed. This is not to say their portrayal of the deep sexism of the miners or of their tendency to gamble is inaccurate. It is simply that Dennis et al. offer no explanation of why these traits are to be found. Paradoxically, the need for description robs their analysis of any attempts at even a functionalist explanation, wherein the handling the existence of such 'working class' behaviours would be in terms of what functions they performed for the community. Still less is there any Marxist or radical interpretation of these behavioural features, although Henriques' commentary from 1969 in the second edition appears to be written much more from this sort of stance. Anthropology does not tend to offer radical politics in most cases (Birx 2010). What are we to use then as concepts to offer some analysis of these two villages, perhaps at the peak of their powers?

The concept of the 'isolated mass'

This was a notion developed by two American sociologists, Clark Kerr and Abraham Siegel, in 1954 to explain the high level of strike activity in mining villages around the world. It looks at first sight to be some form of geographical determinism in maintaining that any spatial location of a population which places it in isolation from other communities is creating a 'mass' that will exhibit unusual behaviour and think differently from those workers found in more interconnected and thus 'conventional' places.

> These communities have their own codes, myths, heroes, and social standards. There are few neutrals in them to mediate the conflicts and dilute the mass. All people have grievances, but what is important is that all numbers of each of these groups have the same grievances.... The employees form a largely homogeneous, undifferentiated mass – they all do about the same work and have about the same experiences. (Kerr and Siegel 1954, 68)

Of course, the concept is not only germane to mining communities. Docklands, logging camps and especially fishing villages are 'isolated' from larger populations by virtue of their positions within forests or on the coast, often in inaccessible harbours and these too are to be seen as isolated masses. Kerr and Siegel (1954) then have the problem of connecting high levels of industrial militancy to isolated masses (Rimlinger 1959). They argue that these communities, in the case of coal mining, rely on fixed locations within, or more accurately above, coalfields and with their highly visible and noxious spoil heaps are patently very unattractive to live in for reasons outlined above. This creates one-industry, homogenous groups of workers who are fixed in space by geology and isolated from the outside by aesthetics. Mobility into other occupations is severely restricted. The work is dangerous and accident rates are high. Group norms are strong, often based on interpersonal needs 'to watch each other's backs'. These mining communities thereby are characterised by collectivism, strong trade unionism and intensively shared cultures based on occupation (Salaman 1971). This cultural and institutional set of arrangements create a defensive and often successful position with regard to opposing management initiatives regarding output control, via strike behaviour in particular but also by manipulating absenteeism.

Within the isolated mass, there is an emphasis on educational achievement and 'male' sports as escape routes from dirt, disease and danger. The Hirst North School in Ashington is the only English educational establishment to have produced three captains of the England football team. Educational achievement often takes the form of moves into regional and national political activism and coal mining is often a centre of labourist politics. Pit villages formed a 'vanguard' of the labour movement with annual galas such as that in Durham acting as ceremonial rites at a national level for Labour and Socialist supporters. In Ashton and in Ashington, there is some evidence of political activism but nothing like to the same extent as in Wales and Scotland (Knowles 1960). The isolated mass concept, however, does seem to explain something of the inward looking nature of the communities and begins to address some of the 'why' questions which Dennis et al. seem unwilling to address.

The political centrality of such isolated masses to the Left in Britain and elsewhere in the form of pit villages however carries with it many disadvantages. Some 'modernisers' within left-wing groups saw defensive labour militancy as a block to 'progress' within the 'new working class' (Lockwood 1960; Hyman and Price 1983). The 'new working class' was produced by the 'new division of labour' that required international thinking in a differentiated way (Frobel 1977; Charnock and Starosta 2016). The very isolation of the pit village was seen as its worst feature, making it dependent upon inward looking, anti-managerialist rhetoric. As 'archetypal proletarians' they were something from the past. In the need for 'new' versions of labourist politics, mining was seen as a drag from the past. Thus, there were sections of the Left that were not likely to support mining communities when they came under real threat because of their presumed resistance to change. And so it came to pass in the mid-1980s in the United Kingdom (Beech 2006; Bevir 2005).

The isolated mass in the twenty-first century

Thirty years later,

> That capitalism has undergone a series of transformations over the last few decades and that these transformations have been reflected- at least to some extent- in a qualitative change in the nature, form and organization of labour is increasingly undisputed. Also widely recognised is that these developments have in turn had a reconfigurative effect on the political organization of workers and their resistance. (Dowling, Nunes, and Trott 2007, 1)

If we accept that the notion of the 'precariat' (Standing 2016; Johnson 2015) will bear some analytical weight upon it, it is easy to see that coal mining in the United Kingdom in the 1950s was not inhabited by the precariat. Of course, men were likely to be killed, industrial disputes could easily send miner's families into penury and periodic fluctuations in the demand internationally for coal could lay pit workers off for long periods. However, miners were relatively well paid and were not burdened usually by having to find roofs over their heads or solid fuel to light and heat their homes. These came with working down the pit. Life was not a constant struggle to exist – in the main. Figure 1 might be helpful in expressing the differences between miners in the 1950s in Britain and the state of precariousness today. This comparison might allow us later on to reconsider coal-mining villages in 2017 in the United Kingdom through the lens of precariousness.

Of course, coal mining is by no means the only form of *Industrial Labour*. Across Britain by the 1970s were to be found Fordist, large scale, fully integrated processes

Coal Mining	Precariousness at work
'Secure', predictable, repetitious	Insecure, contingent, flexible
Regulated, permanent	Illegal, casualised, temporary
Routinised, stable and endowed	Precarious, unstable, insecure
Available access to political system	Non-traditional forms of politicisation
Masculinist	Requiring new subjectivities
Central and strategic role in energy	Non-central place in economy
Identity is fixed and bounded	Identity is rendered fluid

Figure 1. A comparison of precariousness at work and coal mining.

being undertaken on single factory sites. The size and complexity of these factories offered opportunities to the work force to unionise through the factor of scale and the homogeneity of (semi-skilled) work levels (Milkman 1997; Rinehart, Huxley, and Robertson 1997). Single employment contracts with single employers were offered in order to enhance centralised managerial control and there was a predictability of regular repetitious work with a predictable wage at the end of it. Sometimes these factories were placed in former mining areas such as Nissan's plant near East Bolden in County Durham (Garrahan and Stewart 1992). Resistance where it occurred was through strikes, absenteeism and sabotage. This meant there was at least a degree of affinity between mass production workers and coal miners over several decades of the twentieth century, even if this was not totally solid. Then, however, came the rise of *Cognitive Capitalism and Immaterial Labour*.

First in this analysis (Vercellone 2007; Gill and Pratt 2008; Boutang 2011), it is argued that transformations take place in the workplace itself. The factory becomes a network of disparate productions of knowledge. The principal source of value comes to rest in the knowledge produced by workers and not in capital, nor their material labour on things. Workers willingly exploit themselves as individuals who are possessed of separable knowledge and not as part of a collectivity. This form of capitalism empowers those placed in strategic positions in the economy. This approach to immaterial labour is typically found in theorists and activists from France and Northern Italy. They tend to prefix discussions with 'neuro' (as in 'neuro-capitalism', Larsen 2014) indicating the focus upon *the mind* of the worker. Thus, it is felt acceptable to term this 'cognitive capitalism' and since the gold for the capitalist owner is in the mind of the worker with symbols, rather than workers with shovels, it is deemed acceptable to call this 'immaterial labour' (De Angelis and Harvie 2009).

Outside of the factory, perhaps simultaneous processes are seen to have created both *Affective Labour and Precarious Labour*. The position is taken (Dowling, Nunes, and Trott 2007) that class and class struggle have been altered by the shift of gravity of employment from large-scale production sites (back) into the home. Thus, such forces mean that elements of class have to be seen as possessing twilight status. It is foreseen that we are about to face class de-alignment, class fragmentation and divisions based on a schism between those exhibiting poverty and unemployment versus 'valued persons' who have valuable jobs and resources of value. Because Post-Fordist regimes of production (Milkman 1997) spread production away from the factory and into much smaller, geographically dispersed production units, collectivism wanes dramatically. Systems today highlight the individual as both the unit of production *and* consumption. Individuals are given 'permission to think' and to act as entrepreneurs, freed perhaps of the conformity of the isolated mass and the large, homogenising factory. It becomes acceptable to utilise emotion within employment to sell products, design workplaces and produce 'designer workers' (Casey 1996). The 'affective worker' is sought who will offer up her or his mind, body and soul to the corporation. Individuals become required to demonstrate high levels of intimacy, care or emotions as labourers and consumers. The drive is to make the 'worker's *soul* to become part of the factory' (Lazzarato 1996). Resistance where it does take place takes the form of refusal to work entirely. The affective worker has to withdraw themselves from work completely to disengage from their own internally generated scopic regime of self-surveillance.

Biffo Baredi in *The Soul at Work* (2009) maintains that Humanity expressed in and through the form of the body is no longer the measure of the world. Whilst Da Vinci could draw the human male with legs and arms outstretched as the measure of all that surrounded him, today control is no longer exercised at a human level but at the level of nanotechnology and what is invisible to the human eye. What organisations reflect upon are psychopharmacology, algorithms and forms of mass communication. In the first, key workers are not discouraged from experimenting with smart drugs. Indeed, they may be encouraged, just as pilots in the Luftwaffe were, to take amphetamines in the form of 'pilot's chocolate', to keep their concentration levels high whilst flying over Britain (Bloomfield and Dale 2015). Algorithms which change and transform data and produce decisions that humans have to depend upon and use in everyday corporate life remove decision-making from the operative. And with mass communications between organisations and their customers, consumers and clients, linked to constant searches for feedback on your rating of your experience of the corporation's offering, social media have become a key part of employment practices. These govern the soul at work. In the twenty-first century then it might be possible to say that bodies, minds and souls have had their traditional places overturned – both in work and outside work. What we are short of are models of the body, mind, soul triad set in employment.

What we do know is the traditional centrality of work to our 'identity' (Brown, Kirpal, and Rauner 2007). In prisons, as Goffman (1959) showed, one of the first processes a new inmate undergoes is identity stripping. One becomes a number, one's clothing and hair have to become standardised into a uniform way of being, one is forced to wear a uniform and freedom of movement is withdrawn. In the movie 'I, Daniel Blake', the expression of individuality in the title contrasts deeply with Mr Blake's experience in Newcastle of dealing with the social security system. He is far from being an individual and is merely fodder for the maw of the system which appears to be about *not* paying benefits. It is Kafkaesque in the original sense where Kafka worked in industrial insurance himself and obtained therein many ideas of how the system was designed not to pay out.

If prisons are places where identity is stripped from all inmates, and identity stripping is likely to be a part of the processes facing members of the precariat, might it be possible to ask in what ways these two elements interconnect? In both institutional locations, for the prisoner and the member of the precariat, options are very limited.

Economic activity for either is highly constrained by management and the state of the economy. Without resources or because of incarceration, mobility is highly constrained. In these locations, many shared values are likely to develop which are anti-authority, for the only representatives from the outside who are ever seen by those imprisoned are the forces of the state apparatus. This may well create a sense of abandonment and isolation, leading perhaps to something akin to an 'isolated mass'.

Thus, we have come full circle. Isolated masses may be produced by specific economic and geographical circumstances but once these circumstances have changed and disappeared, the isolated mass is in a very poor position to find any form of renewal. In many cases, the isolated mass is a form of prison, enforcing uniformity, reinforcing poverty and ensuring a lack of mobility for 'inmates' across the twenty-first century.

If the twenty-first century is characterised by Cognitive Capitalism, Immaterial Labour, Affective Capitalism and Precariousness then, what role can the pit village play anywhere in the future? We have seen that there is a very high dependence of the pit village upon world markets. There has been the rise of environmental groups warning of the dangers of global warming as a result of carbon emissions, particularly from coal fired power stations (Meij and Te Winkel 2007). There is a glut of cheap and dirty coal from Poland, India, China and Australia, yet pressure to secure fuel supplies is sometimes a national obsession. There has been a very noticeable move to oil and then gas as fuels of choice. All this has allowed a circumvention of the power of domestic miners in what was perceived to be a strategic industry 'bottleneck' where pit villages were seen as pinch points to national economic security. In the United Kingdom of course, we should never forget Thatcher's revenge against the miners through the deliberate closure of virtually every deep pit in the country. This set of closures led to the dismantling of old labour, and as we have seen not all on the Left were entirely unhappy about it (Beech 2006).

The effect on pit villages was and is to be seen in bodies, minds and souls of the community. There were massive changes to subjectivity, understood both as an objective feature of miners as a whole, and as meaning the inner beliefs and self-awareness of the individual miner. Manufacturing a new identity for each and every member of the community became essential for their psychic survival. Key here was the deliberate policy of destruction of pit heads so that the past was buried. In Woodhorn colliery, the day before the pit was to be handed back to the NUM for use as a museum, the NCB blew up the chimney which had stood for over 100 years. One does not have to be a Freudian to see the emasculation that this was meant to symbolically represent. Thus, pit closure brought with it, in many cases, the emasculation of masculine values. The wage earner in the household became much more likely to be the wife because there was the availability locally of 'women's work' in light industry. Many of the men immediately became unemployed. Unemployment of a prolonged nature is associated with crime, drug use and other escape attempts (Cohen and Taylor 1971). There was a marked flight of resources outwards, as capital expenditure reduced, and money in the form of weekly wages no longer circulated in the community. Ashington and no doubt Ashton became sites of enormous socio-economic neglect, wherein its community members lived life on the edge. And these processes of immiseration, polarisation and alienation identified by Marx are to be found in many places outside of the Great Northern Coalfield.

What this produces is a 'precariousness without work' for former coal miners that has certain features to note within it, as in Figure 2.

Precariousness without work

unpredictability

economic deprivation

insecurity

crises in identity

marginalisation

reduction in life chances

Figure 2. Precariousness without work.

The pit village globally

So is this a tale then of the demise of the pit village and all its heritage? Not if we consider Colliery Towns today – but not in the West. For example, in India and China, pit 'villages' have developed and then faced economic uncertainty as the vicissitudes of the market hit home. However, many of these colliery towns are not deep pit ones but are often opencast where there are far fewer workers required and where working conditions are considerably less dangerous. But where deep coal mining is to be found, there are many dangers for the miner to face.

In China, it is said (Andrews-Speed, Ma, et al. 2003; Andrews-Speed et al. 2005; Wright 2004) that over 4300 small, inefficient coal-mining operations have been earmarked for closure in addition to the 7250 that have been closed in the previous 5 years, slashing a further 560 million tonnes from Chinese production. In total, it is forecast that 1.3 million coal-mining jobs and 500,000 steel jobs will be lost as part of a broader economic restructuring. Losses on this scale are suggestive of a huge coal-mining workforce over the last decade, some if not all, of whom will be living in settlements that approximate pit villages. But these villages are very recent inventions in most cases and a tradition around coal extraction may not yet have gained any foothold.

Figures from January 2015 in India (BBC 2015) show that a strike was called by five unions representing some 3.7 million coal workers employed with the state-run Coal India, which has a near monopoly over production. India is opening a coal mine a month in order to double production by 2020. Its goal is to produce 1.5 million metric tons by 2020 exceeding US coal production, and becoming the second largest coal producer in the world, after China. This expansion requires a huge number of new workers, all of whom through the use of company and state carrots or sticks, are willing to become coal miners. Consider the figures in Figure 3 (by kind permission of Vasumathi and Narayana 2016). These are from 2012 and were produced for my use by staff in Basix Ltd in April 2016. They show in the column labelled 'mining and quarrying' that 1908,000 workers were to be found in this category in that year. Yet compare this to the news item above, which claimed that in January 2015, 3.7 million coal miners were on strike. Clearly this means that nearly 2 million new miners have been added into the Indian coal-mining industry in 5 years, dwarfing the expansion in European counterparts more than a century ago. The

Indian Workforce categories

Industrial category	Main Workers ('000s)	Percentage (%)
Total main workers*	312,972	100.0
Agricultural & allied activities	176,979	56.6
Mining & quarrying	1,908	0.6
Manufacturing	41,848	13.4
Electricity, gas and water supply	1,546	0.5
Construction	11,583	3.7
Wholesale, retail trade & repair work, Hotel and restaurants	29,333	9.4
Transport, storage & communications	12,535	4.0
Financial intermediation, Real estate, business activities	6,109	2.0
Other services	31,131	10.0

Source: Industrial classification data based on sample.

Agriculture sector employs largest number of workers : out of 313 million main workers, 166 million (56.6%) are engaged in 'Agricultural and allied activities'.

Figure 3. Indian workforce categories.
Source: M.Vasumathi and DV Narayana; Basix 2016 Ltd, Koti, Hyderabad.

contraction of coal getting in Ashington and Ashton has been compensated by enormous expansion in Indian coalfields.

Of course, the USA continues to have a coal-mining industry. Indeed President Trump has claimed that the industry in West Virginia, for example, will be expanded in his presidency (Loh 2016). It is interesting to note that peak coal production in the United States occurred in 2006 and by 2014, coal production was 14% lower than this, particularly in the coal-producing states of West Virginia, Kentucky, Colorado, Indiana and Utah. Just as India is opening up new coal mines, across the USA coal mines have closed so that according to data from the Mine Safety and Health Administration, the number of operating coal mines in the United States fell by 13% to 1700 pits (https://www.msha.gov/data-reports).

Thus, American Exceptionalism is again a possibility in which the Western trend of colliery closure might well be turned back by the Trump Administration. So globally, communities are arising that are dedicated to coal production whilst elsewhere communities are in steep decline, despite producing a very similar product. The world is a patch quilt of closing and opening coal mines and what one sees is not a uniform picture of the end of the pit village (Rimlinger 1959). Consider, for example, a case of Tianfu township, located within Beibei county, 30 km north of Chongqing city in the People's Republic of China with a population of 47,000 (Andrews-Speed et al. 2005).

Tianfu township

Since the seventeenth century, coal mining has provided an important source of wealth in Tianfu itself. China has the largest small-scale mining industry in the world in terms of production and employment. In 1999, coal production was valued at US$24 billion, and employment in the mining sector exceeded 4 million men (not women). However, these figures are likely to represent vast underestimates (Andrews-Speed, Ma, et al. 2003). Just under a half of this production, approximately 650 million tonnes, came from 75,000–

80,000 township and village coal mines (TVCMs), which are often owned and controlled at the township and village level by local government. A substantial minority of these mines are privately owned but other state companies and agencies maintain ownership including even the army and prison service.

In 1998, because of overproduction of coal and the threat this offered to state controlled coal mines, China began a programme to close thousands of small-scale coal mines over a 3-year period. According to Andrews-Speed, Yang, et al. (2003, 190),

> The removal or deterioration of these economic components of life around the mine site will not only affect the economic strength of the community but substantial economic decline will almost certainly result in a range of social problems (Rocha and Bristow 1997, Mining Minerals and Sustainable Development, 2002a). Common symptoms include unemployment, crumbling infrastructure, failing social services and rising crime.

Because of the recent expansion in Chinese coal production, the labour force has been supplemented by migrant rural workers, just as it was in the United Kingdom 150 years ago. Indeed, the TVCMs are largely composed of migrant 'underemployed' rural workers and hundreds of thousands lost their jobs as the number of TVCMs closed. For government officials in these coal-mining areas, this part of the labour force was not seen as their responsibility and there were pronouncements that these migrant workers should return to their villages just as huge flows of rural workers into the cities was taking place.

Tianfu, our Ashington in the PRC, had 32 mines before the government induced programme of closures. Afterwards, the number of small-scale mines in the township was 18. With a population of 47,000, the town is not huge when compared to Ashington 50 years ago, but the size of the mines must be much smaller. After closure, it appears that few new jobs had been created by local government, but some laid-off workers were able to find jobs elsewhere in Beibei County. As for Tianfu township itself, 'the village has reduced coal output through mine closure, but has failed to generate new economic activities within the boundaries of the township because of its location and its historic dependency on coal mining and quarrying for construction materials' (Andrews-Speed, Ma, et al. 2003) The township government of Tianfu received very little support from the county government of Beibei and many residents of Tianfu had to leave their homes to find employment in other parts of the county. Migration flows in China have been massive and it may be that pit closures are dealt with by movements of the population to other areas of economic activity in the country. The city of Chongqing, which has a population exceeding 10 million, lay close by. For the residents of Ashington in the late 1980s, this set of economic circumstances was a luxury not afforded to them.

> Most small-scale mining provinces elsewhere in the world lack these advantages and will therefore be unable to react so effectively to an enforced programme of mine closure unless higher levels of government become directly involved in the formulation of policies and the provision of resources to implement these policies. (Andrews-Speed et al. 2005, 52–53)

From the brief details of the case of Tianfu, the reader should be able to discern that the isolated mass concept may not be a good fit with Chinese experiences in the twenty-first century. The growth in Chinese coal production was achieved by massive inward migration of peasants from the land – as it was in the United Kingdom much earlier. But the rapid dynamism of the Chinese economy has meant that these are not so much 'settlements' because large sections of the population of Tianfu are both incomers and outgoers within 10 years. The culture of the isolated mass may be thought to require at least a generation to 'bed in' and take root. Whilst Tianfu has been a source of coal production since the seventeenth century and therefore has a true longevity, this local enduring mining culture was quickly transformed by a wave of inward migration in the late 1990s. Maybe the old culture of Tianfu remains unchanged by the events of the last 20 years, but such is the level and depth of social transformation in the PRC that this would be doubtful (Andrews-Speed, Yang, et al. 2003).

Conclusions; unsettled settlements

For Bulmer (1975, 87–88),

> The traditional mining community is characterised by the prevalence of communal social relationships among miners and their families which are multiplex in form. The social ties (of work, leisure, family, neighbourhood and friendship) overlap to form close knit and interlocking locally based collectivities of actors. The solidarity of the community is strengthened not only by these features themselves but by a shared history of living and working in one place over a long period of time. From this pattern derives the mutual aid characteristic in adversity and through this pattern is reinforced the inward-looking focus on the locality, derived from occupational homogeneity and social and geographical isolation from the rest of society. Meaningful social interaction is confined almost exclusively to the locality.

Today, locality has become an impellor for enforced enclosure not social solidarity. Mining villages in the United Kingdom, Belgium and France (*inter alia*) today are, in many senses, places of the unemployed male precariat. The very nature of the isolated mass, with which many pit towns are associated, has created a form of imprisonment for men and women formerly earning their living from coal production. The pit village has had a history of danger, dirt, destruction and dire living conditions. It still does – but elsewhere in the world's political economy. These produce in the present time, albeit in the East, very specific conditions for an isolated mass with class motivations and access to resistance. Yet as we have seen in Tianfu, the pace of change may well prevent the conditions for an isolated mass from developing in the twenty-first century. The fluidity and liquidity of social structures and processes in rapidly transforming societies, where transport systems make travel much easier and allow few settlements to settle, may preclude isolated masses from forming. Yet, strikes of 3.7 million miners in India 2 years ago show that mass strikes are still associated with such forms of employment and it would be interesting to have seen how Kerr and Siegel would have attempted to explain that today.

Coal has not disappeared then from the world economy and perhaps some of the same forces which affected the Atlantic economies historically are today at work outside the West. Moreover, Trump has claimed he will revive the US coal industry and this seems to have won to his side West Virginia in the Presidential election of 2016. The pit village, of course, may not be the same as we imagine looking at English villages in the North of England (in so far as we can) around the mid-1950s. For after all, colliery towns in Wales look quite different due to local geology and geography. The mining valleys produce different types of coal and social arrangements of a linear type along river bottoms when compared to the mining plains of the northern part of the Great Northern coalfield. This is to say nothing of the US coal settlement reflected in 'The

Deer Hunter' where more differences between coal towns raise their heads. No pit village is the same. As Bulmer (1975, 70–71) notes of the isolated mass concept,

> Though miners in Britain and America hold to certain common values, internal cross-currents exist within mining communities, and environmental conditions may be reacted to in different ways. It is precisely this pattern of variation which the concept cannot allow for.

Thus, Ashton coal-face workers seemed to see deputy overmen (Deputies) as agents of management. In Ashington, this feeling was much less in evidence (Trist and Bamforth 1951). No two pits share exactly the same history, geology, settlement patterns, experience of major accidents and union leadership. If there are differences between mining communities, certainly there are complex relations *within* these isolated masses with different inter-twinings of the body, mind, soul found throughout the population. It was certainly *never* homogenous – yet it was patterned. As Gluckman (1961) put it, 'The African newly arrived from his rural home to work in a mine, is first of all a miner (and possibly resembles miners everywhere)'.

But the question to end on perhaps is 'what politico-economic role will pit villages play this century?' In the United Kingdom, the coal-mining town has a long and honourable tradition of playing a role in left-wing politics. Seen as bastions of class consciousness and traditional collectivist values, the pit village entered social science as a place of anthropological interest and what was found there was certainly different from metropolitan life styles. In some senses, the mining community was seen as a piece of exotica, tribally based and closer to home than small Pacific islands. But those days have gone as relatively secure miners have become insecure members of a precariat, living day to day on the edge of a way of life that collapsed in front of them (Warwick and Littlejohn 1992; Waddington et al. 2001).

What can be done to reconcile village inhabitants to the collapse of their ways of life? Is it to embrace retrospection and to fall back upon deeper political resistance and masculinist values? Or is the best strategy for these dispossessed community members to welcome modernity and show openness to new ways of thinking? Does education still have a key role to play? But as I tried to point out at the beginning of this piece, upper middle class values are always the blinkers by which visiting anthropologists blind themselves to the reality of the lives of others. How can we say what are the best strategies for those whom we have little understanding, despite our best efforts? And 'strategies' are future-oriented devices of the powerful. If one feels that the future matters not, why strategise about it at all?

But, for what it is worth, my experience of pit life in a period now located firmly in history is to suggest that community members may have to think of new bodies, new minds and new souls in order to accommodate to the future. The precise meaning of such a gnostic statement is open to much interpretation but in Ashington today, health is a crucial dimension to the everyday lives of people. Without much money, one buys cheap food. Without everyday comforts, one buys cigarettes and booze. The pleasures of the working class have always been 'bed and beer'. Without good GP's clamouring to work in one's area, health care provision is limited. The precariat face poor health every day and so new bodies are required by them for them. Not because these are needed to bring them into production and 'use' but because of their rights to health. New minds and new mind sets are easy to articulate as desirable in the safety of a middle class home but re-creation of selves and identities would be helpful to all within the ex-coal town. To have a future, the future – any future – must be conceivable and it need not be utopian. Finally, new souls would imply the rediscovery of affect for others, where emotional expressions of fellow feeling become the everyday again, and self-possessed individualism (Macpherson 2010) is rebuffed. And how can these conditions of possibility be realised? From investment in and by the community, much of it financial but also in the realm of civil society which was ripped asunder in the mid-1980s.

But, like China today, it is surely not possible for ex-miners to move out and, in emulating many a Cornish tin mining song, emigrate to where jobs at the lode are still available? For nearly all the last generation of miners are no longer able to work, having been crippled, maimed and occupied (Dale and Burrell 2014) by their time underground. The West may have exported jobs but we have also exported deadly occupation by coal dust in the form of silicosis and pneumoniconiosis. On 27 November 2005, Dongfeng Coal Mine, one of China's national key mines, suffered a major coal dust explosion, which claimed the lives of 171 workers. What's more, this accident was the 21st in which more than 100 employees' lives were lost (Zheng et al. 2009). Perhaps the closing of the last deep coal mines in the United Kingdom brings with it some less dangerous 'occupation' of what is rapidly becoming a post-industrial workforce. But this takes us into regional geography and the specific, non-generalised location of the post-industrial bases of cognitive capitalism, immaterial labour and affective capitalism. Precariousness may be what is left elsewhere, not only – but with certainty, within the once bustling mining villages of the twentieth century (Johnson 2015).

Disclosure statement

No potential conflict of interest was reported by the author.

References

Andrews-Speed, P., G. Ma, B. Shao, and C. Liao. 2005. "Economic Responses to the Closure of Small-Scale Coal Mines in Chongqing, China." *Resources Policy* 30 (1): 39–54. doi:10.1016/j.resourpol.2004.12.002.

Andrews-Speed, P., G. Ma, X. Shi, and B. Shao. 2003. "The Impact Of, and Responses To, the Closure of Small-Scale Coal Mines in China: A Preliminary Account." In *The Socio-Economic Impacts of Artisanal and Small-Scale Mining in Developing Countries*, ed. G. Hilson, 511–530. Rotterdam: Balkema.

Andrews-Speed, P., M. Yang, L. Shen, and S. Cao. 2003. "The Regulation of China's Township and Village Coal Mines: A Study of Complexity and Ineffectiveness." *Journal of Cleaner Production* 11: 185–196. doi:10.1016/S0959-6526(02)00038-0.

BBC (2015) 'India Coal Miners Strike Called Off', *BBC News* (Online), 8 January. http://www.bbc.co.uk/news/world-asia-india-30721875. Accessed 20 January 2017.

Beech, M. 2006. *The Political Philosophy of New Labour*. London: I. B. Taurus.

Berardi, F. B. 2009. *The Soul at Work*. Los Angeles: Semiotext(E).

Bevir, M. 2005. *New Labour: A Critique*. London: Routledge.

Birx, H. J. 2010. *21st Century Anthropology: A Reference Handbook, Volume 1*. London: Sage.

Bloomfield, B., and K. Dale. 2015. "Fit for Work? Redefining "Normal" and "Extreme" through Human Enhancement Technologies." *Organization* 22 (4): 552–569. doi:10.1177/1350508415572507.
Boutang, Y. M. 2011. *Cognitive Capitalism*. Cambridge: Polity.
Brown, A., S. Kirpal, and F. Rauner, eds. 2007. *Identities at Work*. Dordrecht: Springer.
Bulmer, M. I. A. 1975. "Sociological Models of the Mining Community." *The Sociological Review* 23: 61–92. doi:10.1111/j.1467-954X.1975.tb00518.x.
Casey, C. 1996. "Corporate Transformations: Designer Culture, Designer Employees and Post-Occupational Solidarity." *Organization* 3 (3): 317–339. doi:10.1177/135050849633002.
Charnock, G., and G. Starosta. 2016. *The New International Division of Labour*. London: Palgrave.
Cohen, L., and L. Taylor. 1971. *Escape Attempts*. London: Penguin.
Conell, C., and S. Cohn. 1995. "Learning from Other People's Actions." *American Journal of Sociology* 101 (2): 366–403. doi:10.1086/230728.
Cronin, J. 1979. *Industrial Conflict in Britain*. Basingstoke: Macmillan.
Dale, K., and G. Burrell. 2014. "Being Occupied." *Organization* 21 (2): 159–174. doi:10.1177/1350508412473865.
De Angelis, M., and D. Harvie. 2009. "'Cognitive Capitalism' and the Rat Race: How Capital Measures Immaterial Labour in British Universities." *Historical Materialism* 17 (3): 3–30. doi:10.1163/146544609X12469428108420.
Dennis, N., F. Henriques, and C. Slaughter. 1956. *Coal is Our Life*. London: Eyre and Spottiswoode.
Dennis, N., F. Henriques, and C. Slaughter. 1969. *Coal is Our Life*. 2nd ed. London: Tavistock.
Dowling, E., R. Nunes, and B. Trott. 2007. "Immaterial and Affective Labour: Explored." *Ephemera* 7: 1–7.
Evans-Pritchard, E. 1937. *The Nuer*. London: Clarendon Press.
Frobel, F. 1977. *The New International Division of Labour*. Cambridge: Cambridge University Press.
Garrahan, P., and P. Stewart. 1992. *The Nissan Enigma*. London: Mansell.
Gill, R., and A. C. Pratt. 2008. "In the Social Factory? Immaterial Labour, Precariousness and Cultural Work." *Theory, Culture & Society* 25 (7–8): 1–30. doi:10.1177/0263276408097794.
Gluckman, M. 1961. "Anthropological Problems Arising from the African Industrial Revolution." In *Social Change in Modem Africa*, ed. A. Southall. London: Oxford University Press.
Goffman, E. 1959. *Asylums*. London: Penguin.
Hyman, R., and R. Price, eds. 1983. *The New Working Class: A Reader*. Basingstoke: Macmillan.
John, A. V. 1980. *By the Sweat of Their Brow*. London: Routledge.
Johnson, M. 2015. "Introduction." In *Precariat: Labour, Work and Politics*, ed M. Johnson, 1–5. London: Taylor and Francis.
Kerr, C., and A. Siegel. 1954. "The Inter-Industry Propensity to Strike: An International Comparison." In *Industrial Conflict*, eds. A. Kornhauser, et al., 189–212. New York: McGraw Hill.
Knowles, K. G. J. C. 1960. "'Strike-Proneness' and its Determinants." In *Labor and Trade Unionism*, eds W. Galenson and S. M. Lipset, 309–310. New York: Wiley.
Korpi, W., and M. Shalev. 1980. "Strikes, Power and Politics in Western Nations 1900-1976." *Political Power and Social Theory* 1: 45–61.
Larsen, S. N. 2014. "Compulsory Creativity." *Culture Unbound* 6 (4): 159–177. doi:10.3384/cu.2000.1525.146159.
Lazzarato, M. 1996. "Immaterial Labour." In *Radical Thought in Italy: A Potential Politics*, eds M. Hardt and P. Virno, 133–147. Minneapolis: University of Minnesota Press.
Lockwood, D. 1960. "The New Working Class." *Sociological Review* 1 (2): 248–259.
Loh, T. (2016) "Trump May 'Dig' Coal, but Industry's Outlook is Flat at Best." *Bloomberg.com* (Online), 10 November. https://www.bloomberg.com/news/articles/2016-11-10/trump-may-dig-coal-but-industry-s-outlook-is-flat-at-best. Accessed 20 January 2017.
Macpherson, C. B. 2010. *The Political Theory of Possessive Individualism: Hobbes to Locke*. Ontario: Oxford University Press.
McManners, R., and G. Wales. 2002. *Shafts of Light: Mining Art in the Great Northern Coalfield*. London: Gemini.

Meij, R., and H. Te Winkel. 2007. "The Emissions of Heavy Metals and Persistent Organic Pollutants from Modern Coal-fired Power Stations." *Atmospheric Environment* 41: 9262–9272. doi:10.1016/j.atmosenv.2007.04.042.

Milkman, R. 1997. *Farewell to the Factory*. Berkeley: University of California Press.

Rimlinger, G. V. 1959. "International Differences in the Strike-Propensity of Coal Miners: Experience in Four Countries." *Industrial and Labor Relations Review* 13: 389–405. doi:10.1177/001979395901200304.

Rinehart, J., C. Huxley, and D. Robertson. 1997. *Just Another Car Factory?* Ithaca: ILR Press.

Rocha, J., and J. Bristow. 1997. "Mine Downscaling and Closure." *Minerals & Energy: Raw Materials Report* 12 (4): 15–20. doi:10.1080/14041049709409110.

Salaman, G. 1971. "Some Sociological Determinants of Occupational Communities." *Sociological Review* 19: 53–77. doi:10.1111/j.1467-954X.1971.tb00619.x.

Shorter, E., and C. Tilly. 1974. *Strikes in France 1830-1968*. Cambridge: Cambridge University Press.

Standing, G. 2016. *The Precariat: A New Dangerous Class*. 2nd ed. Bloomsbury: London.

Trist, E., and K. Bamforth. 1951. "Some Social and Psychological Consequences of the Longwall Method of Coal Getting." *Human Relations* 4(1): 3–38. doi:10.1177/001872675100400101

Vasumathi, M., and D. V. Narayana. 2016. *Private Communication*. Koti, Hyderabad: Basix Ltd.

Vercellone, C. 2007. "From Formal Subsumption to General Intellect." *Historical Materialism* 15: 13–36. doi:10.1163/156920607X171681.

Waddington, D., C. Critcher, B. Dicks, and D. Parry. 2001. *Out of the Ashes?: The Social Impact of Industrial Contraction and Regeneration on Britain's Mining Communities*. London: HMSO.

Warwick, D., and G. Littlejohn. 1992. *Coal, Capital and Culture*. London: Taylor and Francis.

Wright, T. 2004. "The Political Economy of Coal Mine Disasters in China: 'Your Rice Bowl or Your Life'." *The China Quarterly* 179: 629–646. doi:10.1017/S0305741004000517.

Zheng, Y. P. et al. 2009. "A Statistical Analysis of Coal Mine Accidents Caused by Coal Dust Explosions in China." *Journal of Loss Prevention in the Process Industries* 22(4): 528–532. DOI:10.1016/j.jlp.2009.02.010.

REPLY

The isolated mass and contemporary social theory

Paul Edwards

This is a reply to:

Burrell, Gibson. 2017. "The role of coal-mining towns in social theory: past, present and future." *Global Discourse*. https://doi.org/10.1080/23269995.2017.1332473

It is a pleasure to comment on Gibson Burrell's (GB's) (2017) essay, for two reasons. The first, like GB's, is autobiographical, though of a merely intellectual kind: my first substantial paper was published 40 years ago on the Kerr–Siegel hypothesis, and I thus return to it (Edwards 1977). The second is that I offer some wider reflections on social theory; these are inspired by GB's essay, and I have little specific and even less critical to say about it.

The isolated mass

The key question about the concept of the isolated mass is what it is intended to explain. For Kerr and Siegel, it addressed differences in strike rates across industries. But as commentators, such as Rimlinger in the piece cited by GB, soon established, strike rates in coal mining varied massively not only between countries but also within them. Shorter and Tilly (1974, 287–294) indeed report that strikes in France had the opposite pattern to that predicted. If the concept has value, it is to identify one among a number of features of industrial communities that may lead to class solidarity and then, if other factors are also present, to strikes. The most sustained assessment of the combination of factors is that of Church, Outram, and Smith (1991). They stress that, despite the many efforts at explanation from economics, sociology and history, miners' militancy has been extremely 'difficult to resolve'. Their preferred approach is an application of Hyman's (1972) three-level model. Firstly, there are structural factors such as the technical and economic structure of an industry and the social structure of mining communities. Secondly comes organization, in respect of how the work process is organized and the nature and strength of the organizations of employers and workers. Thirdly, we have consciousness in terms of leadership, action and subjective interpretations. Such a framework offers a great deal. To take just one example, some mining communities lacked the solidarity and militancy of 'Ashton' (in fact Featherstone) and Ashington. Thus, Waller (1983) dissects the role of employer paternalism and religion in the development of a relatively quiescent, if still isolated, mining region in Nottinghamshire. As GB tersely remarks, 'no pit village is the same'.

The fact of being an isolated mass was, as GB demonstrates, one part of the structural conditions underpinning miners' solidarity. And local tradition remained influential. Beynon (1973) showed that the solidarity of another 'isolated mass', dockers in Liverpool, sustained local traditions that in turn underpinned the militancy of workers at the car plants introduced to the region. Specifically on Ashington, I studied the nearby Lynemouth aluminium smelter and found that workers carried with them traditions from the mines (Wright and Edwards 1998). There are two important points about the traditions. Firstly, they did not entail simple 'resistance' to management. On the contrary, they gave workers a sense of confidence which allowed them to embrace new forms of work associated with teamwork. These forms indeed had a clear affinity with work group responsibility in the mines. This certainly did not mean acquiescence in managerial policies but rather a robust defence of autonomy and independence along with a willingness to accept some new ideas. Secondly, as with the mines, none of this did any good in the face of the restructuring of the aluminium industry. The smelter closed in 2012 with the loss of over 500 jobs directly, and perhaps up to 3500 in the supply chain.

Social theory

The theoretical conclusion is that being part of a mass can be one factor in sustaining a militant and solidaristic outlook. But that outlook is not necessarily defensive or inward looking. It also promotes a sense of discipline and a commitment to productive norms, as at Lynemouth. The wider conclusion which I reached in 1977 is that sociologists may like the Kerr–Siegel hypothesis because it offers a structural social fact which seems deeper than the kinds of factors stressed by economists or historians. In the intervening period, we have of course had the massive swing away from anything that smacks of determinism so that if anyone now reads Kerr and Siegel, it may be to dismiss them. But the structural fact remains important, and it is good to see GB, as one of the leaders of the turn to Foucault and all that, recognizing it.

I offer two further glosses on what GB says in the latter part of his essay. These turn on models of the contemporary world and emerging social theory.

In relation to the former, GB lays out several perspectives, yet he does not seem to be convinced by any of them. He is right to be doubtful. One point I made in 1977 about Kerr and Siegel, which I had forgotten until rechecking the piece, was that concepts like an isolated mass may characterize, even if they do not explain, polar cases but are much less good at capturing what happens away from the extremes. Many commentators have tried to identify emergent forms of work organization through concepts such as post-Fordism, varieties of capitalism, precariousness or more recent phenomena such as the gig economy. But there is a tendency to write as though the ideal type captures the range of actual cases and as though one world, of the proletarian isolated mass, has been wholly supplanted by another. Models are useful, and indeed essential, for they help us to identify key underlying processes and ask which operate in a given setting. Some economists have usefully developed this idea, thus moving a long way from the market determinism of parts of that field (Rodrik 2015). But models are not a short cut to understanding the complexity of concrete work settings.

If we want to understand this complexity, we need to grasp the kind of factors that GB identifies in his discussion of Tianfu. In terms of the three levels identified by Church and colleagues, structural factors include the economic globalization of the industry and technological change, notably the use of opencast techniques which have allowed mechanization and a production process far removed from that of underground mines with teams of autonomous workers. Organizational factors include, as GB stresses, the use of migrant workers, who are likely to be far more individualized and dependent on managements than were members of the isolated mass. Finally, we have consciousness and action, on which GB says little. There is, however, a growing body of research in labour relations in China which points to elements of militancy and collective organization despite a challenging social and economic context. Workers' consent can never be taken for granted (e.g. Human Relations 2015) . There is then considerable space for scholars to promote emerging, and possibly better, models of employment governance. The dangers of importing 'upper middle class values' and of anthropological condescension highlighted by GB in his conclusions are important, but they should not stand in the way of critical dialogue between social science and workers (Edwards 2015).

Finally, in terms of an underpinning methodology for the kind of analysis indicated above, I draw attention to the growing uses of realism in social science (Sayer 2000). Realism says that we need to understand the world using a layered ontology that identifies the empirical (things that can be immediately sensed), the actual (things not directly sensed but of which people will be aware, such as hierarchy and authority) and the underlying level of the real (forces of which people may not be aware, such as the ways in which power can be constituted in hidden ways). The affinity with Hyman's model of strikes is evident. The causal powers of unobservable forces can in principle be identified by asking what the world must be like for us to observe what we observe. As the debate on the isolated mass demonstrated, powers may or may not operate in a given context, and they may be counteracted by other powers. In Rodrik's (2015, 143) example, if we want to explain something like growing inequality in countries like the USA, we might identify globalization and what economists call skill-based technological change as possible factors. But these operate in different ways in different conditions rather than having determinate effects. And there are other factors, such as those discussed by GB, that may be hard to include in economists' models. As O'Mahoney (2012) shows, realism enables us to identify some features with causal powers without descending into either essentialism or determinism. The isolated mass was one such feature that can help to say something about some mining communities, and GB's reinterrogation of it in contemporary context is timely and apposite.

Disclosure statement

No potential conflict of interest was reported by the author.

References

Beynon, H. 1973. *Working for Ford*. Harmondsworth: Penguin.

Burrell, G. 2017. "The Role of Coal Mining Towns in Social Theory: Past, Present and Future." *Global Discourse*. doi: 10.1080/23269995.2017.1332473

Church, R. A., Q. Outram, and D. N. Smith. 1991. "The Militancy of British Miners, 1893-1986: Interdisciplinary Problems and Perspectives." *Journal of Interdisciplinary History* 22 (1): 49–66. doi:10.2307/204565.

Edwards, P. K. 1977. "The Kerr-Siegel Hypothesis of Strikes and the Isolated Mass: A Study of the Falsification of Sociological Knowledge." *Sociological Review* 25 (3): 551–574. doi:10.1111/j.1467-954X.1977.tb00304.x.

Edwards, P. K. 2015. "Industrial Relations, Critical Social Science and Reform: I and II." *Industrial Relations Journal* 46 (1 and 2): 173-86 and 275-92. doi:10.1111/irj.12097.

Human Relations. 2015. "Changing Work Labour and Employment Relations in China." *Special Issue* 68 (2): 181–326.

Hyman, R. 1972. *Strikes*. London: Fontana.

O'Mahoney, J. 2012. "Embracing Essentialism." *Organization* 19 (4): 723–741. doi:10.1177/1350508411420901.

Rodrik, D. 2015. *Economics Rules*. Oxford: OUP.

Sayer, A. 2000. *Realism and Social Science*. London: Sage.

Shorter, E., and C. Tilly. 1974. *Strikes in France, 1830-1968*. Cambridge: CUP.

Waller, R. J. 1983. *The Dukeries Transformed: The Social and Political Development of a Twentieth Century Coalfield*. Oxford: Clarendon.

Wright, M., and P. K. Edwards. 1998. "Does Teamworking Work and, if So, Why? A Case Study in the Aluminium Industry." *Economic and Industrial Democracy* 19 (1): 59–90. doi:10.1177/0143831X98191004.

Changing precarities in the Irish housing system: supplier-generated changes in security of tenure for domiciled households

Joe Finnerty and Cathal O'Connell

ABSTRACT
This article examines the changing landscape of precarity in the Irish housing system. The article explores, via desk-based research, supplier-generated changes to security of tenure for three household categories. The article concludes that to varying degrees across all tenures, supplier-generated precarity is evident in respect of access, security and supply. This supplier-generated precarity is the outcome of flawed policy assumptions and expectations on the part of the state, which has abandoned its commitment to direct social housing provision and market intervention.

Introduction

This article examines the changing landscape of precarity in the Irish housing system, focusing on supplier-generated changes in security of tenure for domiciled households. It builds on the authors' analyses of the Irish housing system and housing policy, by applying an analytical framework of risk and precarity. Based on reviews of policy and literature and on analysis of relevant housing statistics, the article explores supplier-generated impacts, and subsequent policy responses, to security of tenure/occupation, for three household categories: owner occupiers in long-term mortgage arrears; low- to middle-income households in the private rented sector; and households in new forms of social housing. In relation to social housing suppliers, the article argues that the increasing reliance on private landlordism dilutes the security of tenure for households in this sector. Fundamental shifts are also occurring in private housing. Further precarity and risk faces owner occupiers in severe mortgage arrears due to the increasing securitisation of mortgage loans. For low- to middle-income private rented tenants not in receipt of rent subsidy, their precarity is increased where their landlords' buy-to-let mortgages are in serious arrears, and where rents are being increased to capitalise on a chronic undersupply of new housing. A further twist is added by the fact that some of these indebted buy-to-let mortgages have been securitised and sold, sometimes to vulture funds with more interest in short-term capital appreciation than in professional landlordism or supplying long-term and secure rental accommodation. Some of these transformations in precarity can be traced to policy shifts dating back over two decades;

however, they have been given added impetus since the impact of the 2008 Global Financial Crisis on Irish economy and society, and the policies of austerity which were imposed in its wake.

The first part of the discussion will first clarify the links between precarity and housing, and discuss the importance of housing in welfare terms. After an overview of the housing and tenure system in Ireland in the second part, the article goes on in the third part to discuss the changing supplier-generated risks faced by three categories of Irish households, and where relevant, the policy buffers to manage these risks. It concludes with a brief consideration of the broader lessons which may have applications in other policy contexts.

Precarity and housing

It has been claimed by Wacquant that 'rampant social insecurity' is a key feature of society today, and indeed there is an extensive social science literature on insecurity, risk, precarity and casualisation in labour markets in particular but also in social protection and other domains (Wacquant 2008). Much of this literature claims that precarity and risk has increased – and/or has been shifted on to individuals and households and/or the state and away from business and capital and neoliberalism is widely seen as the key driver (Herrmann 2011). Hacker, for example, has identified a 'great risk shift' where individuals are becoming increasingly responsible for managing the risks of everyday life (Hacker 2008). This literature suggests that these risks in a variety of key social domains were previously absorbed at a systemic level by labour market regulation, social security provision and housing policy which made provision for the housing needs of the general population and targeted particular welfarebased housing at low income and other disadvantaged segments of the population (Garland 2016). Defenders of an opening to precarity, comprising *inter alia* restructuring of welfare state interventions, theorise it as a pragmatic, 'modernising' response – or embrace it as an explicitly ideological pro-market response – to globalisation, competitive pressures and constraints on public spending. In this view, 'flexibility' in a variety of social domains is viewed as a key virtue/requirement of the worker/household in the modern global economy (Friedman 2005).

The contested meaning and impact of increased risk and precarity has prompted more fine-grained analyses sensitive to mechanisms working to accelerate or buffer these economic, political and ideological forces and working at global, national and regional scales. (For an example, see Marr's (2015) study of exits from homelessness in Tokyo and Los Angeles.)

This article builds on previous analyses of precarity in the Irish housing system by the authors (Finnerty 2010; Finnerty and O'Connell 2014a; Finnerty and O'Connell 2014b; Finnerty, O'Connell, and O'Sullivan 2016). The metaphor of snakes and ladders was used to capture the changing housing landscape stratified according to degrees and trajectories of tenure security ('rungs' on a housing 'ladder') and characterised by different levels of precarity ('snakes') (Finnerty and O'Connell 2014a). The concepts of 'casualisation', 'dilution' and 'social housing offer' were used in subsequent analyses to focus on the less favourable social housing supports available by contrast with the traditional local authority housing offer (Finnerty and O'Connell 2014b; Finnerty, O'Connell, and O'Sullivan 2016).

Housing and well-being

Housing is a fundamental human need, addressing the unavoidable necessity for shelter and the basic requirement for a home (Fox 2007; Kenna 2011). As well as physical security, housing also contributes to psychological well-being by fulfilling a sense of personal space, autonomy and privacy. Security of occupancy, which contributes to subjective feelings of security regardless of tenure, is highly valued by households (Hulse and Milligan 2014). The concept of ontological security is also linked to home. Giddens refers to the

> confidence that most human beings have in the continuity of their self-identity and the constancy of their social and material environments. (Giddens 1991, 92)

Basic to a feeling of ontological security is a sense of the reliability of persons and things. Dupuis and Thorns (1998) assert that the home encompasses a bundle of attributes and as constant space it is the setting for day to day routines, it is a haven from surveillance and acts as a space which enables control and is integral in identity formation.

Deepening precarity in housing has multiple consequences at the level of households and society more broadly. According to Stahre, VanEenwyk, Siegel and Njai (2015), precarity in housing can lead to deepening stress and anxiety, undermine self-esteem and lead to the onset of wider mental health and well-being problems. It is not only adults who are affected, as unstable housing status can also impact more negatively on child welfare and development (Dockery et al. 2013; Finlay 2017; Murphy and Hearne 2017). A poorly functioning housing system will have profoundly negative consequences for households and for the wider economy and society. It will generate the risk of insecure or unsuitable housing arrangements, or will result in homelessness in the most extreme cases. Policy changes which alter the volume, source and conditions attached to social housing can also negatively impact on access and security of households and lead to greater levels of precarity in a policy area widely associated as concerned with security and stability. Given the importance of secure housing, several international bodies such as the UN (1948) and the Council of Europe (2000) have proposed that the goal of housing policy should be to ensure the provision of a sufficient quantity of affordable, secure accommodation that is in a reasonable state of repair and is located where people need it. Morgan (1996, 446, our emphases; also; Morgan 2009) suggests that 'this accommodation should be *secure* so it enables households to have a degree of *control* over their lives. It should enable people to express their *sense of identity* and provide those dependant on them with a *stable home*'.

In terms of risk and precarity manifested in increased insecurity of tenure and of occupancy, our analysis identifies three categories of domiciled households impacted by supplier issues: those in long-term mortgage arrears in owner-occupied housing, tenants in low- to middle-income sector employment in the private rented sector and low-income tenants in receipt of the current social housing offer. Households in the non-domiciled sector, i.e. those 'roofless' or 'houseless' (FEANTSA 2011), are not included in this analysis, nor are travellers living on halting sites or asylum-seekers in 'reception centres', nor are situations of domestic violence.

The following section examines the categories, trends and current distribution of Irish housing tenures, and goes on to discuss the changing supplier-generated risks faced by Irish households, and where relevant, the policy buffers to manage these risks.

Irish housing suppliers: categories, trends and current distribution

Domiciled households in Ireland live in one of four housing tenures: not-for-profit public housing, not-for-profit private housing, for-profit rented housing and owner-occupied housing. The four housing tenures have been the object of a range of direct and indirect interventions and supports by central and local government aimed at both housing production and consumption.

Figure 1 depicts the distribution of Irish households by tenure in the period between 1946 and 2016. The chart illustrates the fluctuations in owner occupation and private renting, with the former peaking and with the latter reaching a historic low market share in the early 1990s. It also shows how market share of social housing (defined as accommodation directly built and managed by local authorities and not-for-profit social landlords as opposed to a social housing offer of subsidised accommodation in the private market) has never risen above 20% of the total the reasons for which will be returned to later in the discussion. Currently, most Irish households (68%) live in owner-occupied housing, with 20% in the private-rented sector and 12% in social housing (Central Statistics Office 2017).

Owner-occupied housing

Owner-occupied housing has been the dominant tenure in the Irish housing system since the foundation of the Irish state in the 1922 and at its peak in the early 1990s

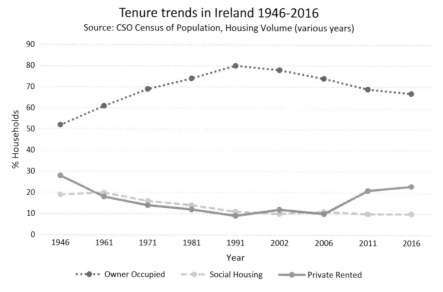

Figure 1. Tenure trends in Ireland 1946–2016.
Source: CSO Census of Population, Housing Volume (various years).

accounted for over 80% of the housing system. Its dominance over the other tenures was driven by its designation as the 'widely preferred form of tenure' (NESC 1988, 4) by the majority of households and was underpinned by a favourable policy regime such as state supports for house purchase, measures to encourage the transfer of dwellings from rental tenures into owner occupation and fiscal supports which have induced households into the sector and encouraged them to stay there (O'Connell 2005). There was also a relatively benign approach to mortgage arrears and households in difficulty could avail of state subsidies to help them meet repayments. Over the past two decades, there has been a scaling back of many of supports as the state has pursued tenure neutral policies and aspiring owner occupiers enter the market with far fewer supports than previous generations. Nonetheless, there is still a deeply rooted aspiration to ownership amongst the population despite the impact of the economic crash which has given rise to phenomena such as negative equity, mortgage arrears and the threat of repossession over a small minority of households.

Social housing

Direct and indirect government interventions in housing systems in advanced capitalist societies typically aim at contributing to the housing welfare of the population (amongst other objectives, such as stimulating economic activity) (Doling 1997). However, some interventions are more overtly 'welfarist' than others as they target the housing needs of low income-renting households. These households typically face insecurities and risks in the labour market such as low wages, temporary or part-time employment or other factors such as disability, long-term illness or old age which place them at a disadvantage in paying for housing from their own means. Social housing, historically understood as rental housing which is provided outside of normal market processes on a subsidised basis by not-for-profit landlords (Fahey 1999), potentially modifies the negative effects of market precarities on the quality, security and residential stability of the housing that such households consume. In recent years, the emergence of a more complex mix of social housing supports have given rise to the term 'social housing offer' to describe the range of interventions and supports to low-income households in the form of directly provided accommodation and also financial measures to assist households pay for housing in the private-rented sector on a long-term basis.

As noted above three categories of landlord – spanning three of the four housing tenures – are involved in the delivery of social housing/the social housing offer, namely local authorities, housing associations and private landlords (Finnerty and O'Connell 2014b). According to the Irish government's *Social Housing Strategy 2020*, the relative housing contribution of these suppliers is set to undergo change under new policy, with a greater emphasis on provision from housing associations [see 'Irish housing suppliers: categories, trends and current distribution' section] and private landlords through a shift to creating, 'flexible and responsive social housing supports' (DoECLG 2014c, 51).

Since the early 2000s, social housing offers from private for-profit and not-for-profit provision have dominated, in a hybrid and complex provision mix when compared to the previous phases (O'Connell 2007). The displacement of direct provision from local authorities and housing associations by private market-based suppliers was clearly signalled in 2009, as Ireland was grappling with a severe economic and fiscal crisis, when the Housing Minister stated that:

> We can no longer rely on the traditional acquisition and construction approach to meeting social housing needs. We must embrace every opportunity for delivering additional supply through market based mechanisms. (Finneran 2009)

This policy shift was given added impetus in the government *Housing Policy Statement* published in June 2011 which envisaged that

> A restructuring of the social housing investment programme to allow for the delivery of new social housing through more flexible funding models will provide key sources of delivery in the period ahead. (Department of Environment, Community and Local Government 2011, 2)

A further policy shift was signalled in the funding regime for social housing which impacted directly on the volume of direct provision by local authorities. Norris notes that the historical model of funding social housing in Ireland was based on long-term loans to local authorities which were repaid incrementally from rents collected from tenants and local authority contributions raised from commercial and domestic rates. It meant that even in economically difficult times, loans could be serviced and capital funding was never a barrier to new building. This regime prevailed until the 1980s when it was replaced by one based on capital grants from central government to local authorities to build social housing. As Norris observes, 'this meant that central government had to meet the full cost of buying or building social housing upfront in a lump sum which was not easily affordable' (Norris 2016, 236). The impact can be seen in the severe fall in output evident from the late 1980s onwards (see Figure 2). As a result of this shift in the funding model, the state became increasingly reliant on utilising the private rented sector to accommodate low-income households.

The cumulative impact of a changed funding model and the economic crisis of 2008 led to a drastic fall in capital-funded direct provision of social housing by local authorities and housing associations depicted in Figure 2. A modest recovery in provision

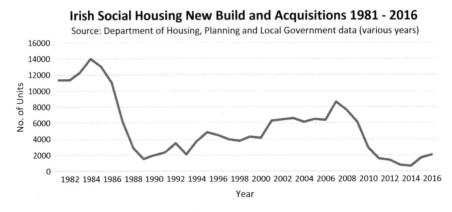

Figure 2. Irish social housing new build and acquisitions 1981–2016.
Source: Department of Housing, Planning and Local Government data (various years).

occurred in 2015, the bulk of which has occurred through local authority acquisitions in the property market rather than building new units.

In contrast, as Figure 3 illustrates, there has been a parallel growth in social housing offers based on current expenditure through the Rental Accommodation Scheme and the Long-Term Leasing Scheme. Both schemes draw heavily on the private rented sector as a source of accommodation and on the Supplementary Welfare Rent Allowance, a form of housing benefit, as a source of funding. A further scheme known as the Housing Assistance Payment (HAP) was introduced as a long-term housing support for households previously reliant on the rent allowance. These trends indicate that there has been a clear shift in emphasis in the nature of social housing policy, away from offers based on capital funded direct build by local authority and approved housing bodies (AHBs) towards offers based on renting and leasing properties sourced from the private market.

Private renting

Until the 1990s, private renting acted as a stepping stone tenure to social housing for many low-income households and a permanent destination for a very small and shrinking minority who mainly occupied rent-controlled dwellings (NESC 1988). By the start of the 1990s, its share of the housing system overall had fallen to 7% from approximately 18% in the early 1960s (Central Statistics Office 1997). Private renting began to grow during the following decades and by 2016 it accounted for a 20% share of the housing system (Central Statistics Office 2017). A combination of factors drove this growth including tax reliefs made available to investors under town and urban renewal schemes, house price inflation and rising rents which made residential property attractive to investors, and increased demand from private renters including a large share of households unable to access directly provided social housing from local authority or housing association landlords as a result of reductions in supply and aspiring home owners who could not access mortgages in the wake of the banking collapse.

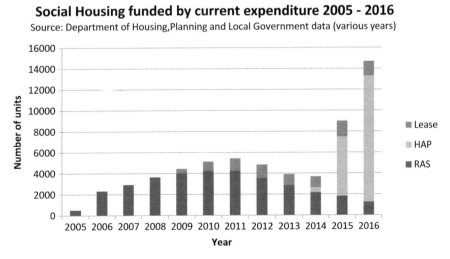

Figure 3. Social housing funded by current expenditure 2005–2016.

Source: Department of Housing, Planning and Local Government data (various years).

AHBs/housing associations

The early 1990s witnessed the emergence of not-for-profit housing association landlords. The primary policy impetus for this was the publication of *A Plan for Social Housing* (DoE 1991) and a follow-up policy document *Social Housing: The Way Ahead* (DoE 1995). *A Plan for Social Housing* presented an analysis of the range of methods by which the needs of low-income households could be met by AHBs in the voluntary and co-operative sector to complement the output of local authorities. A significant growth in visibility and activity in the sector ensued, with the number of registered AHBs or housing associations growing from 75 in the early 1980s to 470 by 2001. By 2016, the regulator for AHBs estimated the total stock of the sector to be approximately 27,000 units which represents approximately 20% of all social housing (Housing Agency Regulations Office 2016).

Households in precarity

In terms of supplier-generated risk and precarity manifested in increased insecurity of tenure and of occupancy, our analysis identifies three categories of domiciled households: (i) households in long-term mortgage arrears in owner-occupied housing; (ii) tenants in low-to- middle income sector employment in the private rented sector; (iii) low-income tenants in receipt of the current social housing offer.

Households in long-term mortgage arrears in owner-occupied housing

For the owner-occupied sector, the Irish housing crash had multiple consequences, the most serious and long-lasting of which was the incapacity of a proportion of households to maintain their mortgage repayments. The primary causes of mortgage arrears were falls in income due to unemployment and reduced working hours, cuts in wages and increases in taxes. For many households which had entered the housing market at its peak, borrowings were sustainable only on the basis of dual incomes so when one or both earners experienced a reduction or loss in earnings vulnerability to mortgage default was heightened. The scale and extent of this form of housing distress is evident in the data on arrears in respect of principal dwelling houses from the latter half of 2009 onwards. Data published by the Central Bank show that the total number of such arrears peaked at 143,851 in December 2012, before gradually reducing over the following number of years. By December 2016, the total number of mortgages in arrears had fallen to 77,500; however, over 40% (33,000) of these were classified as being in long-term arrears, i.e. 2 years or more in duration (Central Bank of Ireland 2017).

The question which arises from this trend is whether such arrear levels are generating what the authors have previously (Finnerty and O'Connell 2014a) referred to as 'snakes' in the housing system as they do in other countries, as measured by key indicators such as house repossessions and rising levels of homelessness. In other words, employing the metaphor of the children's board game, are vulnerable households sliding off the ladder of owner-occupation and down the snake of housing distress to repossession and homelessness? The evidence in Ireland to date regarding house repossessions suggests that the snake has not yet taken hold despite the upward overall trend since 2009. In the period from September 2009 to March 2017, a cumulative total of 7650 dwellings were repossessed by lenders by way of court orders or voluntary surrenders (Central Bank of Ireland 2017). Whether or not this level of repossessions has contributed to homelessness there is as yet no documented evidence (as most family homelessness appears to be generated by evictions from the private rented sector, discussed below). If households whose homes have been repossessed are able to afford to access the private rented sector, the additional demand which this represents will put extra pressure on the sector, especially in urban areas where it is already struggling to cope with demand, and this could lead to even further increases in rents, and ultimately to increases in homelessness.

Policy levers and safety nets

If the conditions for a 'snake' are present in the Irish housing system why has it not materialised to date in the form of mass repossessions? The explanations for this relate to market conditions and public policy levers, each of which is now looked at in turn.

Market conditions since the housing crash have not been conducive to banks repossessing homes as house prices have recovered slowly. However, with recent rises in house prices, evident especially in urban areas, it can be expected that the attitude of lenders will change as it is realised that repossessions can make inroads into arrears and yield returns on outstanding housing debt.

The public policy levers have taken the form of a 'code of conduct' on mortgage arrears issued by the Central Bank of Ireland and the establishment of a personal insolvency service. Under the Central Bank Code of Conduct, mortgage lenders are legally bound to put in place a Mortgage Arrears Resolution Process (MARP) and establish an Arrears Support Unit. Compliance with the Code involves adhering to a moratorium on repossession proceedings against households which fall into arrears so long as they are deemed to be co-operating with the resolution process. As a result, the repossession figures which have been recorded are attributable almost exclusively to foreign lenders who were not party to the State bank bailout, sub-prime lenders who lent money at very high interest rates to borrowers deemed to be too risky by mainstream banks and mainstream bailed-out banks where terms of existing agreements have not been adhered to by borrowers. Given the requirement under the Code of Conduct to put in place a MARP, financial institutions have to operate within a framework in their handling of cases and this has resulted in greater level of engagement when repayment difficulties arise or mortgages are identified as being vulnerable to going into arrears. Most evidently this appears in the form of loan accounts which have been subject to 'restructuring'. This includes a variety of arrangements including interest-only repayments, reduced instalments, loan-term extensions, arrears capitalisation, payment moratoria and deferred interest arrangements. While these arrangements may offer the appearances of a solution, it is questionable whether they will be long-term remedies in many cases, as they do not address the underlying problem of unsustainable debt. The other public policy lever is the personal insolvency service, which was established by the Government in 2012, and allows for the implementation of personal insolvency arrangements including secured debts such as mortgages. However, the personal insolvency provisions have been criticised as dealing with low numbers relative to the scale of the housing and general debt problem and because they give financial institutions a veto on any resolution arrangements. Amendments to the original legislation have been proposed to address this power imbalance.

A tidal wave of repossessions?

A question which arises is what will happen if and when the attitude of lenders changes in respect of mortgage arrears? The Central Bank of Ireland has revealed that 'non-bank entities' now control 45,638 mortgages in Ireland and almost 15,000 of those are held by unregulated loan owners such as foreign vulture funds. Many financial institutions regulated by the Central Bank of Ireland have sold non-performing loans to overseas investors in an effort to improve their balance sheets. The Central Bank has found that around 38% of mortgage accounts held by unregulated loan owners are in arrears of over 720 days, compared to just 19% of accounts held by retail credit firms and in the final quarter to December 2016, 455 dwellings were taken into possession which was the highest recorded since the onset of the financial crisis which suggests that the vulnerability of such households to proceedings for repossession is growing (Central Bank of Ireland 2017).

Households in low- to middle-income sector employment in the private rented sector

Shortcomings in relation to tenant security, the quality of accommodation and rental uncertainty have been endemic in the Irish private rented sector. The Housing Act 1992 was a preliminary attempt to address the most egregious problems in the sector (Ryall 1999; Galligan 2005). This legislation introduced limited reforms in the areas of quality of accommodation, provision of rent books and the requirement to register tenancies with a residential tenancies board and the establishment of minimum notice to quit periods. The private rented sector has been subject to more recent reforms aimed at introducing minimum standards and bolstering tenants' legal rights. Over the past decade, regulations for housing standards have been phased in to ensure that tenants have access to individual sanitary facilities, food preparation facilities and independently controlled heating to each bedsit unit (Government of Ireland 2017). Though the justification of minimum standards is self-evident, some property owners have argued that their impact has been to eliminate the 'bedsit' segment of the private rental market which was predominantly accessed by low-income households (e.g. single person households) without making provision for alternative supply at a time of severe competition for affordable accommodation especially in urban areas; however, there has been no empirical validation of this assertion (Irish Property Owners Association 2016).

Following the *Commission on the Private Rented Residential Sector* (2000), the *Residential Tenancies Act* of 2004 introduced significant legal improvements to the legal protections for private renters, particularly in relation to the 'Part IV' reforms in security of tenure. In essence, Part IV of the 2004 Act gives tenants who have observed the conditions of the lease during a six-month probationary period security of tenure for the remainder of a 4-year period, subject to certain qualifications, such as where the landlord is selling the property or where major renovation is to be carried out. In these cases of sale or renovation, the legislation requires a notice to quit period which lengthens depending on how much of the 4-year period has elapsed (Ryall 2012). Adjustments to Part IV have been introduced to extend the 4-year period to 6 years under the Planning and Development (Housing) and Residential Tenancies Act 2016. The 2016 legislation also introduced rent caps in designated Rent Pressure Zones where rents can be increased to a limit of 4% per annum and also introduced restrictions on terminating tenancies with 10 or more units in a development.

Despite these legislative measures, the available evidence indicates that insecurity of tenure is on the increase in this sector with the chief mechanisms being the capacity of landlords and financial institutions who acquire mortgages in arrears from banks to circumvent the tenant security measures to raise rents and terminate existing tenancies. However, there is also concern that a significant rise in repossessions from buy to let landlords who have gone into arrears will lead to greater tenant insecurity. A total of 14,518 properties which are in the buy-to-let sector are more than 2 years in arrears in mortgage repayments with arrears of more than €1.5 billion (Central Bank of Ireland 2017). Given the lack of supply of local authority housing, tenants who live in dwellings which are repossessed will likely have to turn to the private rented sector for new accommodation. However, increases in rents over the past number of years, particularly in the larger urban areas, have meant that low-income households, and especially those dependent on Rent Supplement, are unable to afford the rents being demanded.

Households in receipt of the current social housing offer: RAS, HAP, lease

Direct and indirect government interventions in housing systems in advanced capitalist societies typically aim at contributing to the housing welfare of the population (amongst other objectives, such as stimulating economic activity) (Doling 1997). However, some interventions are more overtly 'welfarist' than others as they target the housing needs of low-income renting households. These households typically face insecurities and risks in the labour market such as low wages, temporary or part-time employment or other factors which place them at a disadvantage in paying for housing from their own means such as disability, long-term illness or old age. Social housing or the more recently coined term 'social housing offer', understood as rental housing which is provided outside of normal market processes on a subsidised basis (Fahey 1999), potentially modifies the negative effects of market precarities on the quality, security and residential stability of such housing.

As noted above three categories of landlord – spanning three of the four housing tenures – are involved in the delivery of Irish social housing namely local authorities, AHBs also called housing associations, and private landlords whose tenants receive some form of rental subsidy (Finnerty and O'Connell 2014b). According to the Social Housing Strategy 2020, the relative housing contribution of the latter two suppliers is set to undergo change under new policy, with a greater emphasis on provision from housing associations discussed below and private landlords through a shift to creating, in an echo of Standing's (2011) description of the precariat, 'flexible and responsive social housing supports' (DoECLG 2014b, 51).

Until the early 1990s in Ireland social housing was almost exclusively anchored in the local authority sector and its overall market share had stabilised at around 10% after several decades of gradual decline. A local authority tenancy is the longest established form of social housing offer in Ireland, and these are legislated for under the 1966 Housing Act. Although a local authority could apply to the District Court to secure possession of a dwelling under Section 62 of the 1966 Act, occupancy was in practice viewed as being lifetime in duration, and there is currently no obligation on registered tenants to move dwellings if or when their household circumstances change (Kenna 2011). Local authority tenants are charged a differential rent calculated according to household income and it evident that there was a high degree of stability in rents charged as a percentage of total household expenditure. There was no probationary period for local authority tenant once a tenancy was established, and the tenancy succession by family members of the primary tenant was the norm. Tenants were also entitled to apply to purchase their dwellings on a generously discounted basis under successive right to buy schemes.

A qualification in relation to security of tenure was contained in a set of provisions of the 1997 Housing (Miscellaneous Provisions) Act allowing a local authority to issue an exclusion order to a named person on the grounds of anti-social behaviour (s3.2) or refuse or defer the making of a letting (s14). However, in practice, the 1997 measures have proved to be a convoluted and contested route to invoke to terminate tenancies in comparison to Section 62 of the Housing Act 1966 which is much more straightforward, and the 1997 legislation has been used only in extreme instances of criminality and anti-social behaviour. Research undertaken in the late 1990s showed that, apart from minority of failing estates, local authority housing was generally successful in offering secure settled accommodation to tenants (Fahey 1999).

Private renting is assuming a longer-term housing role for increasing numbers of low-income households and there are a number of aspects to this. First, the rent supplement scheme has unintentionally become a permanent housing support as many low-income households rely on it on an ongoing and long-term basis to meet their rent payments. A large proportion of rent supplement claims now extend beyond 1 year in duration which implies that the established trajectory towards permanent settled social housing is no longer occurring as it did when directly provided local authority housing was the main type of social housing offer.

In recognition that the original purpose of rent supplement as a short-term income support had effectively evolved into a long-term housing support, the Housing (Miscellaneous Provisions) Act 2014 provided for the replacement of rent supplement for long-term recipients by HAP and its administration will be transferred from the Department of Social Protection to local authority housing departments. Such payments will conform to the income-related rent setting scheme in operation for local authority tenants. Under the banner of 'tenure neutrality' this aims to effectively integrate that payment with the local authority differential rent scheme. However, an unwelcome aspect of the official interpretation of tenure neutrality is its giving effect to the kind of casualisation analysed in Finnerty et al. (2014b), as the HAP offer is deemed equivalent to the traditional local authority offer since households in receipt of the HAP are deemed to have their housing needs adequately met and will be removed from the local authority waiting list. A qualification to this is that while such households are not entitled to be on the social housing list, they are entitled to transfer their waiting time on the social housing waiting list to the housing transfer list, an option taken up by over 95% of HAP recipients which indicates their preference for 'traditional' social housing over options sourced in the private market.

Risk shift in the social housing offer

The question arises as to whether the changed social housing offer is a short term but reversible aberration arising from the austerity measures imposed in the aftermath of the financial crash from 2008 onwards or a structural departure from historic role of the state as a direct provider of homes to low-income households? An analysis of long-term policy trends and data suggests the latter, as direct provision by local authorities has been falling for over two decades in real and relative terms while the output levels of AHBs have remained modest.

Over the past decade the shift away from capital investment in social housing by local authorities and AHBs has become pronounced as new supply is almost total reliant on turn key acquisitions by local authorities and AHBs under the Capital Assistance Scheme.

This long-term decline in direct provision of accommodation contrasts with the growth based on the private market as leasing and renting from private landlords now outweighs direct provision by social landlords as the main source of social housing offers (Figure 3). An effect of the risk shift in social housing has been the creation of a sliding scale of social housing offers which are defined not by household needs but by who supplies the accommodation, and by what financial mechanism it is paid for. At the top of this scale is social housing provided by a local authority which is qualitatively stronger than any of the others especially in respect of security and affordability and inheritance. This is followed by a tenancy with AHB which equates with a local authority tenancy except for inheritance rights though these are destined to be diluted over time as tenancies in the AHB sector are realigned with tenancies in the private rented sector. Currently there is a clear distinction between offers made by non-market suppliers and offers sourced from suppliers in the private market. The latter do not equate to the former in terms of security, rent certainty or inheritance with the result that the overall social housing offer regime now varies according to when households presented with a housing need with established tenants of local authorities enjoying the most secure and least precarious tenancies and newly presenting applicants facing fare less attractive prospects in private renting.

Conclusion

This article set out to examine whether supplier-generated precarity and insecurity has emerged over the past two decades in the respective tenures which comprise the Irish housing system. It concludes that to varying degrees across all tenures, supplier-generated precarity is evident in respect of access, security and supply. This supplier-generated precarity is the outcome of flawed policy assumptions and expectations on the part of the state which has abandoned its historic, albeit pragmatic, commitment to direct social housing provision and market intervention. In social housing, the cumulative effect of the long-term policy changes dating from the early 1990s and compounded by the economic crisis of 2008 has been the collapse of local authority provision, historically the most secure form of social housing. This collapse has been predicated on a conscious policy preference favouring not for profit and private market suppliers to meet social housing needs. Neither of these sources has proven up to the task set for them. Capital investment by AHBs has not reached the levels anticipated by government policy and its performance illustrates clear capacity limits. Despite the role expected of it in social housing policy, the private market has effectively rejected the complexities of a state-subsidised hybrid social housing in preference for more profitable free market opportunities. Furthermore, low-income and medium-income households in the private rented sector who do not qualify for state subsidies face an increasingly competitive housing environment where legislative reforms aimed at strengthening security are systematically undermined by landlords. Supplier-generated precarity is also evident in the other tenures. In the owner-occupied sector, households which fall into arrears with their mortgage repayments are more likely to face proceedings for repossession of their homes than they did in previous years. This is because social policy levers restraining lender behaviour were phased out and lightly regulated vulture funds have acquired the non-performing loans of home owners and private landlords from financial institutions.

The most salient lesson the Irish case offers which may have wider application concerns matters of policy formation and implementation. Policy reformers must recognise that the environment in which major policy adjustment occurs is shaped by historical and contemporary factors that must be taken into account when changes are being devised and implemented. In the case of Irish housing policy, the long term shift away from direct provision of social housing by local authorities (i.e. the historical context) since the early 1990s was based on overly optimistic assumptions about the capacity of alternatives sources (AHBs and private market suppliers) to deliver social housing. AHBs have clear capacity limits on how much they can or want to expand to meet social housing needs, while the private market has clearly signalled that it prefers to accommodate profitable minimally regulated tenancies from unsubsidised households. In relation to the owner occupier sector, policymakers made unrealistic assumptions about the capacity of light touch regulation to ensure a well-functioning system of credit for the Irish mortgage market where that market was exposed to global actors and the process of financialisation. Where policymakers make overly optimistic assumptions about reform, the impact on housing welfare and the potential for negative impacts is substantial as evidenced above in relation to precarity and insecurity of tenure for the three categories of household discussed. Furthermore, policy reformers must be cognisant of the potential for unforeseen events such as economic crisis and market and system failure, or they may well end up with a self-inflicted perfect storm, as the Irish case demonstrates, caused by the abandonment of historically effective policies and the failure of their replacements.

Disclosure statement

No potential conflict of interest was reported by the authors.

References

Central Bank of Ireland. 2017. "Residential Mortgage Arrears and Repossessions Statistics: Q1 2017." Statistical Release 8th June 2017. Dublin: Central Bank of Ireland.
Central Statistics Office. 1997. *Census of Population 1991, Volume 10, Housing*. Cork: CSO.
Central Statistics Office. 2017. *Census 2016 Profile 1 - Housing in Ireland*. Cork: CSO.

Commission on the Private Rented Residential Sector. 2000. *Report of the Commission on the Private Rented Residential Sector*. Dublin: Stationery Office.
Council of Europe. 2000. "Recommendation No. R 3 of the Committee of Ministers to the Member States on the Right to the Satisfaction of Basic Material Needs of Persons in Situations of Extreme Hardship." http://fra.europa.eu/fraWebsite/frc2011/docs/CoE-standards-hr-protection-irreg-migrants.pdf.
Department of Environment. 1991. *A Plan for Social Housing*. Dublin: Department of the Environment.
Department of Environment. 1995. *Social Housing: The Way Ahead*. Dublin: Department of the Environment.
Department of Environment, Community and Local Government. 2011. "Housing Policy Statement." http://www.environ.ie/en/DevelopmentHousing/Housing/PublicationsDocuments/FileDownLoad,26867,en.pdf.
Department of Environment, Community and Local Government. 2014a. "Government Approves Publication of Housing Bill." http://www.environ.ie/en/DevelopmentHousing/Housing/News/MainBody,37939,en.htm.
Department of Environment Community and Local Government. 2014b. "Social Housing Strategy 2020." http://www.environ.ie/en/Publications/DevelopmentandHousing/Housing/FileDownLoad,39622,en.pdf.
Department of Environment, Community and Local Government. 2014c. "Social Housing Strategy 2020: Support, Supply and Reform." http://www.housing.gov.ie/sites/default/files/publications/files/social_strategy_document_20141126.pdf.
Dockery, M., R. Ong, S. Colquhoun, J. Li, and G. Kendall 2013. "Housing and Children's Development and Wellbeing: Evidence from Australian Data." AHURI Final Report No. 201. Melbourne: Australian Housing and Urban Research Institute. https://www.ahuri.edu.au/research/final-reports/201.
Doling, J. 1997. *Comparative Housing Policy*. London: Macmillan.
Dupuis, A., and D. C. Thorns. 1998. "Home, Home Ownership and the Search for Ontological Security." *The Sociological Review* 46 (1): 24–47. doi:10.1111/1467-954X.00088.
Fahey, T. 1999. "Introduction." In *Social Housing in Ireland: Success, Failure and Lessons Learned*, edited by T. Fahey. Dublin: Oaktree Press.
FEANTSA 2011. "Updated European Typology on Homelessness and Housing Exclusion." http://www.feantsa.org/en/toolkit/2017/09/11/updated-ethos-typology-on-homelessness-and-housing-exclusion.
Finlay, F. 2017. "Launch of Respond Family Hub." https://vimeo.com/209909593.
Finneran, M. 2009. "Ministerial Address to Irish Council for Social Housing Annual Conference." www.icsh.ie/eng/news/2011_biennial_national_social_housing_conference_housing_ireland.
Finnerty, J. 2010. "A New Model of Social Housing?" *Cornerstone* 42: 11–13.
Finnerty, J., and C. O'Connell. 2014a. "Housing Ladders and Snakes: An Examination of Changing Residential Tenure Trajectories in the Republic of Ireland." In *Contemporary Housing Issues in a Globalized World*, edited by P. Kenna, 251–266. Farnham: Ashgate.
Finnerty, J., and C. O'Connell. 2014b. "50 Years of the Social Housing 'Offer' in Ireland: The Casualisation Thesis Examined." In *Public and Private Renting in Ireland*, edited by L. Sirr. Dublin: IPA.
Finnerty, J., C. O'Connell, and S. O'Sullivan. 2016. "Social Housing Policy and Provision: A Changing Regime?" In *The Irish Welfare State in the Twenty First Century: Challenges and Change*, edited by M. Murphy and F. Dukelow. Basingstoke: Palgrave Macmillan.
Fox, L. 2007. *Conceptualising Home: Theories, Laws and Policies*. Oxford: Hart Publishing.
Friedman, T. 2005. *The World Is Flat: A Brief History of the Twenty-First Century*. New York: Farrar, Straus and Giroux.
Galligan, Y. 2005. "The Irish Private Rented Sector." In *Housing Contemporary Ireland*, edited by M. Norris and D. Redmond. Dublin: IPA.
Garland, D. 2016. *The Welfare State: A Very Short Introduction*. Oxford: Oxford University Press.

Giddens, A. 1991. *Modernity and Self-Identity: Self and Society in the Late Modern Age*. Stanford: Stanford University Press.

Government of Ireland. 2017. *S.I. No. 17/2017 - Housing (Standards for Rented Houses) Regulations 2017*. Dublin: Stationery Office.

Hacker, J. 2008. *The Great Risk Shift: The New Economic Insecurity and the Decline of the American Dream*. Oxford: Oxford University Press.

Herrmann, P. 2011. "Precarity: Fundamental System Change or Only a New Form of Poverty: An Introduction." In *Precarity – More than a Challenge of Social Security Or: Cynicism of EU's Concept of Economic Freedom*, edited by P. Herrmann and S. Kalaycioglu. Bremen: Verlag.

Housing Agency Regulations Office. 2016. "The Regulation of Approved Housing Bodies (AHBs) in Ireland 2015." *Annual Report and Sectoral Analysis*. https://www.housingagency.ie/Regulation/Regulatory-Structure/Regulation-Office.

Hulse, K., and V. Milligan. 2014. "Secure Occupancy: A New Framework for Analysing Security in Rental Housing." *Housing Studies* 29: 5. doi:10.1080/02673037.2013.873116.

Irish Property Owners Association. 2016. "Submission to the Oireachtas Housing Committee." Accessed May 2016. http://www.oireachtas.ie/parliament/oireachtasbusiness/committees_list/housingplanningandlocalgovernment/.

Kenna, P. 2011. *Housing Rights, Law and Policy*. Dublin: Clarus.

Marr, M. 2015. *Better Must Come: Exiting Homelessness in Two Global Cities*. Ithaca: Cornell University Press.

Morgan, J. 1996. "The Casualisation of Housing." *Journal of Social Welfare and Family Law* 18 (4): 445–460. doi:10.1080/09649069608410189.

Morgan, J. 2009. "Housing and Security in England and Wales: Casualisation Revisited." *International Journal of Law in the Built Environment* 1 (1): 42–58. doi:10.1108/17561450910950241.

Murphy, M., and R. Hearne. 2017. *Investing in the Right to Home: Housing, HAP and Hubs*. Maynooth: National University of Ireland.

(NESC) National Economic and Social Council. 1988. *A Review of Housing Policy*. Dublin: NESC.

Norris, M. 2016. *Property, Family and the Irish Welfare State*. London: Palgrave MacMillan.

O'Connell, C. 2005. "The Housing Market and Owner Occupation in Ireland." In *Housing Contemporary Ireland: Policy, Society and Shelter*, edited by M. Norris and D. Redmond. Dublin: Institute of Public Administration.

O'Connell, C. 2007. *The State and Housing in Ireland: Ideology, Policy and Practice*. New York: Nova.

Ryall, A. 1999. "A Review of Housing Legislation since 1992." In *Private Rented Housing: Issues and Options*. Dublin: Threshold.

Ryall, A. 2012. "Strengthening the Regulation of Residential Tenancies: Revision of Residential Tenancies Acts 2004 and 2009." *Conveyancing and Property Law Journal* 17 (4): 74.

Stahre, M., J. VanEenwyk, P. Siegel, and R. Njai. 2015. *Housing Insecurity and the Association with Health Outcomes and Unhealthy Behaviors, Preventing Chronic Distress*. Washington State. doi:10.5888/pcd12.140511.

Standing, G. 2011. *The Precariat*. London: Bloomsbury Academic.

United Nations. 1948. "Universal Declaration of Human Rights." http://www.un.org/en/universal-declaration-human-rights/index.html.

Wacquant, L. 2008. *Urban Outcasts: A Comparative Sociology of Advanced Marginality*. Cambridge: Polity.

REPLY

Understanding housing precarity: more than access to a shelter, housing is essential for a decent life

Kelly Greenop

This is a reply to:
Finnerty, Joe and C. O'Connell. 2017. "Changing precarities in the Irish housing system: supplier-generated changes in security of tenure for domiciled households." *Global Discourse* 7 (4): 473–488. https://doi.org/10.1080/23269995.2017.1399708

Joe Finnerty and Cathal O'Connell's paper 'Changing precarities in the Irish housing system: supplier-generated changes in security of tenure for domiciled households' (2017) is a careful analysis of changing Irish housing policy settings in recent decades, that sheds rare light on the specific policy mechanisms which increase housing precarity. While examining the Irish system specifically, the observation of policies directly affecting housing precarity reflects a global trend towards precarity which is both worrying and drives us to consider its long-term consequences and remedies.

Finnerty and O'Connell unmask common housing policy terms such as 'flexibility' and 'market-based mechanisms', as ultimately serving banks and investors, far more than residents, as they draw together the dispersed statistics to demonstrate the policies' effects. Precarity is the key term of analysis because of its focus on residents themselves and their circumstances rather than a focus on economics and finance. While a precarity analysis is not unique to Finnerty and O'Connell, indeed, precarity is a key term across academic and activist discourses, to which Finnerty and O'Connell refer, maintaining a focus on how policies affect people is vital if we are to see the policy changes required to alleviate human suffering and prevent the perpetuation of disadvantage.

Here, I address some issues raised by, but not within the scope of, Finnerty and O'Connell's analysis: In what other locations does housing precarity exist and within the housing precariat, who are the most vulnerable? If certain policies cause housing precarity to be worsened, what are the possible effects? What might be the opposite of housing precarity, what policies could lead to this and what evidence is there for their efficacy? Being an Australian-based researcher, I will use examples from Australia, and elsewhere, to expand the discussion beyond Ireland and read in the wider implications of growing housing insecurity.

Establishing the extent of housing precarity in Ireland and beyond

Unsurprisingly, housing precarity is not unique to Ireland, and is an increasing problem around the world (for example, Dwyer and Phillips Lassus (2015) in the USA; Smith (2014) in China; Colic-Peisker, Ong, and Wood (2015) in Australia; and Vasudevan (2015) looking globally).

Housing precarity, Finnerty and O'Connell argue, is one of the steps towards what they describe as a 'snake' – analogous to a 'snakes and ladders' game of housing – contrasted with a 'ladder' of opportunity towards better housing. This concept aligns with descriptions of homelessness into which extreme housing precarity can be categorised, as secondary or tertiary homelessness. Secondary homelessness is experienced when people must stay with friends or family through lack of other accommodation; while tertiary homelessness is experienced where people are not roofless but have no security of tenure, for example long-term boarding house accommodation (Chamberlain and MacKenzie 2008:vii). On the housing precarity spectrum, these forms of homelessness are part of the slide down the snake, and the housing 'ladder' becomes more difficult to access and risks to housing security increase. Finnerty and O'Connell provide compelling evidence of the specific policies that increase these risks.

Who are the most vulnerable within the housing precariat?

Like Ireland and many other countries, inequality within Australian society is growing (UN Sytems Task Team 2012), as is housing precarity. What is important to tease out within these contexts is which specific categories of people are most vulnerable, and therefore in need of targeted housing policies.

Australian Indigenous people are at particular risk of housing precarity: they are discriminated against by landlords, real estate agents and neighbours, 35% of Indigenous people reporting discrimination in their housing (Ferdinand, Paradies, and Kelaher 2013). Indigenous Australians are less likely to be able to afford their own homes than the rest of the population, and often rely on State Housing. Australian government investment in directly owned state housing has diminished over decades and has become increasingly residualised (Morris 2015), and has become housing only for those with 'the greatest need'. Anecdotally, waiting times are typically over 5 years long in parts of Australia. As a result, people face crowding in with family members, who may then be at risk of breaching their own rental agreements, or undertake other risky coping strategies (Memmott, Birdsall-Jones, and Greenop 2012). For Indigenous people who do have homes, they are more often of poorer quality, and lower proximity to employment, education and health services (Pink and Allbon 2008). While urban Indigenous people's housing is generally better than that in the most remote areas, both remote and urban Indigenous people remain at a substantial housing disadvantage compared with non-Aboriginal people (Memmott, Birdsall-Jones, and Greenop 2012).

In Australia, an emerging vulnerable category is older women, now recognised as being increasingly at risk of homelessness. As women age and some become single – through widowhood, or separation and divorce – their previous two-income household is lost, and increasing numbers of women find that they cannot afford private rental or mortgage payments on a single income (Petersen and Parsell 2015; Petersen 2015). A report by Homelessness Australia states 'One of the most disadvantaged demographic profiles for a person to have is to be old, single, poor, female and in private rental accommodation' (Homelessness Australia 2015).

Another group precariously housed in Australia is that of young people aged 18–35. Their rate of homeownership has been dramatically reduced in recent years as incomes have stagnated and housing prices have escalated (HILDA Report 2017, 88). Many live still with their family of origin – seeing them unfairly accused of enjoying an extended adolescence – but also many live precarious housing lives in privately rented accommodation, often shared with relative strangers and subject to housing discrimination and poor terms. As housing purchase is one of the main paths to wealth accumulation in Australia, delaying or not participating in this housing 'ladder' will have future society-wide consequences. Targeted policy changes are needed to address housing precarity for older women, Indigenous people, migrants, people of colour, young people and other vulnerable groups.

Consequences of housing precarity: lessons from history and the globe

An important factor to bear in mind when discussing housing precarity is its broader implications, which are addressed by research that examines the effects of financial disadvantage identifying poverty, violence and family dysfunction, but the stability of housing itself is also a major factor in being able to access services and form supportive networks especially for culturally and linguistically diverse groups. Moving residence often breaks these networks, and this can lead to isolation and further disadvantage (Johnstone et al. 2016). We know from research that childhood disadvantage can last a lifetime and take various forms (Murayama et al. 2017; Kallio, Kauppinen, and Erola 2017; Marsland 2017) and that protective factors include having attentive and engaged parents and carers, who are not continually preoccupied with survival and solving fundamental issues such as housing stability. This should be in front of the mind for policymakers: removing housing stability factors has flow-on costs in terms of educational achievement for children, mental and physical health for entire families, and results in the failure of people to reach their potential. This affects the whole of society, as well as being a personal tragedy for individuals affected.

A global and historical perspective on housing is also enlightening to this discussion. Informal settlements are increasing globally (Beattie, Mayer, and Yildirim 2010), the result of a complex set of factors including migration to cities which increases urbanisation, unaffordable housing within those rapidly growing cities and global financial markets influencing both city shapes and land values. These slums and shanties are far below current Western standards and represent situations much worse than faced by those in the West, often lacking running water, electricity, security of tenure or access to municipal services like garbage collection. Yet some slum dwellers are still compelled to participate in the formal, market economy despite their informal housing status (Härmä 2013). In other words, the market does not care where people are housed, only that they are available as labour. Once living within informal housing, transitioning people to decent housing is difficult without government or institutional intervention and this is considered one of the world's 'wicked problems'.

The century of growth and social progress in the West may seem to be part of an inevitable upward trajectory, but historical perspectives from within the 20th Century tell us that this trajectory itself may be precarious. Harry Leslie Smith's memoirs describe his childhood life of poverty in 1920s Yorkshire, and flesh out the impact of severe poverty and an insecure existence. In the West too, people have lived lives of extreme poverty, within living memory.

> As a child and teenager, I never felt secure in my housing or whether I'd be able to get a decent meal at the end of the day. The tenement we fled to in Barnsley in 1927 was smaller than the hovel we had left just one hurried step ahead of the bailiff…In truth, the house we moved into was no better than a stall for an animal in a poor farmer's paddock. That we were forced to live this way in the past was unjust, but if you don't think it is happening in today's Britain, think again. (Smith 2017)

A chilling housing example in our times already exists through *Poor Kids*, the 2006 BBC documentary (BBCTV 2006) that gave voice to, and vision of, the poorest children in Britain. This film documented the structural inequalities that perpetuated poverty across generations, poverty that at the time was being endured by 3.5 million children in Britain. Housing was a key element shown in this documentary: mould-infested tower blocks causing serious health consequences, power to the home affordable only for limited times, lack of basic cooking, bedding and studying furnishings. Their lives were – and are – defined by their precarious financial and therefore housing circumstances.

A glance at the YouTube comments on clips from the *Poor Kids* video indicates that many people still believe that poverty is a choice, drug addiction can be overcome through willpower rather than health services, and that many people fall into the category of the 'undeserving poor'. This term is a hangover from 19th Century attitudes about morality and poverty based in an unwillingness to work and a lack of moral fibre (Katz 2013). Finnerty and O'Connell's analysis demonstrates that, on the contrary, structural forces operate to put housing out of reach, and there is clear evidence of the role this plays in entrenching poverty.

What is the opposite of housing precarity and what can it teach us?

The UN Universal Declaration of Human Rights (UN 1948) inscribes housing as an essential human right in Article 25, but it is seldom used as a call for direct action to provide these important rights. Yet we know that there is a real price paid by those who experience housing precarity and homelessness. The costs to society at large and people individually both economically and in terms of opportunity cost are significant. The opposite of housing precarity is housing security. In the USA, Australia and other places, small forays into 'Housing First' programs have been made in recent decades. These programs provide unconditional housing for primary homeless (roofless) people, in (often purpose built, good quality) social housing where they are securely tenanted, as well as able to access to a range of optional social, health and community supports. The false binary of the 'deserving' and 'undeserving' poor can impinge on attitudes about the ethical value of these programmes which do not require a prior show of compliance to sobriety or other requirements. But recent work in Australia has evaluated the cost savings of these Housing First programs, and they work. Housing people who were previously sleeping rough, in decent accommodation, is cheaper than servicing them living on the streets (Parsell, Petersen, and Culhane 2017), reinforcing existing data from the USA (Culhane 2008; Wright et al. 2016). While I also strongly agree that housing (like health care and education) is a fundamental human right, it is important to stress – to policymakers in particular – that we all benefit when we all advance access to these essential rights for all.

It would seem then that ideological or moral factors may be at play in determining housing policies across much of the West, where the role of housing more recently is emphasised in its role as providing investment opportunity rather than as the provision of shelter within a community. Policies and market settings that produce less secure, less affordable housing – such as the case in Ireland – seem to be driving people out of the spending middle class, which is an overall negative for economies. Parsell and Jones point out that even 'those not convinced by the moral necessity to address homelessness could support government policy to address homelessness on the basis that doing otherwise is financially irresponsible' (Parsell and Jones 2014, 434). I would argue that housing precarity is also worthy of such policy attention, in order to prevent the stepping towards the risky 'snakes' that Finnerty and O'Connell identify, lest we return to chronic housing shortage and deeper intergenerational disadvantage, hampering the possibilities for future generations.

Disclosure statement

No potential conflict of interest was reported by the author.

ORCID

Kelly Greenop http://orcid.org/0000-0003-2145-5277

References

BBCTV. 2006. Poor Kids. J. Neumann (Director).
Beattie, N., C. Mayer, and A. B. Yildirim. 2010. *Incremental Housing: Solutions to Meet the Global Urban Housing Challenge Network Session*. Brazil: Global University Consortium, SIGUS-MIT UN World Urban Forum. http://web.mit.edu/incrementalhousing/WUF-Rio/pdfs/networkSessionSUMMARY.pdf.
Chamberlain, C., and D. MacKenzie. 2008. "Counting the Homeless, Australia, 2006." ABS Catalogue No. 2050.0. Canberra: Australia Bureau of Statistics, Commonwealth of Australia.
Colic-Peisker, V., R. Ong, and G. Wood. 2015. "Asset Poverty, Precarious Housing and Ontological Security in Older Age: An Australian Case Study." *International Journal of Housing Policy* 15 (2): 167–186. doi:10.1080/14616718.2014.984827.
Culhane, D. 2008. "The Cost of Homelessness: A Perspective from the United States." *European Journal of Homelessness* 2: 97–114.
Dwyer, R., and L. Phillips Lassus. 2015. "The Great Risk Shift and Precarity in the U.S. Housing Market." *The ANNALS of the American Academy of Political and Social Science* 660 (1): 199–216. doi:10.1177/0002716215577612.

Ferdinand, A., Y. Paradies, and M. Kelaher. 2013. *Mental Health Impacts of Racial Discrimination in Victorian Aboriginal Communities: The Localities Embracing and Accepting Diversity (LEAD) Experiences of Racism Survey*. Melbourne: Lowitja Institute.

Finnerty, J., and C. O'Connell. 2017. "Changing Precarities in the Irish Housing System: Supplier-Generated Changes in Security of Tenure for Domiciled Households." *Global Discourse* 7 (4) : 473–488. doi: 10.1080/23269995.2017.1399708.

Härmä, J. 2013. "Access or Quality? Why Do Families Living in Slums Choose Low-Cost Private Schools in Lagos, Nigeria?" *Oxford Review of Education* 39 (4): 548–566. doi:10.1080/03054985.2013.825984.

Homelessness Australia. 2015. "Ending and Preventing Older Women's Experiences of Homelessness in Australia, Joint Submission of Homelessness Australia and Equality Rights Alliance to the Economic Security of Older Women Inquiry." http://www.homelessnessaustralia.org.au/sites/homelessnessaus/files/2017-07/Economic_Security_of_Older_Women_Inquiry.pdf.

Johnstone, M., C. Parsell, J. Jetten, G. Dingle, and Z. Walter. 2016. "Breaking the Cycle of Homelessness: Housing Stability and Social Support as Predictors of Long-Term Well-Being." *Housing Studies* 31 (4): 410–426. doi:10.1080/02673037.2015.1092504.

Kallio, V. J., T. M. Kauppinen, and J. Erola. 2017. "Intergenerational Accumulation of Social Disadvantages across Generations in Young Adulthood." *Research in Social Stratification and Mobility* 48: 42–52. doi:10.1016/j.rssm.2017.02.001.

Katz, M. B. 2013. *The Undeserving Poor America's Enduring Confrontation with Poverty*. Oxford: Oxford University Press.

Marsland, A. L. 2017. "The Cost of Childhood Disadvantage for Future Generations." *Brain, Behavior, and Immunity* 65: 9–10. doi:10.1016/j.bbi.2017.06.004.

Memmott, P., C. Birdsall-Jones, and K. Greenop. 2012. *Australian Indigenous House Crowding*. Melbourne: Australian Housing and Urban Research Institute.

Morris, A. 2015. "The Residualisation of Public Housing and Its Impact on Older Tenants in Inner-City Sydney, Australia." *Journal of Sociology* 51 (2): 154–169. doi:10.1177/1440783313500856.

Murayama, H., T. Fujiwara, Y. Tani, A. Amemiya, Y. Matsuyama, Y. Nagamine, and K. Kondo. 2017. "Long-Term Impact of Childhood Disadvantage on Late-Life Functional Decline among Older Japanese: Results from the JAGES Prospective Cohort Study." *The Journals of Gerontology: Series A*. doi:10.1093/gerona/glx171.

Parsell, C., and A. Jones. 2014. "Bold Reform or Policy Overreach Australia's Attack on Homelessness: 2008–2013." *International Journal of Housing Policy* 14 (4): 427–443. doi:10.1080/14616718.2014.967923.

Parsell, P., M. Petersen, and D. Culhane. 2017. "Cost Offsets of Supportive Housing: Evidence for Social Work." *The British Journal of Social Work* 47 (5): 1534–1553. doi:10.1093/bjsw/bcw115.

Petersen, M. 2015. "Addressing Older Women's Homelessness: Service and Housing Models." *Australian Journal of Social Issues* 50 (4): 419–438. doi:10.1002/(ISSN)1839-4655.

Petersen, M., and C. Parsell. 2015. "Homeless for the First Time in Later Life: An Australian Study." *Housing Studies* 30 (3): 368–391. doi:10.1080/02673037.2014.963522.

Pink, B., and P. Allbon. 2008. "The Health and Welfare of Australia's Aboriginal and Torres Strait Islander Peoples 2008." ABS Catalogue No. 4704.0. Canberra: Australian Bureau of Statistics

Smith, H. L. 2017. *Don't Let My Past Be Your Future*. London: Little, Brown Book Group.

Smith, N. R. 2014. "Living on the Edge: Household Registration Reform and Peri-Urban Precarity in China." *Journal of Urban Affairs* 36: 369–383. doi:10.1111/juaf.12107.

UN Systems Task Team. 2012. "Addressing Inequalities: The Heart of the Post-2015 Agenda and the Future We Want for All." UN Systems Task Team on the Post-2015 UN development agenda. New York: United Nations Systems Task Team.

United Nations (UN). 1948. "The Universal Declaration of Human Rights." http://www.un.org/en/universal-declaration-human-rights/.

Vasudevan, A. 2015. "The Makeshift City: Towards a Global Geography of Squatting." *Progress in Human Geography* 39 (3): 338–359. doi:10.1177/0309132514531471.

Wilkins, R. 2017. *The Household, Income and Labour Dynamics in Australia (HILDA) Survey: Selected Findings from Waves 1 to 15*. Melbourne: Applied Economic & Social Research Institute, The University of Melbourne.

Wright, B., K. Vartanian, H. Li, N. Royal, and J. Matson. 2016. "Formerly Homeless People Had Lower Overall Health Care Expenditures after Moving into Supportive Housing." *Health Affairs* 35 (1): 20–27. doi:10.1377/hlthaff.2015.0393.

Precarious living in liminal spaces: neglect of the Gypsy–Traveller site

Joanna Richardson

ABSTRACT
Gypsy and Traveller sites are precarious and liminal spaces to live. Insufficient in number and below standard in management and maintenance, the impact can result in poorer health and education outcomes, but also reduced community cohesion in society where conflicts occur over perceived values of spaces and of people. This article explores the precarious lives of Gypsies and Travellers who pursue a nomadic or semi-nomadic lifestyle and seeks to show how neglected or insufficient accommodation impacts on their perceived identity and exclusion. It examines the problems created by the neglect of the Gypsy–Traveller site and attempts to develop a framework for better understanding the precarity of such groups, who are seen to be different because of the spaces they inhabit. In developing a more nuanced framework of precariousness, particularly focusing on the overlap of relative and perceived precarity in liminal spaces, the article highlights the marginal position of Gypsies and Travellers resident on sites and suggests that control is still exercised by the state over these 'ghetto-like' spaces, sometimes through neglect and sometimes through a move towards 'mainstreaming' management. The article helps to develop an understanding of Gypsy–Traveller site management, marginalisation and control, through the lens of precarity and within a frame of emerging theoretical concepts of the ghetto.

Introduction

Many Gypsies and Travellers live in precarious situations. Those on the roadside and in unauthorised encampments can sometimes be located in dangerous places, close to traffic or subject to surveillance, hostility and eviction (Richardson 2006). For Travellers who live on local authority or housing association sites, these are often in marginalised spaces on the outskirts of settled communities close to railway lines, sewage works or rubbish dumps – locations where there was least objection when the sites were originally planned – and they can be perceived as marginal spaces by the wider community. Those Gypsies and Travellers who have bought their own land and built a site, but who have not got the required planning permission, are subject to conflict with the local authority and judgement by planning inspectors; sometimes being given temporary permission after temporary permission – stability and security of accommodation hanging in the balance. Some Gypsies and Travellers have their own sites with full planning permission, but even then there is a precariousness of acceptance and inclusion by their local community and more so in wider societal, political and media discourse.

Insufficient accommodation results in poorer outcomes and lower levels of community cohesion. There has been structured repression of Gypsy and Traveller culture through lack of accommodation for years: 'Repression has taken many forms, from murder to displacement to various measures of assimilation and sedentarization' (Kabachnik 2009, 461). Recent accounts show how consequences of state-organised control – such as through housing and planning legislation in England – continue to marginalise Gypsies and Travellers, creating unequal outcomes and life chances for them (see further Richardson and Ryder 2012).

Precarity of equality leads to insufficient accommodation, neglected site management and exclusion from communities. There is a precarity of security linked to management of existing sites which is interesting to explore further, as there is a gap in the current literature on site management. This article looks at the more domestic and routine construction of precarity and conflict that occurs in the structures, management, policy-making discourses and processes surrounding Gypsy and Traveller site delivery and management by local authorities and housing associations in England.

It is argued that the liminal spaces inhabited by official and temporary sites and encampments occur because of the self-reinforcing negative discourse around Gypsies and Travellers, but also because of the nexus between relative and perceived precarity of Gypsy/Traveller lives. This powerful discourse needs to be understood within a longer history of persecution and stigmatisation (Richardson 2006). The argument of the article is that liminal, marginalised spaces such as Traveller sites can be improved through renewed focus on maintenance and management; low-level conflicts can be reduced when physical surroundings are improved, and community cohesion can be improved when there is better contact between sites, encampments, local agencies and communities. However, ultimate 'mainstreaming' of sites could lead to an undermining of Gypsy and Traveller culture and community diversity which is one of the strengths of a 'ghetto-like' status (which is explored in the article). There should be a space in accommodation provision and management, and in wider discourse practices, that recognises the nexus of relative and perceived precarity and which addresses specific issues where equality of provision needs to be mainstreamed, but where diversity of culture and the embrace of difference are accommodated and encouraged.

The article helps to develop an understanding of Gypsy–Traveller site management, marginalisation and control, through the lens of precarity and within a frame of emerging theoretical concepts of the ghetto. It is structured as follows – the first section, briefly, sets out the methodological approach to a study which informs part of the later argument on the challenges of the historical neglect and more recent mainstreaming of site management, which further raises questions over their ghetto-like status. Second, the article frames a debate on 'precariousness' in which there is an attempt to offer a typology of precariousness relating to marginalised groups. Third, the article moves to a discussion on liminality in spaces and places and a debate on the ghetto-like status of Gypsy–Traveller sites. In the fourth part of the article, examples from the findings of a research project, funded by the Joseph Rowntree Foundation (JRF) and since published

(Richardson and Codona 2016), are analysed through a series of themes emerging from the conceptual framework on precarity and liminality. It examines whether traditional 'neglect' of the issue and specifically of the sites physically as a method of control has made way for a mainstreaming of management which may have the effect of 'absorbing' part of the 'ghetto-like' status of sites, also controlling through its erosion of 'community' and (re)action. The fifth and final part of the article will offer some conclusions.

Methodological approach

In part, this article draws on a standard literature search and review process, followed by presentation and debate of ideas on precarity and liminality of Gypsy and Traveller sites with a small British Academy-supported conference of academics from a range of disciplines across the UK. It draws upon recent research findings from a specific project which ran from 2014 to 2016 and which built knowledge on some of the problems and conflicts faced by Gypsy/Traveller site residents. The article also reflects on a framework of understanding constructed from a variety of research undertaken since 2001.

Building on previous research with Gypsy and Traveller communities, a project to further examine the conflict inherent in site delivery and management was developed in 2014, in conjunction with a PhD student/Traveller advocate. Following subsequent close working in three case study city areas to further develop the research question with Gypsy and Traveller advocacy organisations, the project was successfully funded by the JRF (Richardson and Codona 2016). The research sought to understand the different levels of conflict within Gypsy site delivery and management in order to suggest how the challenges, complexities and in some cases improved outcomes could be negotiated. The original plan for the research was extended by the research project advisory group to focus on the ingredients for good practice in site delivery and management across the country. What was originally envisaged to be a study based on three (anonymised) case study cities became a national level piece of work. For the JRF research, the team visited 54 Traveller sites, spoke to 122 Gypsies and Travellers and 95 professionals from across the range of public services, in the four countries of the UK. The original selection of the three case study city areas was achieved in discussion with JRF colleagues and project advisors, based on knowledge of existing challenges, conflicts and communication breakdowns hampering delivery and management of sites. The extension of the study to areas outside of the original cases – and across the UK – was based upon learned knowledge from Gypsy and Traveller community members and advocacy groups advising the researchers that 'you must visit x place – their sites are great/awful'.

Precarious lives: a conceptual model for precarity

> Precarity also characterises that politically induced condition of maximised vulnerability and exposure for populations exposed to arbitrary state violence and to other forms of aggression that are not enacted by states and against which states do not offer adequate protection. (Butler 2009, ii)

Waite (2008) discussed that the term precarity '... implies both a condition and a possible rallying cry for resistance'. Standing (2011) echoes this point for resistance and notes that the precariat are a new 'dangerous class' ready to mobilise through collective action.

Yet 'precarity' is complex and still difficult to define as it is relational and changing according to wider contexts. Beer et al. (2016) attempt to define 'the precariously housed' in Australia according to three specific measures – anyone suffering from the effects of two or more of these three is deemed to be in housing precarity. Summarising Beer et al.'s three measures in the study, they are (1) housing costs in excess of 30% of income (this is a standard measure across housing studies of 'affordability'), (2) living in private rented accommodation (the authors explain that in Australia this tenure is insecure, which is in common with England but less so with other mainland European countries) and (3) the third measure in Beer et al.'s study was whether the survey respondent had been 'affected by a recent forced move'. Coupled with housing precarity, Beer et al. (2016) also included 'the precariously employed' which included households where all adults were in casual labour contracts.

The study by Beer et al. (2016) is interesting for housing studies generally as it highlights the way precarity is structured into housing and employment systems. The private rented sector in certain countries, with a lack of regulation and scrutiny is seen as a whole tenure to be precarious – and seeing as that sector is growing in market share in England, that must be a concern. Affordability in many cities in the rented and owner-occupied markets sees residents spending significantly more than 30% of their income on their accommodation, and the broader political and economic system is dependent on a market where house values constantly increase. Employment precarity is also seen to be on the increase in England in spite of challenges by Uber drivers and others in the temporary and shadowy corners of the 'flexible' employment market. The same people, vulnerable people, those with precarious lives, inhabit these realms – they live in the private rented sector with high rents, poorly regulated landlords, prone to revenge evictions or extreme rent hikes and at the mercy of employers who can call them in or cancel work at a moment's notice. The same people inhabit the various and multiple precarious realms.

Within the mutually reinforcing cycles of deprivation and marginalisation, it is possible to see how 'super marginalised' groups like Gypsies, Roma and Travellers can live extremely precarious lives. More prone to eviction – such as Roma economic migrants living in tented camps on the outskirts of cities, or English Gypsies or Irish Travellers constantly evicted and moved on from one roadside layby to another car park, to another deep verge, for as long as it takes a council to liaise with police and go to court to evict, or to draw up a public space protection order or injunction. Even when 'settled' Gypsies, Roma and Travellers are seen as 'other' and discriminated against in schools where children face bullying or (in)access to public services and broader acceptance and accommodation in communities. Gypsy and Traveller sites may be seen in popular media, political and social discourse as 'ghetto-like' spaces of deviance.

The argument resulting from the JRF study (Richardson and Codona 2016) and other studies, (Richardson 2006; Richardson and Ryder 2012) is that Gypsy and Traveller sites' ghetto-like image results from discursive exclusionary practices, insufficient physical and social accommodation and poor/neglectful site management. And so a range of responses are needed to match these multifaceted problems which can occur in these liminal spaces of precarity. Whilst it is evident against a number of criteria that many Gypsy and Traveller sites are spaces of absolute precarity, these are also spaces of relative and perceived precarity and even where physical and economic improvements are made, if Gypsy and Traveller site residents still believe they live more precarious lives this can lead to self-segregation – an element of ghettoisation. It is important then, through responses to exclusionary discourse, through better communication strands between site managers and residents to attempt inter-group contact approaches in order that communities see precarity can be a point of unity and similarity rather than difference. Whilst Kauff et al. (2016, 23) noted from their studies that '… intergroup contact may work via different processes for majority and minority members', there is evidence that 'cross-group friendship' could help reduce 'in-group distancing'. In his work evaluating culture, Johnson (2013, 132) noted that 'it is the interaction between people working within different (and differently realised) social institutions which shapes possibilities for well-being within the two groups'.

In terms of understanding the lives of Gypsies and Travellers in need of accommodation, this article suggests there are two broad areas of precarity, related to (1) equality and (2) security – and linked to security, there is a third level of (3) 'perceived precarity'. The first type (equality) is a well-rehearsed area of analysis in relation to Gypsies and Travellers (for example, see further Richardson and Ryder 2012) amongst others. There are examples of absolute poverty, but also relative measures which create relational inequality and also perceived inequality. The second type (security) links to the feelings associated with safety of current accommodation – for example on an unauthorised encampment, there may be an absolute danger related to situation on the roadside, but there is also relative insecurity even where one might be living on a permanent site safer, at least, from highway traffic. Examples were found in the JRF research where there were deficiencies in the road surface, or broken drain covers, or lack of fencing around pitches; whilst there was not necessarily the level of danger as on a roadside encampment, there were fears of relative insecurity and safety. Finally (the third level of precarity), there could also be perceived insecurity even when on the surface things seemed to be stable: perceived precarity.

Precarity itself is multifaceted and complex. It might be useful to consider a typology of precarity which helps to explain how social exclusion and poverty or physical and perceived insecurity affects marginalised groups so that different social policy response measures can be examined.

- Absolute precarity/adversity – based on measures of poverty or physical insecurity applicable to anyone, a static measure based on income, tenure type, physical environmental or health standards.
- Relative precarity/adversity – based on feelings of unfairness, where outcomes of poverty or physical insecurity are relative to others, such as comparative insecurity of tenure within one tenure type or one geographical area.
- Perceived precarity/adversity/fear – it is particularly this that enforces bonding capital and 'gating in' and can be seen to exist in groups where there is already predefined absolute and/or relative precarity. An additional element of insecurity might be felt where all things considered there was a level of relative stability, but based on individual and in-group experiences both recent and historic, a level of anxiety and fear heightened notions of precarity, amplifying the effects.

This process of the amplification of fear and anxiety as a result of the third type – perceived precarity – could be found in a number of individuals and groups living and working in conditions of deprivation, but this article argues that for individuals and groups who are 'seen to be' different, because the accommodation they live in looks different or is imagined to be 'other', then the impact of this amplification can worsen. So, in the case of Gypsies and Travellers who live on a site (seen to be different) and who are talked about by politicians and the media as being different (imagined to be other), it is argued that the impact of perceived insecurity (insufficient street lighting, poorly maintained road, lack of fencing around pitch) is felt differently – it is amplified and increases anxiety and perceptions of 'otherness' and unfairness.

It is the perceived element of the precarity conceptual framework which is particularly appropriate for considering Gypsy and Traveller lives. The spaces in which they live are part of the overarching marginalising discourse through which they are controlled. The look of the site – the location, the quality of repair and maintenance – is part of the overall appearance of the Gypsy and Traveller perceived identity. When sites are perched on the edges of towns and cities, or hidden central industrial areas, when they look shabby and unloved, there is an assumption made about the residents in that space. After a while of such negative scrutiny, the impact appears to be increased anxiety on an individual level, but also across whole sites – creating low-level tension and heightening the potential for conflict on and outwith the site. Not all sites, though, are 'seen' by wider communities, they are tucked away out of sight on the periphery. Many people will have limited experiences of seeing sites first hand, because they have been spatially confined to the outskirts as part of a technique of governance control – the first experience some may have of the image of a site, separated by geography, is an image filtered through the lens of press or political discourse.

Contested dwelling: liminal, ghetto-like spaces

A central argument of this article is that Gypsies and Travellers are confined and controlled through site marginality and neglect. In the next section, findings from the research will show how site residents view neglectful management and how it can undermine presumptions of beneficial increased solidarity that may occur in ghetto-like spaces. It is important first though to explore notions of liminality and spatial confinement. McCabe and Briordy (2016, 2) discuss liminality as '… a transitory stage through which the social person or community passes' and to which there is an end-point once the stage has passed through (for example puberty) and emerged reintegrated in society. But McCabe and Briordy (2016, 2) suggest that understandings of liminality in anthropology allow for a broader meaning now which allows us to '… conceive liminality as a fluid state, or situation, where one is constantly moving between different worlds'. Meier and Frank (2016, 363) say:

> But dwelling is also an issue of power and contestations – as it is realized in processes such as segregation, gentrification and displacement and in socio-spatial forms such as gated communities or shanty towns.

Liminal spaces also move through lifecourse transitions of perception, moving between different worlds of inhabitants and visitors. Shields (1990) talks about this transitory nature of liminal spaces through history, through his case study of Brighton Beach which moved from being seen as a medicalised beach in 1800 towards a 'carnivalisation' of that towards a mass tourist destination – the pleasure beach, then on to 'deviance and violence' of the 'dirty weekend' phase from the 1920s. The perception of Brighton, in this case, was of a liminal space then moving through varying phases of use.

In the context of Gypsy and Traveller sites then, 'liminal' spaces are both transitions of perception, both of themselves by themselves or by wider community members, politicians and press; and they are physical spaces on the margins gated out (but may perceive through an amplified anxiety lens the need to be gated in) and more likely than not (in public planning debates on providing new sites in an area) perceived as 'ghetto-like' spaces. McGarry (2017, 251) notes:

> Roma frequently are consigned to liminal, dangerous, marginal, polluted spaces that are separate from the majority. This is an expression of the socio-spatial power of the state, asserting its sovereign authority over a given space and people.

'Ghetto' is an interesting lens through which to consider Gypsy and Traveller sites accommodation and there is a growing body of literature on the spatial confinement, marginality and ghettoisation of Roma in Europe. Whilst clearly not a ghetto in the traditional sense of the word (with approximately two-thirds of UK Gypsy–Travellers living in housing and not on sites or on the roadside), there are some useful characteristics for a frame of reference in this work. The ghetto can be seen as a tool for confinement and ethno-racial domination; Marcuse (1997) suggested that a ghetto was 'a spatially concentrated area used to separate and to limit a particular involuntarily defined population group ... treated as inferior by the dominant society'.

It is possible to see that a Gypsy–Traveller site could sit within this definition to a degree, being spatially concentrated (often on the margins, but sometimes tucked away in central industrial parts of the city) and those living on the site being involuntarily defined as 'other' and often judged as inferior. The balance of power in relation to Gypsy–Traveller sites is very heavily in favour of the dominant society, outside the site; but there are degrees of power and control being exercised within too.

Wacquant (2014) highlights the challenges inherent in attempting to transplant the notion of the 'ghetto' into other urban realities where they do not directly translate. Pointing instead to the marginality of an urban precariat – socially, spatially and economically, but not strictly ghettoised. He says:

> I thus refute the fashionable thesis of a transatlantic convergence of dispossessed districts on the pattern of the African-American ghetto and instead point to the emergence, on both sides of the Atlantic, of a new regime of poverty in the city, fuelled by the fragmentation of wage labour, the retrenchment of social protection and territorial stigmatization. I conclude that the state plays a pivotal role in the social as well as the spatial production and distribution of urban marginality: the fate of the urban precariat turns out to be economically underdetermined and politically overdetermined. (Wacquant 2014, 1692)

Wacquant's framework for understanding the ghetto (Wacquant 2008, 2014) has been analysed through examples of Gypsy–Traveller sites by Powell (2013) who makes clear that sites are not ghettos but that exploration of the ghetto framework can help to better understand their exclusion and marginalisation in society. In saying that, Powell (2013) suggests that:

> Key characteristics in the definition of the ghetto are shown to hold true for Gypsy-Traveller sites such as: ethnic homogeneity, spatial confinement, shared cultural identity, mutual distancing and retreat into the private sphere of family.

Powell (2013) goes further to say that three characteristics, whilst they may hold true for Roma ghettos in Central and Eastern Europe, do not hold so for UK Gypsy–Traveller sites, namely parallel institutionalism, state retreat and loss of economic function. In the traditional understanding of ghetto, there have been contentious debates over definitions and changing indices (Peach 2009). In discussing this challenging recent history in definition, Peach refers to key texts and makes clarifications:

> Philpott showed that the ghetto was dually exclusive: nearly everyone in the ghetto was Black and nearly all Blacks lived in the ghetto. The enclave, on the other hand, was dually dilute: only a minority of minorities lived in their groups' enclaves; rarely did the minority form a majority of the enclave's population. (Peach 2009, 1388)

In Peach's (1996) work on analysis of the 1991 census to establish levels of discrimination and segregation, she concludes that 'Ghettos on the American model do not exist [in Britain]'. Taking Peach's (2009) comparison between ghettos and enclaves, one can see that Gypsy and Traveller sites are neither dually exclusive nor dually dilute. Whilst the majority of Gypsies do not live on sites, but in bricks and mortar (not often out of choice when asked to reflect on their accommodation preferences), sites comprise, in the vast majority of cases, 100% Gypsy and Traveller residents – a hybrid ghetto-like space.

A strict application of 'ghetto' to a number of different marginalised spaces, including Gypsy and Traveller sites, is problematic, as shown in the arguments within the evolving literature on this subject. Nonetheless, it is a useful frame for discussion to take debates forward, rather than continue in a circular argument of what exactly a ghetto is based on an American-type model. Indeed, Agier (2009) points to this usefulness if we look to an evolution of the term, rather than strict application of ghetto criteria.

> Moreover, researchers today use it as an urban marker for continuously confirmed marginalization at the social, economic and political levels – as a place that one cannot but want to escape from, yet where a certain identification with the 'place' nonetheless takes shape. (Agier 2009, 855)

Wacquant (2012) refers to ghetto as a 'fuzzy and evolving notion' and points to the role of the ghetto

> as organizational shield and cultural crucible for the production of a unified but tainted identity that furthers resistance and eventually revolt against seclusion … the ghetto is best analogized not with districts of dereliction … but with other devices for the forcible containment of tainted categories, such as the prison, the reservation and the camp.

He returns to this double-edged definition of ghetto 'as *sword* (for the dominant) and *shield* (for the subordinate)' (Wacquant 2012, 23) but discusses that the defensive protective properties of ghetto are subsumed by its "exclusionary modality". The protective properties of ghetto are held in the communal strands of everyday living and historical, cultural norms. A site of protest, of defence, "shield" and protection is contingent on the collective values and cultures of those residing on the site, albeit with additional recruits to physically enforce the defence (Richardson 2016). The defensive properties of a ghetto-like site are broken if individual responses come to the fore. Powell (2016) notes this in his understanding of Elias' 'We-I balance'.

> It is this feature [subordination of the I to the we] of many Gypsy-Traveller/Roma groups which has enabled their preservation and cultural continuity, despite the persistence of asymmetric power relations and assimilatory hostility from wider society. (Powell 2016, 150)

This hostility from wider society (sword) can cause marginalised groups to further retreat behind their shield, to strengthen the capital which bonds their community and to weaken the ties that bridge to wider society. Powell and Lever (2015, 11) note this can happen through 'development of parallel institutions' and state 'the educational segregation of Roma as an exemplar of this process'. In recent years, in Britain, however, one could suggest that further to segregation through 'education otherwise' – often homeschooling, there has been a wholesale undermining of the potential for a parallel system of education which protects Gypsy–Traveller cultural values. Traveller Education Services have been vastly reduced in the implementation of local government austerity measures meaning those parents who wish to educate their children 'otherwise' don't have the supportive infrastructure to allow them to properly realise this ambition. It is easy enough for authorities to see the 'education otherwise' box ticked as a method for absolving themselves of responsibility, without too much introspection on how young adults, some with limited literacy skills, can educate their children in a way that doesn't further marginalise them for the future.

Returning to the question of the double-edged nature of the ghetto (sword/shield) – questions are raised by Clough Marinaro (2015) on whether the strengths of the shield (solidarity) are truly there in modern urban camps in Rome. She suggests that the impact in Europe of the modern political context of austerity undermines solidarity – reduces the ghetto properties of defence and protection from the wider world. Following on from this, Clough Marinaro (2017, 1) in her work on 'neo ghettos' analyses how state policies in Italy have pushed a number of diverse Roma groups into two accommodation responses: (1) 'surveillance intensive villages' or (2) 'unauthorized micro encampments', producing 'intertwined informalities in housing and employment that reinforce power inequalities despite Roma's attempts to exert some agency and autonomy through building social capital within and beyond their communities'.

The politics and policies in Rome, Clough Marinaro argues, are producing neo ghettos which constrain Roma, undermine their solidarity and through continued poor management embed marginalisation in a cycle. This is an argument seen in this article, where it was found in the study of Gypsy and Traveller sites in England that (1) poor management or (2) mainstreaming both in their different ways served to devalue the cultural currency of Gypsy/Traveller characteristics of site life and further marginalise and control site (and also roadside) residents.

Also based on research in Rome, Maestri (2014) suggests that community response to crisis and austerity could be a potential for bridging solidarity. Roma could work with non-Roma who are also facing the consequences of crisis (unemployment, difficulty accessing sustainable and affordable housing). This would require less of a focus on the ethnic definition of Roma in a move away from the identity politics approach of Roma, Gypsy and Traveller rights debates in recent decades. Maestri argues that solidarity between Roma and other marginalised Italian people on the basis of their inability to access the employment market shows a more promising future for escape from the ghetto-like villages that were built in response to the original economic crisis.

> Crises, as mentioned before, have an ambivalent character: they can exacerbate social conflicts, they can produce new cleavages, but they can also create the conditions for new forms of solidarity and productive contestations of previous divisions. The second lesson is about the possibility of changing the Roma housing situation by organising mobilisations on the basis of their socio-economic status rather than their ethnic identity. (Maestri 2014, 818)

Maestri (2016) follows up on this argument through her introduction of 'assemblage thinking'. Her concern is that through essentialising Roma we are further marginalising and othering them. Through observation of some Roma families, she saw the circular definition and marginalisation of the Roma ghetto-like space on the people. One group in Maestri's (2016) study 'became' squatters and no longer came under 'nomad policy' remit but under a more mainstream housing response:

> By practicing a movement to a space (a political squat) that falls outside the reach of the Roma policy assemblage, the Roma managed to escape the marginalizing effects of evictions, leading to a rhizomatic rearticulation of their marginalized – rather than marginal – position. (Maestri 2016, 131)

What Maestri is suggesting in her de-essentialising assemblage approach may work on one level, and indeed it is seen in this article in the discussion on 'mainstreaming' of site management in England, but for all of its strengthening of bridging capital and accessing non-specialist responses, there is also the potential for it to undermine the strong bonding capital that so links identity and place on the Gypsy site in the UK.

There is a complicated response to Gypsies, Roma and Travellers – particularly so for Gypsies and Travellers who, in England, live on unauthorised encampments or on the roadside, being moved from place to place. Whilst it cannot be argued that Gypsy and Traveller sites are ghettos in any 'true' sense, there can be a unifying sense made in understanding these liminal spaces as particular and peculiar in the city as spaces which could usefully use a label like 'ghetto' as a way of amplifying collective identity and where (re)action could be performed from and for that place as a particular site of protest (Richardson 2016). For the purposes of better understanding sites as liminal, marginalised spaces where residents are seen as 'other' and are at a disadvantage in the power dynamic with the majority outside the site, then a hybrid ghetto-like framework can be useful. The use of 'ghetto' to frame the argument is not simple though – there is no binary 'good' or 'bad' in relation to sites, or as shall be seen later in approaches to site management. Powell (2007) reminds the ambivalent nature of social relations, and which can be seen on Gypsy–Traveller sites, at any one time site residents may at one and the same time be friends and also in conflict with one another. What the research in this article suggests though is that where sites are particularly poorly managed and there is physically evident neglect, there may be amplified feelings of 'everyday grind conflict', one of the strings of ambivalence but which may be quick to flare.

Controlling liminal ghetto-like spaces: from neglect to 'mainstreaming'

The stigmatisation of Gypsies, Roma and Travellers is a key aspect of 'othering' and marginalising. If we see Gypsies as 'not like us', then it is easier to say no to new site development and to acquiesce to societal marginalisation of their culture and interests (Richardson 2006). Continued stigmatisation is a key ingredient in the ongoing disempowerment of Gypsies and Travellers in our communities (Powell 2008).

In some respects, sites imagined as ghettos are easier to monitor and police (Richardson 2007) and so it is in the interests of the state to maintain separateness in a specific place where inhabitants are easier to keep under surveillance and control. Mulcahy in his (2011) study of policing Travellers in Ireland refers to 'policing strategies of spatial regulation' and the tactics of containment and displacement. Traditionally police would 'contain' the 'problem' of Gypsies and Travellers – leave them be unless there were complaints. Mulcahy (2011) notes one police respondent in his research said 'Travellers are alright in their own place, easily dealt with'. Even in terms of unauthorised encampments, there are some places that are more 'alright' than others and this was noted in the JRF research (Richardson and Codona 2016) in terms of negotiated stopping approaches.

This section of the article examines a number of examples found in the JRF study. The findings from the research included qualitative examples of differing approaches to site delivery and management. In this article, they are analysed through the theme of managing 'ghetto-like' spaces through a spectrum of measures from 'neglect' to 'mainstreaming'.

Neglect

The findings on 'neglect' in Gypsy–Traveller site management ranged from a cumulative effect of lots of small things that were wrong and stayed wrong, leading to low-level conflict, through to really poor management. In the report, the findings on management were categorised into three cultures of management: as 'grasping the nettle' (good management, investing in sites, communicating with residents), 'ticking along' (mostly alright, but not great) and 'ostrich' (pretending the problem will go away). Neglect was found in a small part in the second category and a larger part in the third.

Neglect leading to 'ghetto-like' site

There were two sites in separate areas of the UK, where the neglect was so severe as to make the site seem physically 'ghetto like' as a space to 'separate and limit' those who resided on it. On the first site, in England, there appeared to be dysfunctional relations between site residents themselves, and with the police, as well as run-down utility buildings, burnt-out vehicles near the entrance and serious signs of neglect; on this site visit, the researcher was accompanied by police in a marked car and this would have had an impact on the level of welcome – no residents were spoken to during the visit, it was for the purposes of observing the physical state of the council run site. In this one town, there was a 'dispersal' approach on the one hand in terms of public space protection orders and injunctions against unauthorised encampments, but then on the other hand the presence of a particularly poorly managed public site.

In the second example in a different country of the UK, there was no electricity to the site on the day and had not been for some time and there was flooding on one pitch due to a water tap being stuck on. The site had an overwhelming feeling of neglect and there was rubbish piled near the site entrance and further away on one boundary. The residents on this site were incredibly welcoming and friendly, because of the regard in which the liaison officer, who did not work for the organisation supposed to be managing the site, was held.

Feeling neglected

On other sites visited, even where the site was physically being regenerated, there were feelings of neglect and worry by residents, because of internal conflict on site which was not seen to be dealt with:

> We've just put our names down for a house, love the site – the plot and shed are very nice; but fed up with the violence and feuding. (M17d & F12d)
>
> Been told that they were coming out to do it [put fence around plot] in January and its March now – when is it happening, kids not safe. I'm very frustrated as [the site officer] couldn't give a date [site officer voiced frustration too]. Two weeks ago there was a fire and police came out because of fires and burning of the rubbish along the roadway. (F59d)

There can be a perception that 'Gypsies will sort their own problems' – this approach was noted in the Mulcahy's (2011) work earlier in the article related to police perceptions that conflicts and problems will be resolved 'internally'. This also resonates with the discussion earlier on Wacquant's (2014) work on the Chicago ghetto. It can leave residents on site feeling isolated and neglected when issues are left because they're seen to be a 'Gypsy' issue rather than a site management issue.

> There was an issue of ASB with some visiting kids who threw bricks at a passing bus and now it won't stop at the site. The issue with tipping – CCTV caught it. [Local agency] people see it but think its o.k to do this on the site: they don't report it – different expectations. (F1l)
>
> Would like to see council listen more and things to be more about what the people on the site want who live with the situation day after day. We never get listened to, we never have what we want only what the council wants us to have, sick of asking nobody listens anyway, sick to death. (F21l)
>
> The management is what lets the site down. We have to have rules, but we also have to follow those rules. Travellers are a problem sometimes, they cause the problems by not listening, not behaving themselves, causing the rest of the people on the site to want to move off to get some peace. (F22l)
>
> We need to do a lot more work with vulnerable people, biggest issue is sites/rents and utilities. Disproportionately high costs of rents and bills…. I'm not choosing sides and things like that – its about fairness. You should not be treated differently. (Professional)

'Potholes of doom'

The research team visited very many 'ticking along' sites where there were a number of long-standing, low-level management issues, compounding a lack of longer-term maintenance and investment on the site, and creating feelings of mistrust, amplifying fractures in the lines of communication between organisations managing sites and the residents.

A pothole on one of the sites in case study one became emblematic of a problem being reported but nothing being done. On repeated study visits residents talked to one of the housing association officers about getting it fixed and were told it would be looked at: with no result. Follow-up emails from the research team enquiring about the pothole were met with replies that it was in process and would be fixed. On one visit, a resident showed minor damage to their trailer caused by a car driving fast over the pothole. It became an emblem of poor communication and institutional understanding of site management processes for specific problems that included rubbish near the entrance, small repairs requested repeatedly and issues related to street lights, drain covers and rubbish on a communal area. But it was the pothole which seemed to become a symbol of low-level, 'daily grind' conflict. It also was a perceived threat to physical safety by residents:

> I keep myself to myself, some people get on here: some don't. It's a troublesome site. Sometimes I don't feel safe. Danger of car going into my caravan [as a result of the pothole]. People all time of night, skids, handbrake turns. That's how I got the dent in the caravan. (F39d)

In addition to the insights on site management, this response (and other conflicted Traveller site responses quoted earlier) also challenges notions of internal solidarity in ghetto-like spaces. Clough Marino (2015) questioned the strength of the 'shield' of solidarity in such spaces. The response of F39d in this research also questions the notions of Traveller solidarity on sites where low-level neglect through poor maintenance adds 'low-level grind' conflict that seems to undermine the 'shield'. Officers on subsequent visits were asked who was responsible – which officer and which team – but there seemed to be a lack of management. It got 'reported in', but it was never very clear where. The 'pothole of doom' even prompted the research team to request a meeting across different parts of the organisation to talk about communication (as well as to share emerging findings from the case study and to share wider good practice from elsewhere). Happily, the pothole was finally repaired before the end of the study, the rubbish was cleared and the drain cover fixed; but it was just one example of very many and although the physical presence of the pothole was a perceived threat to safety, it was emblematic of the long-running maintenance issues on many sites, that can cause residents to feel unheard and neglected.

Mainstreaming

A double-edged sword – 'mainstreaming' site management – was found to include physical improvements to sites, but was not always sensitive to specific needs of residents (literacy and standardised communications processes, for example) and also seemed to have the potential to erode the distinct nature of site community characteristics and perhaps diffuse (re)action to marginalisation and control.

However, many residents spoken with showed a preference for mainstream management by the council or housing association than specialist approaches. Residents seemed particularly concerned at council sites being sold to or managed by other Gypsies or Travellers, away from the mainstream scrutiny that could be applied if a local authority or housing association initiated sufficient management and communication practices.

[The site] is run well, I like the council running it – wouldn't want a private Gypsy/Traveller to buy it and manage it. [My husband] used to be a warden on the site … it might be o.k on small sites, but not on bigger sites, open to power and bullying. (F65s)

Mainstreaming of Gypsy–Traveller sites and lives seems to be developing in three ways: (1) not allowing informal (non-mainstream/meanwhile) sites through continuous eviction of encampments and unauthorised developments and (2) encroachment of town and city boundaries onto previously marginal spaces on the outskirts and (3) 'mainstreaming' of site management processes aligned with the rest of the housing stock.

Attempting to 'save' a space from 'meanwhile' liminal use – mainstream sites or nothing (but probably nothing)

The sites where Gypsies and Travellers live are so inherently linked to their identity and their perceived identity that the place takes on an evolving character of its own. It becomes one where the space can be pushed towards the perceived identity of the Traveller residents (brownfield, near a tip, on the edge) or pulled away from them as not being appropriate because it is 'our' space (in the greenbelt) or because it is 'our' common ground where trees are grown or football games are played – not 'theirs'. Land is 'saved' from development, for Gypsy and Traveller sites, and indeed other unpopular land uses such as for social housing more broadly but particularly for hostels and other such spaces where the residents are seen as 'other'. Such land is even protected from 'them' when the use is meanwhile, temporary and unofficial but is amplified if there is a whiff that it will become permanent.

In the JRF research (Richardson and Codona 2016), one example case involved an extended Irish Traveller family who were being moved from place to place around the town. After a period of continuously moving around, it was accepted that the family wanted to reside in the town and the local plan team were asked to identify a site in the masterplan. They found a suitable location for a permanent site in a part of woodland next to a lorry park on county council-owned land within the designated urban extension. The working assumption of the consultant, from discussions with officers at the county, was that planning would be applied for and that the site would be leased to the family. The officers of the borough council suggested that pre-planning advice should be sought, which the consultant and the family duly did; the result being a design for a 5-pitch site, and a bridge building exercise between the family and the planners at the council. This case helps to illustrate the 'meanwhile use' of liminal spaces as part of the circular definition and re-definition of both place and of the people who reside there. The 'meanwhile use' can be related to a temporary use of a space before it is developed into something else or returned to original use – or it can refer to spaces, as found in negotiated stopping examples in the JRF work – which are not used to accommodate transitory groups most of the year round, but in response to key events, or crises, can be used temporarily, in the meanwhile.

The case above – which presented itself during the data gathering for the JRF study – highlights two key considerations – first the 'threat' of an alternative use galvanised reaction from the community to 'save' the space and second the space was not as green as the fantasmatic label; both locations used by the family were quite informal spaces next to existing residential or industrial use. This is not to undermine the argument from residents in the case, but to highlight that 'green belt' can be a mystical label used as an 'empty signifier' as part of any argument. The case was also reminiscent of the arguments for and against the unauthorised development at Dale Farm where one person's 'greenbelt' was another's former scrapyard.

This example from the research is frustrating on a number of levels and demonstrates the importance of 'relative precarity' in understanding the issue. In this case, the officers, some councillors and a religious leader working with the planning consultant and family were attempting to regularise or mainstream an existing liminal site as a method of site provision. The power of the crowd came in when local residents campaigned to 'save' the space from this use. One of the challenges for authorities attempting to move from 'neglect' to 'mainstreaming', particularly in the delivery of sites, is that it can result in tolerated informal use (where that occurs) becoming a negative public debate on the characteristics of already marginalised groups and can result in no provision at all.

'Keeping them in their place' through eviction (but some glimmers of hope)

One example in the findings, in an anonymised town, was particularly stark. Here, the idea of public space protection had amplified to the extent that an injunction was taken out against a list of named Traveller families connected to a large unauthorised development in the region and who were known to travel through the town and stop on the verges and common spaces. However, what was different was that at the bottom of the list was also 'persons unknown', which effectively provided a blanket ban on encampments in the town by anyone known or unknown. This particularly draconian measure was a new turn, although not completely unique as there were a handful of other areas also injuncting Gypsies and Travellers.

This example, and others, provided the flip side to 'negotiated stopping' approaches and the study found this to be much more the expensive and conflict ridden method of 'managing' encampments. The research (Richardson and Codona 2016) also found that where there were existing sites that were managed reasonably well, then this approach was less likely to be used as there would be fewer objections to new site development from existing residents. It was surely no coincidence then that in the same town that used the injunction approach there was an example of an extremely poorly managed, dysfunctional site. Such a schizophrenic strategic climate is not conducive to delivery of appropriate accommodation and wider community cohesion, the study found. However, even in such challenging areas, there were lone voices trying to change things; so in a wider climate of political hostility, the former police and crime commissioner and a senior police officer were trying to reframe the debate, bring local councils together to view the problem of unauthorised encampments through the lens of insufficient accommodation. They tried to move the discussion on to solution through provision of transit accommodation, rather than a discourse of eviction.

There was one high profile good practice example in the study report, where Negotiated Stopping was an official scheme, jointly developed by the advocacy agency and the council with others. In other areas, the approach of negotiation was more low key, in one area the senior local politician not wanting to talk about it explicitly, because it was easier to operate without a light shining on it: 'We do that [negotiated stopping] just go down there and ask them how long they'll be, take bin bags and all that'. In the first nationally recognised example, there was an attempt to regularise and mainstream an informal 'toleration' approach and to share that good practice more widely; there has been a slowing down of political enthusiasm for this in the city, but negotiation is still used in some scenarios. In the second example from the study, it was the informal (invisible) nature of the approach – the provision of accommodation by not doing something (evicting) that seemed to be key to success. In other words what looks like neglect in an area may be a hidden method of providing and that by shining a light on that hidden method the whole approach could be eroded. Mainstreaming may be an answer for local authorities on site delivery and management in some ways, but not in others. The challenge with that though is that the residents 'tolerated' at the whim of an informal, invisible agreement are triply precarious in their housing situation – real, relative and perceived.

Encroachment: 'who's new round here?'

This second example of the blurring of lines between ghetto-like Gypsy and Traveller sites and the dominant group outside through 'mainstreaming' was the encroachment of towns and cities around existing sites. In one of the three case study areas which were evaluated in depth throughout the research, there was an example of one council run site, which was managed well and had generally positive responses from residents on the management. This site had been developed before the neighbouring houses were completed and so the residents grew together as a community; and at one stage during the research, there was even an idea to use a common grassed space leading down from a path between the houses and the site as a play area for all residents to get together – unfortunately the officer proposing this idea and liaising with a charity to enquire if work could be undertaken left and the scheme was never followed through.

There were other examples in other towns where houses were being built near to existing sites as demand for housing grew and blurred boundaries. This seemingly positive accidental approach to bringing communities together can work well, but there are potential hazards too. The permanence of bricks and mortar housing can make residents forget that the new housing development they've moved into is new and the Gypsy site next door has been there for decades. The seeming temporary nature of the Gypsy site gives an air of 'newness' and housed residents in any complaints about neighbouring sites, might forget the site was in fact there first.

During an initial dissemination seminar in December 2016, for the published JRF report (Richardson and Codona 2016), the authors heard verbal evidence from a council officer, which was backed up by others in the room, that banks and other lenders were saying to councils that they would not lend on housing developments where there was provision within the plans to include accommodation for Travellers. During the course of the research interviews with professionals, it was heard that financing sites was increasingly difficult and that as well as burdensome 'value for money' tests in relation to previous grant regimes, there was also the view from lenders that sites were not a good money investment and that they would reduce rather than increase in value – unlike 'mainstream' (bricks and mortar houses) housing development. The encroachment of towns and cities out towards sites may make neighbours out of 'others', but the negative connotations are that housing development to be built near, or including designs for, a Gypsy site may not be funded or that in forgetting the history of a site in an area can lead to site residents being seen as 'newcomers' even when the site was there first – and resulting in potentially managed decline of the site as a precursor to winding it down and selling it on as more valuable real estate potential (as indeed seems to be happening in many inner London social housing estates).

Mainstreaming management processes

In the earlier discussion under 'neglect', an example of the 'pothole of doom' was used as an emblem for a range of low-level conflicts between residents and with site managers. In a bid to combat that a number of organisations were attempting to mainstream services on sites so that they were the same as wider stock management. Echoing Maestri's (2016) calls to de-essentialise Roma, mainstreaming approaches meant that Gypsies and Travellers on sites were to be treated like any other resident of the council or the housing association, in terms of key management issues such as repairs. Rather than site visits resulting in a repair being 'called in' (who knows where), residents were expected to ring the call centre as other tenants in houses were expected to do. Whilst this normally resulted in better record keeping and prompter services, there were down sides, such as one man telling the research team how much he had spent on his 'pay as you go' mobile phone on hold for the call centre, and others saying that they just did not understand the process or have the correct telephone number.

Increasingly, mainstreaming also brought an expectation on contractors as well as residents – for example that where one person was all that was necessary to fix a tap in a house, the same should be true for on-site that there shouldn't be an expectation of double-staff visits for 'security'. There were positive examples during data collection from councils who provided cultural awareness training for contractors to create better understanding and more mainstream approaches.

Conclusions

Whilst it is evident against a number of criteria that many Gypsy and Traveller sites are spaces of absolute precarity, these are also spaces of relative and perceived precarity. Even where physical and economic improvements are made, if Gypsy and Traveller site residents still believe they live more precarious lives, this can lead to self-segregation and perception that sites are 'ghetto-like'. It is suggested that the liminal spaces inhabited by official and temporary sites and encampments occur because of the self-reinforcing negative discourse around Gypsies and Travellers, but also because of the nexus between relative and perceived precarity of Gypsy/Traveller lives. The argument of the article is that liminal, marginalised, ghettoised spaces such as Traveller sites can be improved and site residents listened to and included through renewed focus on maintenance and management. Low-level conflicts can be reduced when physical surroundings (as embodied by the 'pothole of doom') are improved, and community cohesion can be improved when there is better contact between sites, encampments, local agencies and communities. However, the journey from 'neglect' to 'mainstreaming' is not a simple path of 'bad' to 'good'. There are complications around identities; erosion of informal practices which may have been better for Gypsies and Travellers than mainstream practices (for example, around negotiated stopping); and a potential erosion of the feeling of identity, of bonding capital emerging from the marginalisation of the ghetto-like space and the building of a platform from which to (re)act.

The ghetto is a tool for spatial confinement and ethno-racial domination, and the traditional neglect of many sites run by the state has contributed to the ghetto-like separation of residents – countering the wider discourse of integration and cohesion. On the other hand 'mainstreaming' is not necessarily a panacea, as the process can contribute to the undermining of any, albeit ambivalent, platforms of solidarity. The use of 'ghetto' is a useful approach for considering the management of Gypsy and Traveller sites as it provides a space to consider these complex and intertwined identities and issues. Clough Marinaro (2017) challenges the nature of solidarity in Roma 'ghettos' and this article includes similar findings on Gypsy sites in England, but the picture is more complex than that. The social networks on Gypsy and Traveller sites in this study were seen to 'tick along' most of the time but with expressions of low-level or 'everyday grind' feelings of conflict either with management or with other residents. At certain points this intricate balance of social relations could 'flare' in a moment of overt conflict or sometimes in a moment of solidarity. The usefulness of examining Gypsy and Traveller site management through the lens of the 'ghetto' is to allow for expression of such complexity.

Gypsy and Traveller sites can indeed be precarious and liminal spaces to live. Neglected and insufficient accommodation impacts on perceived Gypsy/Traveller identity and subsequent exclusion. The article helps to develop an understanding of Gypsy–Traveller site management, marginalisation and control, through the lens of precarity and within a frame of emerging theoretical concepts of spatial confinement, marginality, neglect and state abandonment of the 'ghetto'. In examining the findings from the JRF research through a more nuanced framework of precariousness, particularly focusing on the overlap of relative and perceived precarity in liminal spaces, this article has highlighted the marginal position of Gypsies and Travellers resident on sites and suggested that control is still exercised over these 'ghetto-like' spaces, sometimes through neglect and sometimes through a move towards 'mainstreaming' management.

Disclosure statement

No potential conflict of interest was reported by the author.

References

Agier, M. 2009. "The Ghetto, the Hyperghetto and the Fragmentation of the World." *International Journal of Urban and Regional Research* 33 (3): 854–857. doi:10.1111/ijur.2009.33.issue-3.

Beer, A., R. Bentley, E. Baker, A. D. LaMontagne, K. Mason, and A. Kavanagh. 2016. "Neoliberalism, Economic Restructuring and Policy Change: Precarious Housing and Precarious Employment in Australia." *Urban Studies* 53 (8): 1542–1558. doi: 10.1177/0042098015596922.

Butler, J. (2009) *Performativity, Precarity and Sexual Politics*. Lecture given at Universidad Complutense de Madrid, June 8, http://www.aibr.org 10.11156/aibr.040303e

Clough Marinaro, I. 2017. "The Informal Faces of the (Neo)-Ghetto: State Confinement, Formalization and Multidimensional Informalities in Italy's Roma Camps." *International Sociology* Online http://journals.sagepub.com/doi/abs10.1177/0268580917706629 32: 545–562. doi:10.1177/0268580917706629.

Clough Marinaro, I. 2015. "The Rise of Italy's Neo-Ghettos." *Journal of Urban History* 41 (3): 368–387. doi:10.1177/0096144214566958.

Johnson, M. 2013. *Evaluating Culture: Wellbeing, Values and Institutions*. Basingstoke: Palgrave Macmillan.

Kabachnik, P. 2009. "To Choose, Fix, or Ignore Culture? The Cultural Politics of Gypsy and Traveller Mobility in England." *Social and Cultural Geography* 10 (4): 461–479. doi:10.1080/14649360902853247.

Kauff, M., K. Schmid, S. Lolliot, A. Al Ramiah, and M. Hewstone. 2016. "Intergroup Contact Effects via Ingroup Distancing among Majority and Minority Groups: Moderation by Social Dominance Orientation." *PLoS ONE* 11 (1): e0146895. doi:10.1371/journal.pone.0146895.

Maestri, G. 2014. "The Economic Crisis as Opportunity: How Austerity Generates New Strategies and Solidarities for Negotiating Roma Access to Housing in Rome." *City: Analysis of Urban Trends, Culture, Theory, Policy, Action* 18 (6): 808–823. doi:10.1080/13604813.2014.962895.

Maestri, G. 2016. "From Nomads to Squatters: Towards a Deterritorialization of Roma Exceptionalism through Assemblage Thinking." In *Rethinking Life at the Margins: The Assemblage of Contexts, Subjects and Politics*, edited by M. Lancione. London: Routledge.

Marcuse, P. 1997. "The Enclave, the Citadel, and the Ghetto: What Has Changed in the Post-Fordist US City." *Urban Affairs Review* 33 (2): 228–264. doi:10.1177/107808749703300206.

McCabe, M., and E. Briordy. 2016. "Working in Liminal States: Fluidity and Transformation in Organizations." *Journal of Business Anthropology* 2: 1–12.

McGarry, A. 2017. *Romaphobia: The Last Acceptable Form of Racism*. London: Zed Books.

Meier, L., and S. Frank. 2016. "Dwelling in Mobile Times: Places, Practices and Contestations." *Cultural Studies* 30: 362–375. online. doi:10.1080/09502386.2015.1113630.

Mulcahy, A. 2011. ""Alright in Their Own Place": Policing and the Spatial Regulation of Irish Travellers." *Criminology and Criminal Justice* 12 (3): 307–327. doi:10.1177/1748895811431849.

Peach, C. 1996. "Does Britain Have Ghettos?" *Transactions of the Institute of British Geographers* 21 (1): 216–235. doi:10.2307/622934.

Peach, C. 2009. "Slippery Segregation: Discovering or Manufacturing Ghettos?" *Journal of Ethnic and Migration Studies* 35 (9): 1381–1395. doi:10.1080/13691830903125885.

Powell, R. 2007. "Civilising Offensives and Ambivalence: The Case of British Gypsies." *People, Place & Policy Online* 1 (3): 112–123. doi:10.3351/ppp.0001.0003.0002.

Powell, R. 2008. "Understanding the Stigmatization of Gypsies: Power and the Dialectics of (Dis) Identification." *Housing, Theory and Society* 25 (2): 87–109. doi:10.1080/14036090701657462.

Powell, R. 2013. "Loïc Wacquant's "Ghetto" and Ethnic Minority Segregation in the UK: The Neglected Case of Gypsy-Travellers." *International Journal of Urban and Regional Research* 37 (1): 115–134. doi:10.1111/ijur.2013.37.issue-1.

Powell, R. 2016. "Gypsy-Travellers/Roma and Social Integration: Childhood, Habitus and the "We-I Balance"." *Historical Social Research* 41 (3): 134–156.

Powell, R., and J. Lever. 2015. "Europe's Perennial "Outsiders": A Processual Approach to Roma Stigmatization and Ghettoization." *Current Sociology* Online. doi:10.1177/0011392115594213.

Richardson, J. 2006. *The Gypsy Debate: Can Discourse Control?* Exeter: Imprint Academic.

Richardson, J., and A. Ryder, Eds. 2012. *Gypsies and Travellers: Empowerment and Inclusion in British Society*. Bristol: Policy Press.

Richardson, J., and J. Codona. 2016. *Providing Gypsy and Traveller Sites: Negotiating Conflict*. York JRF/Coventry CIH.

Richardson, J. 2007. "Policing Gypsies and Travellers." In *Travellers, Gypsies, Roma: The Demonisation of Difference*, eds M. Hayes and T. Acton, pp.104-116. Cambridge: Cambridge Scholars Press.

Richardson, J. 2016. "Gypsy and Traveller Sites: Performance of Conflict and Protest; Sites of Protest." In *Sites of Protest*, eds S. Price and R. Sanz Sabido, 179–194. London: Rowman and Littlefield.

Shields, R. 1990. "The 'System of Pleasure' Liminality and the Carnivalesque at Brighton." *Theory, Culture and Society* 7 (1): 39–72. doi:10.1177/026327690007001002.

Standing, G. (2011) *The Precariat – the New Dangerous Class*, policy network essay online www.policy-network.net May 2011

Wacquant, L. 2008. *Urban Outcasts: A Comparative Sociology of Advanced Marginality*. Cambridge: Polity Press.

Wacquant, L. 2014. "Marginality, Ethnicity and Penality in the Neoliberal City: An Analytic Cartography." *Ethnic and Racial Studies* 37 (10): 1687–1711. doi:10.1080/01419870.2014.931991.

Wacquant, L. 2012. "A Janus-Faced Institution of Ethnoracial Closure: A Sociological Specification of the Ghetto." In *The Ghetto: Contemporary Global Issues and Controversies*, eds R. Hutchinson and B. D. Haynes, 1–32. Boulder: Westview.

Waite, L. 2008. "A Place and Space for a Critical Geography of Precarity?" *Geography Compass* 3 (1): 412–433. doi:10.1111/j.1749-8198.2008.00184.x.

REPLY

Gypsy-Traveller sites in the UK: power, history, informality – a response to Richardson

Ryan Powell

This is a reply to:

Richardson, J. 2017. "Precarious living in liminal spaces: neglect of the Gypsy–Traveller site." *Global Discourse.* 7 (4): 496–515. http://doi.org/10.1080/23269995.2017.1389232.

Jo Richardson's article on the relationship between precarity and the neglect of accommodation and maintenance on Gypsy-Traveller sites provides a renewed focus on their substandard living conditions in the United Kingdom. This is indeed a neglected area in contemporary terms with the accommodation situations of Gypsy-Travellers slipping further and further down the social policy agenda in recent years since the Global Financial Crisis of 2007/8. This paper provides an overview of the contribution of the research before some critical reflections on how this line of inquiry might be further enhanced. It then discusses the potential of situating Gypsy-Traveller experiences on sites in the United Kingdom within wider international debates on housing informality, which could aid urban scholars in moving beyond the unhelpful, static binary of Global North/Global South.

Richardson's contribution is important in several respects. Firstly, it shines light on the ongoing struggle of many Gypsy-Traveller groups who wish to retain their connection to a nomadic (or semi-nomadic) mode of existence. The ability to move and move freely is central to the employment practices and cultural expression of many Gypsy-Traveller groups, despite intense pressures towards sedentarisation and the incessant stigmatisation that comes with a nomadic orientation within the contemporary period; nomadism being associated with 'uncivilised' and pre-modern standards of living (Powell 2011). For some households and groups, mobility can be fairly limited and confined to the summer months, such as travel to fairs or weddings. Yet living on a designated Gypsy-Traveller site (i.e. as a permanent base) plays a central role in the social organisation of family and community life, with research showing how once nomadic (or semi-nomadic) Gypsy-Travellers confined to bricks and mortar can suffer psychologically as a result (Greenfields and Smith 2010). The close proximity and communal spaces afforded by sites are central to the socialisation of Gypsy-Traveller children, intergenerational mixing and the transmission of cultural practices crucial to identity formation (Powell 2016). Secondly, the central theme of neglect adds further evidence to the inferior treatment of Gypsy-Travellers with their accommodation needs somehow less important than those of other groups in society exposing the political and societal lack of will in accommodating nomadism (Niner 2004). Wacquant's (2008a,

2008b) analytical concept of the ghetto is utilised here in illustrating the peculiar urban formation that constitutes the Gypsy-Traveller site and draws attention to spatial confinement. Thirdly, the article makes an insightful contribution in tentatively suggesting that there is a link between the relative neglect and poor maintenance of site environments and the propensity for internal conflict within them. In this sense the renewed focus on site management issues points to the environmental exclusion of Gypsy-Traveller groups (Filčák and Steger 2014) as a neglected aspect of Gypsy-Traveller marginality, with much of the UK literature centred on social and spatial processes of marginalisation and stigmatisation. This notion also chimes, to some extent, with Wacquant's insights on the 'institutional desertification' which is a key characteristic of ghettoisation in his schema (Wacquant 1997; Wacquant 2008a; Wacquant 2008b). Finally, situating experiences of UK Gypsy-Travellers alongside those of European Roma, drawing on the impressive scholarship of Isabella Clough Marinaro (2015, 2017) and Gaja Maestri (2014, 2016), is helpful in showcasing the potential and analytical power of international comparison in appreciating the wider European context of anti-Gypsyism. Reference to Maestri's (2016) work on the emergence of new squatter solidarities between Roma and non-Roma, in response to austerity in Rome, also captures more positive dynamics of urban relations.

A frustration of the article, and of wider research on Gypsy-Travellers and Roma in general, relates to the lack of an explicit and historically informed power perspective (see Powell 2008, 2016; Powell and Lever 2017; Cretan and Powell forthcoming). Richardson (2006) and Lucassen, Willems, and Cottaar (1998) has developed crucial insights on the role of discourse in controlling Gypsy-Travellers but the power imbalance they invariably face begs for a deeper, longer-term analysis and understanding of *group stigmatisation* which goes beyond notions of 'othering', one which acknowledges the remarkable continuity across Europe in the positioning of Gypsy-Travellers/Roma as an often dehumanised inferior social group (Cretan and Powell forthcoming; Van Baar 2012). Of course, there are contexts in which relations are more harmonious, reciprocal and convivial (as Richardson hints at and Maestri captures), but it is difficult (and can be pernicious) to ignore the long-standing and deep-rooted anti-Gypsy-Traveller and anti-Roma sentiment that predominates; which has done so for centuries, and which has arguably been more freely and overtly expressed in recent years (Fox and Vermeersch 2010; Cretan and Powell forthcoming). While Richardson is right to state that people experience Gypsies as 'not like us' and that powerful discourses must be understood within a (much, much) longer history of stigmatisation, there is a need to elaborate further on this fundamental issue.

A historical sensitivity to the experiences of Gypsy-Travellers and Roma in Europe serves as a crucial counter to the present-centred, static conceptualising which blights much research in the peculiar field of 'Romani Studies'. This historical viewpoint is implicit within Richardson's argument but there is certainly scope here for her, and others, to develop the insights in this article in much longer-term perspective. For example, such an endeavour would inform of the fact that precarity is far from a new phenomenon and has shaped life on the margins for many Gypsy-Traveller and Roma groups, often subsumed within a wider category of landless vagrants and paupers, throughout history (Geremek 1997; Mayall 1988). A further problem with present-centred accounts is their tendency to contribute to the production of static concepts, which are simply inadequate in capturing the dynamics of interdependent relations. For instance, I have argued elsewhere (Powell 2008) that the dialectics of identification and disidentification, as put forward by De Swaan (1995, 1997), provide for a more dynamic, and therefore reality-congruent, framework in approaching the relations between Gypsy-Travellers and wider society. This can also help expose the 'invisibilisation of Roma racism' through which poorer Roma tend to be blamed for their own marginalised predicament: Roma are decoupled from a history of persecution and constructed as 'the problem' (Powell and Van Baar forthcoming; see also Wacquant 2009). This historical and dynamic lens could bring much to bear on the important issues raised by Richardson here. A dynamic framework of power can also shed light on the relationship between Gypsy-Traveller stigmatisation and their *relative* lack of social integration (i.e. the persistence of a psychological, social and spatial separation) vis-à-vis other 'outsider' groups in society, while also informing of in-group power dynamics. This latter issue raises thorny questions for academics and welfare professionals such as the resolution of internal conflict among the Gypsy-Traveller community, gendered divisions of labour and domestic violence (Casey, 2014; Powell 2011; Okely and Ardener 2013). The frustration here is that Richardson could go much further and deeper in her analysis in contributing to an understanding of these neglected areas, which would be extremely valuable.

Richardson's contribution refocuses attention on the continued marginalisation of Gypsy-Travellers and the way in which site accommodation maintains social and spatial separation and perpetuates perceptions of inferiority. But it is also the case that Gypsy-Travellers in conventional housing (Greenfields and Smith 2010) and 'wealthy Roma' households residing in large dwellings in more affluent locations also face intense stigmatisation (Crețan 2015; Cretan and Powell forthcoming; Ruegg 2013). As well as the increased attention to historical processes and power relations called for above, this suggests the need to also incorporate the experiences of upwardly mobile Gypsy-Traveller/Roma groups into future research. This would allow for a more comprehensive understanding of the relational dynamics of group stigmatisation and marginalisation and can also challenge the essentialisation of the 'Gypsy condition' or the 'Roma category', which Maestri and Richardson call for.

Finally, though beyond the scope of the article, Richardson's insights also connect to recent debates on housing informality. For instance, she touches upon the informal responses of municipal authorities to unauthorised encampments (i.e. non-enforcement), which can help facilitate nomadism. Furthermore, Richardson's argument that 'mainstreaming' on Gypsy-Traveller sites may undermine the positive social relations and cultural exchange within them chimes, to some degree, with ongoing debates about the consequences (intended and unintended) of the formalisation of 'slum' housing in many parts of the world (see Meth and Buthelezi 2017; Meth and Charlton 2017). Recent research has challenged the notion of housing informality as a phenomenon of the 'Global South' in calling for a processual and relational approach (Clough Marinaro 2017; Durst and Wegmann 2017; Boudreau and Davis 2017; Lancione 2016; Pasquetti and Picker 2017). Gypsy-Travellers, Roma and other semi-/nomadic groups across Europe have long operated within the context of housing informality it could be argued. For example, Roma ghettos in Romania and Slovakia exhibit many attributes that we might more readily associate with informal settlements in the likes of Indian mega-cities. A wider, comparative perspective might therefore help challenge the artificial binary between Global North/Global South, formality/informality, compliance/non-compliance, etc. Again, here a long-term perspective would inform of the relatively recent process of human sedentarisation (that is, in the long sweep of human history) and help challenge conceptualisations which tend to (re)produce unhelpful static binaries. It would perhaps be profitable then, to consider the experiences of Gypsy-Travellers in the UK with those of other such marginalised groups in different urban and international contexts, and in long-term perspective.

Disclosure statement

No potential conflict of interest was reported by the author.

References

Boudreau, J. A., and D. E. Davis. 2017. "Introduction: A Processual Approach to Informalization'." *Current Sociology* 65 (2): 151–166. doi:10.1177/0011392116657286.

Casey, R. 2014. "'Caravan Wives' and 'Decent Girls': Gypsy-Traveller Women's Perceptions of Gender, Culture and Morality in the North of England." *Culture, Health & Sexuality* 16 (7): 806–819. doi:10.1080/13691058.2014.911961.

Clough Marinaro, I. 2015. "The Rise of Italy's Neo-Ghettos." *Journal of Urban History* 41 (3): 368–387. doi:10.1177/0096144214566958.

Clough Marinaro, I. 2017. "The Informal Faces of the (Neo-)Ghetto: State Confinement, Formalization and Multidimensional Informalities in Italy's Roma Camps." *International Sociology* 32.4: 545–562. doi:10.1177/0268580917706629.

Crețan, R. 2015. 'Get out of Traian Square'! The triadic nexus of anti-Romaism, territorial stigma and backdoor nationalism. Unpublished manuscript.

Cretan, R., and R. Powell. forthcoming. "The Power of Group Stigmatisation: Wealthy Roma, Urban Space and Strategies of Defence in Post-Socialist Romania." *International Journal of Urban and Regional Research*.

De Swaan, A. 1995. "Widening Circles of Identification: Emotional Concerns in Sociogenetic Perspective." *Theory, Culture and Society* 12,: 25–39. doi:10.1177/026327695012002002.

De Swaan, A. 1997. "Widening Circles of Disidentification: On the Psycho- and Sociogenesis of the Hatred of Distant Strangers - Reflections on Rwanda." *Theory, Culture and Society* 4 (2): 105–122. doi:10.1177/026327697014002010.

Durst, N. J., and J. Wegmann. 2017. "Informal Housing in the United States." *International Journal of Urban and Regional Research* 41: 282–297. doi: 10.1111/ijur.v41.2.

Filčák, R., and T. Steger. 2014. "Ghettos in Slovakia: The Environmental Exclusion of the Roma Minority." *Analyse and Kritik* 36 (2): 229–250.

Fox, J., and P. Vermeersch. 2010. "Backdoor Nationalism." *European Journal of Sociology* 50 (2): 325–357. doi:10.1017/S0003975610000159.

Geremek, B. 1997. *Poverty: A History*. London: Blackwell.

Greenfields, M., and D. M. Smith. 2010. "Housed Gypsy Travellers, Social Segregation and the Reconstruction of Communities." *Housing Studies* 25 (3): 397–412. doi:10.1080/02673031003711022.

Lancione, M., ed. 2016. *Rethinking Life at the Margins: The Assemblage of Contexts, Subjects, and Politics*. London: Routledge.

Lucassen, L., W. Willems, and A. Cottaar. 1998. *Gypsies and Other Itinerant Groups: A Socio-Historical Approach*. New York: Palgrave.

Maestri, G. 2014. "The Economic Crisis as Opportunity: How Austerity Generates New Strategies and Solidarities for Negotiating Roma Access to Housing in Rome." *City: Analysis of Urban Trends, Culture, Theory, Policy, Action* 18 (6): 808–823. doi:10.1080/13604813.2014.962895.

Maestri, G. 2016. From Nomads to Squatters: Towards a Deterritorialisation of Roma Exceptionalism through Assemblage Thinking. In *Rethinking Life at the Margins: The*

Assemblage of Contexts, Subjects and Politics, edited by M. Lancione, 227–249. London: Routledge.

Mayall, D. 1988. *Gypsy-Travellers in Nineteenth Century Society*. Cambridge: CUP.

Meth, P., and S. Buthelezi. 2017. "New Housing/New Crime? Changes in Safety, Governance and Everyday Incivilities for Residents Relocated from Informal to Formal Housing at Hammond's Farm, eThekwini." *Geoforum* 82: 77–86. doi:10.1016/j.geoforum.2017.03.026.

Meth, P., and S. Charlton. 2017. "Men's Experiences of State Sponsored Housing in South Africa: Emerging Issues and Key Questions." *Housing Studies* 32 (4): 470–490. doi:10.1080/02673037.2016.1219333.

Niner, P. 2004. "Accommodating Nomadism? An Examination of Accommodation Options for Gypsies and Travellers in England." *Housing Studies* 19 (2): 141–159. doi:10.1080/0267303032000168568.

Okely, J., and S. Ardener. 2013. "Gypsy Women: Models in Conflict." *Introductory Readings in Anthropology*, edited by H. Callan, B. Street and S. Underdown, 166–173. Berghahn Books

Pasquetti, S., and G. Picker. 2017. "Urban Informality and Confinement: Toward a Relational Framework." *International Sociology* 32: 532–544. doi: 10.1177/0268580917701605.

Powell, R. 2008. "Understanding the Stigmatization of Gypsies: Power and the Dialectics of (Dis) Identification." *Housing, Theory and Society* 25 (2): 87–109. doi:10.1080/14036090701657462.

Powell, R. 2011. "Gypsy-Travellers and Welfare Professional Discourse: On Individualization and Social Integration." *Antipode* 43 (2): 471–493. doi:10.1111/j.1467-8330.2010.00759.x.

Powell, R. 2016. "Gypsy-travellers/Roma and Social Integration: Childhood, Habitus and the 'We-I Balance." *Historical Social Research* 41.3: 134–156.

Powell, R., and H. Van Baar. forthcoming. The Invisibilization of Roma Racisms. In *The Securitization of the Roma in Europe*, edited by H. Van Baar, A. Ivasiuc, and R. Kreide. London: Palgrave Macmillan

Powell, R., and J. Lever. 2017. "Europe's Perennial "Outsiders": A Processual Approach to Roma Stigmatisation and Ghettoization." *Current Sociology* 65 (6): 680–699. doi:10.1177/0011392115594213.

Richardson, J. 2006. *The Gypsy Debate: Can Discourse Control?* Exeter: Imprint.

Ruegg, F. 2013. "Gypsy Palaces: A New Visibility for the Roma in Romania." *Urbanities* 3.1: 3–21.

Van Baar, H. 2012. "Socio-Economic Mobility and Neo-Liberal Governmentality in Post-Socialist Europe: Activation and the Dehumanisation of the Roma." *Journal of Ethnic and Migration Studies* 38 (2): 1289–1304. doi:10.1080/1369183X.2012.689189.

Wacquant, L. 2008a. "Ghettos and Anti-Ghettos: An Anatomy of the New Urban Poverty." *Thesis Eleven* 94: 113–118. doi:10.1177/0725513608093280.

Wacquant, L. 2008b. *Urban Outcasts: A Comparative Sociology of Advanced Marginality*. Cambridge: Polity Press.

Wacquant, L. 2009. *Punishing the Poor*. Durham (NC): Duke University Press.

Wacquant, L. J. 1997. "Elias in the Dark Ghetto." *Amsterdams Sociologisch Tijdschrift* 24 (3–4): 340–348.

REPLY

Traveller precarity, public apathy, public service inaction, a reply to Jo Richardson's article from a community work perspective

Denis Barrett and Siobhan O'Dowd

This is a reply to:
Richardson, J. 2017. 'Precarious Living in Liminal Spaces: Neglect of the Gypsy-Traveller site.' *Global Discourse*. 7 (4): 496–515. http://doi.org/10.1080/23269995.2017.1389232.

In this short response to Jo Richardson's (2017) article on precariousness and the housing situations on Gypsy/Traveller/Roma sites in the UK, we seek to evaluate and apply the ideas within our own experience and that of relevant communities in Ireland by bringing perspectives based on community work and a rights-based approach. Our response will focus on the situation relating to Irish Travellers[1] and will incorporate a reflection on the most significant recent development relating to Traveller rights in Ireland – the official recognition in March 2017 by the Irish Government that Travellers are a distinct ethnic minority, following similar recognition by the UK Government. 2017 also marked the publication of a new National Traveller & Roma Inclusion Strategy in Ireland (Department of Justice and Equality 2017). Our response will also consider perspectives based on recent coverage of these issues by mass media.

Absolute precariousness and the traveller accommodation crisis

Richardson's article outlines the precarious situation relating to the accommodation of Travellers, Gypsies and Roma in the UK. The analysis is supported by the recent research undertaken with Codona (Richardson and Codona 2016), bringing a rich source of direct experience and personal testimonies of over 120 people on sites through England, Scotland, Wales and Northern Ireland. Richardson considers absolute, relative and perceived precariousness that applies to the experiences of these communities.

In October 2015, a tragedy occurred in Carrickmines, a suburb of Dublin City, that brings the absolute precariousness of Travellers' accommodation in Ireland into sharp focus. A sudden fire broke out at night on a local authority halting site, killing 10 Travellers, including 5 children, from an extended Traveller family. The incident was sympathetically reported widely in the media, with the funeral service shown on the evening news. When the family was moved from the site to be housed by the

Council in a liminal space nearby – a Council owned vacant car park in a *cul de sac* – the residents nearby objected and formed a blockade. Despite voices in the media calling for empathy and tolerance, and public assurances from Council officials that the site would not become a long-term or permanent site, the blockade continued. After a few weeks the Council caved in to this pressure and opted for a less appropriate site. The extended family at the heart of the tragedy have now moved back in to the redeveloped site but ensuing fire inspections in local authority halting sites have been followed by closure of other sites. This experience mirrors some of the findings in Richardson's paper that public discriminatory attitudes are often exasperated by local authority inaction or actions that further underscore discrimination towards Travellers.

Richardson's description of an ongoing accommodation crisis for Travellers in the UK is mirrored in Ireland. She (2017, 508) references a difficult case: 'in a wider climate of political hostility, the former police and crime commissioner and a senior police officer were trying to reframe the debate, bringing local councils together to view the problem of unauthorised encampments through the lens of insufficient accommodation'. The right to accommodation and the current situation where there is insufficient accommodation for Travellers/Gypsies/Roma may be implicit but worth repeating as a necessary underlying factor in this analysis. In the Census 2016 analysis, Traveller accommodation in caravans, mobile homes or other temporary shelters increased just over 10% in the years from 2011 to 2016, having previously shown a substantial decline. Almost 40% of traveller households met the definition of overcrowding (where number of persons exceeds number of rooms) compared to 6% of households overall (Census Statistics Office 2016). This is especially concerning, given that Article 25 of the Universal Declaration of Human rights states that 'everyone has the right to a standard of living adequate for the health and well-being of himself and of his family, including […] housing and medical care and necessary social services' (UN General Assembly 1948).

On 5 May 2017, 2 months after the March announcement of official recognition of Traveller ethnicity, *The Irish Times* published an article outlining how local authorities in Ireland failed to spend more than €1.2 million provided to them by the Department of Housing to build Traveller accommodation in 2016, failing to fulfil the legislative obligations of the Housing (Traveller Accommodation) Act 1998 (Power 2017). The article cited examples of serious concern, including one of the largest halting sites in the country, which was described as being in 'shocking condition', having originally being built for 10 families and now housing 34 families and 150 people. The article reflects Richardson's findings of sites in liminal spaces being managed by local authorities in ways that range from neglect through 'ticking along' to well managed, and where poorly managed sites can generate greater public objections to any proposed accommodation solutions.

The Richardson and Codona JRF (2016) study highlights another aspect that is familiar in the Irish context, the sad observation by individual public servants that low-key or under the radar approaches to accommodation needs (for example, through negotiated stopping where services are provided and unofficial temporary encampments are tolerated) are necessary, because by shining a light on that hidden method the whole approach could be eroded. It speaks to an acceptance that the current housing response is dysfunctional and normalises responses that are unconventional and outside public policy. But it also speaks a little to the humanitarian and public service instincts of individuals and some 'lone voices' whom Richardson found to be attempting to improve situations locally against a background of challenging realities. This is important, if only because a recent Behaviour and Attitudes Traveller Community National Survey found that 78% of people would not have Travellers as neighbours. This points to local authority difficulties in providing suitable accommodation against enormous push-back from settled communities. The same survey finds these same attitudes replicated by public agencies with 33% of Travellers reporting having experienced discrimination from local authorities and housing bodies (O'Mahony 2017).

In considering the significance of the state recognition of Travellers as a distinct ethnic group, being made up by people who share certain characteristics such as culture, language, religion or traditions, it may be worth asking whether the analysis of the housing and accommodation needs of Travellers/Gypsies/Roma should be viewed through this lens, rather than the lens of the settled majority population, from which the policy makers, decision makers and academics come.

Emily Logan, chief commissioner of the Irish Human Rights and Equality Commission (IHREC) that reports to the UN, reflected this view when she said that Travellers as a recognised ethnic minority have a 'right to culturally appropriate housing' (Power 2017). This would mark another significant departure from a policy of 'assimilation', the key recommendation from the first Government policy relating to Travellers – A report of a Commission on Itinerancy in 1963, and fulfil some of the spirit of the Irish Housing (Traveller Accommodation) Act in 1998, which obliges local authorities to meet the current and projected needs of the Traveller community in consultation with Travellers locally.

This question of providing 'culturally appropriate housing' is at odds with the observation posed by the finding of the Richardson and Codona JRF (2016) study that the current response to accommodation needs in the UK generate self-reinforcing negative discourse around Gypsies and Travellers. The National Traveller & Roma Inclusion Strategy attempts to strengthen central government efforts on provision of Traveller Accommodation by robust monitoring and reviews to prevent the underspend by local authorities as referenced in *The Irish Times* article (Power 2017).

Richardson's article mentions but does not directly address other aspects of precariousness affected by housing, such as health, wellbeing and education. The All Ireland Traveller Health Study of 2010 (Institute of Public Health 2010) also co-produced research, found significant health disadvantage particular to the Traveller population while a more recent ESRI (Economic and Social Research Institute) Report in Feb 2017 highlighted extreme disadvantage suffered by Travellers in Ireland across a range of indicators, including health, housing, education, employment and mortality (Holland 2017). Travellers surveyed for the Behaviour & Attitudes Survey cited 'mental health, accommodation and unemployment as the aspects of life which they perceive to have declined over the past five years' (O'Mahony 2017). In O'Mahony's survey, over 90% of Travellers agree that mental health issues are common within the community but also that there is general discomfort in discussing mental health issues. Most shockingly perhaps 82% of Traveller community members report that they have been affected by suicide. A traveller woman responding to this survey captured vividly the toll this has enacted on the community: 'We've a pain in our shoulders from carrying coffins' (O'Mahony 2017).

Significantly, the ESRI stated that the recognition of ethnicity could be of considerable benefit ensuring respect for the cultural identity of Travellers in the context of targeted services. Given that the report also stated that 70% of Travellers live in caravans or overcrowded housing, and that there is a higher birth rate among the Traveller population, the need for an appropriate housing response is urgent and growing.

Richardson, in introducing the idea of liminal spaces, mentions that these spaces are often located near roadsides, dumps or power lines. These spaces are uninhabited and available for temporary encampments because they are unsafe or unfit for human habitation. The fact that these are often the only spaces available for Traveller/Gypsy/Roma accommodation, and the effect of this on the health, education and well being of those who live there, in particular the youngest and the oldest in the population, needs to be set against the background of insufficient accommodation provided by the local and national Government. The voice and visibility of Travellers in these processes needs to be mentioned here. In Ireland organisations such as the Irish Traveller Movement and Pavee Point operate at national level, while, locally, organisations such as the Traveller Visibility Group[2] (TVG) in Cork, are Traveller-led for Travellers. These organisations act as advocates for Travellers' needs and rights and represent Travellers on consultative committees including the Local Traveller Accommodation Action Committee LTAAC. A response from such organisations in the UK to the findings of the Richardson and Codona (2016) survey would add usefully this perspective to the analysis.

The cultural identity of Travellers is strongly connected to their tradition of nomadism, and the dynamics around their housing needs can be viewed as distinct to those of other groups. In the Irish context, Travellers often maintain possession of caravans, enabling their tradition of nomadism to be still relevant and practised, often seasonally, within Ireland and also across to the UK. Most sites that Travellers live on, both official and unofficial, are adapted or in some cases designed to have space for these caravans. In addition, in keeping with their history, the horse has a central role in Traveller culture and ownership of horses is still prevalent. This brings other challenges both for Travellers themselves, for the settled community and for local government in terms of the use of liminal spaces for grazing, and brings up questions of animal welfare. While some good practice projects have been supported in Dublin and Tralee, there remains local opposition to other such initiatives. A recent Horse Project in Cork, which would have supported horse grazing and some training for young Travellers in horse welfare was supported by an interagency grouping including Traveller Projects and The Local Authority. The site identified for this project did not require planning permission. However, when the local authority decided to seek it anyway, they were met by 128 objections in an area where there are perhaps 30 residents. Predictably perhaps in light of this, planning permission was refused, but those same residents are appealing this decision on the grounds that the refusal wasn't strong enough!

Richardson suggests that the use of the term 'ghetto' or 'ghetto-like' is useful as a means of analysing the control of this minority by the dominant sector of society and the poor maintenance of sites in this light. The comparison of Traveller-specific sites to ghettos is a challenging one, but the observed effects of poorly managed and maintained sites contributing to the creation of self-perpetuating perceptions among the settled population, while troubling, cannot be ignored. However, the usefulness of the term to critique attempts at state control may need to be balanced against its being imposed from a different setting and reflecting quite different social dynamics. An alternative way of looking at this that reflects another analysis is to recognise the origin of the word 'site' as camp-site, and to recognise that Travellers live in extended family groupings, or 'clans', separate from other family groupings, with a range of complex inter-family social norms that are a much stronger factor in determining individual behaviour than the factors that typically apply to individuals or families in the settled community or, indeed, in city 'ghettos'. As such, the idea of a 'ghetto' or 'ghetto-like' may not always be useful, and if it is to be used we would advocate consultation with Travellers themselves.

In conclusion, the article poses a number of useful, if challenging and troubling, questions that have a strong resonance in Ireland. If the vision of a diversity of culture and the embracing of difference that Jo Richardson poses is to be achieved then shining a light on the current situation is both necessary and urgent. However, if the observed effect of current public housing policy in action in the UK in relation to Travellers/Gypsies/Roma is as Richardson suggests, through either neglect (e.g. the pothole of doom) or in mainstreaming management, it is instead generating self-reinforcing negative discourse around Gypsies and Travellers and this vision is further away than ever. The space provided by the cross-cultural working group has brought these questions up in a new way and has provided the authors with a sense that there is solidarity around addressing the precariousness that Travellers/Gypsies/Roma and Aboriginal people face than was previously unimagined.

Notes

1. Since the 1990s the term Traveller is preferred by Travellers and is used almost exclusively in Ireland, while the term Gypsy is no longer in common use. Minceir a cant word, is used by many younger traveller activists.
2. The TVG are members of CESCA (Cork Equal and Sustainable Communities Alliance) and were participants in the cross-cultural working group in Cork, hosting one of the sessions featuring a presentation by Mary Graham, a representative of the aboriginal people in Australia. This generated a rich exchange on the values shared by both peoples. NASC (The Irish Immigrant Support Centre), an NGO is another member of CESCA that supports people from the Roma community in Cork and throughout the country.

References

Census Statistics Office. 2016. 'Profile 8 Irish Travellers, Ethnicity and Religion', *Census of Population 2016*, Dublin: Statistics Office. Accessed November 3, 2017. http://www.cso.ie/en/releasesandpublications/ep/p-cp8iter/p8iter/p8itseah/

Department of Justice and Equality. 2017. *National Traveller and Roma Inclusion Strategy: 2017-2021*. Dublin: Department of Justice and Equality. Accessed November 3, 2017. http://www.paveepoint.ie/wp-content/uploads/2015/04/National-Traveller-and-Roma-Inclusion-Strategy-2017-2021.pdf

Holland, K. 2017. 'Travellers Suffer "Extreme Disadvantage", Report Shows', *The Irish Times*, 17 January, Accessed November 3, 2017. https://www.irishtimes.com/news/social-affairs/travellers-suffer-extreme-disadvantage-report-shows-1.2939444

Institute of Public Health. 2010. *All Ireland Traveller Health Study (AITHS)*. Dublin: Department of Health and Children. Accessed November 3, 2017. http://www.ucd.ie/issda/data/allirelandtravellerhealthstudy/

O'Mahony, J. 2017. *Traveller Community National Survey 2017*. Dublin: National Traveller Data Steering Group & The Community Foundation for Ireland. Accessed November 3, 2017. https://drive.google.com/file/d/0B60RQ_OxViAVVFUxVkg5amRrVTJ1eHJPLUdHb2ZxZWZEbVVZ/view

Power, J. 2017. 'Over €1.2m in Traveller Housing Funding Left Unspent', *The Irish Times*, 5 May, Accessed November 3, 2017. https://www.irishtimes.com/news/social-affairs/over-1-2m-in-traveller-housing-funding-left-unspent-1.3071590

Richardson, J. 2017. "Precarious Living in Liminal Spaces: Neglect of the Gypsy-Traveller Site." *Global Discourse* 7 (4): 496–515.

Richardson, J., and J. Codona. 2016. *Providing Gypsy and Traveller Sites: Negotiating Conflict.* York: JRF.

UN General Assembly. 1948. "Universal Declaration of Human Rights" (217 [III] A). Paris: UN. Accessed December 14, 2017. Retrieved from http://www.un.org/en/universal-declaration-human-rights/

Universities as key responders to education inequality

Siobhán O'Sullivan, Séamus O'Tuama and Lorna Kenny

ABSTRACT
This paper explores the responsibility of the university sector to respond to educational inequality and to those with precarious relationships to education. The paper explores how although there are considerable benefits to be attained from higher education and lifelong learning, many people are dislocated from the university sector and feel that the university is not for them. It argues that the university sector must develop a community mission to respond to these issues and explores the approach of the Centre for Adult Continuing Education in University College Cork, Ireland, in developing such a community mission. Through working with communities and supporting inclusive and diverse learning opportunities, the paper argues that universities can contribute to tackling the ongoing persistence of educational inequality.

Introduction

At the outset, this paper has to address two central questions. Firstly, what is the wider function of the university. Secondly, to what extent can the university ameliorate current challenges around educational inequality, the consequences of economic and social marginalisation and precarity. The first question is a perennial one, and has to remain so as no institution's societal meaning remains static. In the past, the role of the university was famously articulated by Humboldt and Newman and in more recent times by Boyer (1990). All such discussions invariably reflect both internal organisational and mission questions as well as the broader societal purpose. Rather than rehearse these discussions, the persistent challenge of the university is contemporary relevance. Fitzgerald et al. (2016) describe the university as a social entity which inheres a responsibility to serve a public good function. The exact nature of this public good function is obviously contestable, but the premise of this paper is that, however described, the university has a public good responsibility.

This paper assumes that a key university public good is wider community engagement and the amelioration of societal inequalities in order to enable full participation by all. It is important to acknowledge that formal education is only one element in human learning and that within formal education the university is just one type of provider. Access to university education will never be universal nor should it be seen as the ultimate goal for all learners. In this regard it differs significantly from primary education, where a target for achieving universal access is an international objective being pursued by the United Nations. There is significant progress in the primary school education sector, even if it still lags behind agreed targets. Likewise, lower secondary and higher secondary education participation rates are increasing, but participation rates decline as students move up the educational ladder. There are still significant pockets of inequity for instance around gender, ethnicity, religion and geography (UNESCO 2015). Universal access is critical at foundational level education not only in providing (most often) the child with basic numeracy and literacy skills but also as Mahlo (2017) points out it is a phase for enhancing life skills and when 'the foundation of learning is laid effectively, a critical time for promoting interest in education and positive attitudes toward school' (pp. 1–2). Failure at this stage may see a learner alienated from the education system. However, educational needs diverge as learners progress through life, therefore at university level the challenge is not about universal access, but equity of participation across the population. Equity of participation can have significant individual and collective benefits socially and economically.

Some pilot projects have been designed by University College Cork to tackle issues of inequality and provide both individual and collective benefits. These are still at an early stage, but they are adopting inclusive methodologies that have potential to bring the university closer to groups and individuals that currently have low levels of engagement with the university. The paper begins by exploring the benefits of education, and then highlights the extent of inequality and the dislocation of marginalised communities from the university. It goes on to argue that universities have a social responsibility to address this inequality, and to widen the orientation of the university sector through community engagement. Finally, we present some pilot projects being pursued in University College Cork in the Centre for Adult Continuing Education (ACE) to address equity of access.

The benefits of education and lifelong learning

Adult education is delivered in a range of settings and at varying levels, including the community, further education training centres and colleges and by universities. In the wider educational context, the benefits for individuals, families and communities from adult education and lifelong learning are both direct and indirect as highlighted by Field (2009) in his work on well-being. The direct benefits are 'capabilities and resources which influence their well-being' and the indirect ones enhance 'their resilience in the face of risk' (Field 2009, 7). A key point he makes is that these benefits are both individual and collective as they deliver broader community good.

Investment in adult education delivers both social and economic goods such as reduced welfare and health costs, reductions in crime and the related costs of the criminal justice system. Beaven et al. (2011) estimate a return of £35–£40 for each pound invested in further education apprenticeships in the UK. Proficiency in literacy, numeracy and problem solving is positively associated with general well-being including health and social cohesion. The Organisation for Economic Co-operation and Development (OECD 2009, 171) reports that 'educational attainment is positively associated with self-reported health, political interest and interpersonal trust' and reiterates the strong relationship between educational attainment and health indicators in its 2013 report (OECD 2013). Bailey, Breen, and Ward (2009) indicate that adult education promotes both physical and mental health, thereby enhancing people's self-confidence, self-esteem and dignity as a purposeful member of the community.

University education is a significant factor in determining people's life chances including the likelihood of employment, income levels (termed the graduate premium), risk of poverty, and health and well-being (OECD 2013). Children tend to emulate the educational attainment of parents, thus the further a parent progresses in education the further the child is likely to progress. Fragosa (2014, 61) in his analysis of the Portuguese 2006 survey on the transition to retirement by the National Institute of Statistics says 'there is an intergenerational "transmission" of education... educating adults has the immediate effect of increasing their children's educational levels'. Irish data from the European wide Survey on Income and Living Conditions demonstrate that respondents whose parents were educated to primary level or below had a 21% rate or risk of poverty, three times that of respondents whose parents had a primary degree or higher (Central Statistics Office, CSO 2007). The 2011 Irish Census shows that 20-year-olds with both parents educated to university or equivalent level have an 89% propensity to pursue similar levels of education against 45% for those whose parents have lower levels of education (CSO 2012).

Like other forms of education, university education also enhances social capital, i.e. the networks and associations that an individual participates in, and the shared values, contribution to common goals and social support from this participation. According to Putnam (1995), social capital is important to social cohesion since it facilitates coordinated action and mutual trust. While social capital is generated in all aspects of life, it can be strengthened through education. Granovetter (1983) claims that education gives socio-economically disadvantaged communities bridging weak ties to well-placed individuals outside their normal networks who can open up opportunities and contacts. A second dimension is that all closed communities 'suffer a lack of cognitive flexibility' (Granovetter 1983, 205). Basically the views of one's own group reinforce already held views. Bridging weak ties forces individuals to see the other in a new light and to modify their thinking to facilitate new opportunities and more open ways to see the world.

The benefits of bridging ties generated by education can be significant factors in building new networks and thus reduce precariousness and enhance resilience. Lin (1999) states that 'social resources or social capital enhances an individual's attained statuses'. Put simply an individual with stronger social capital will do better in terms of income, career and status than someone with lower social capital with similar education, family and community context. However, as the next section demonstrates, marginalised communities are often dislocated from the university and this limited access restricts their opportunities to benefit from higher education (HE).

Dislocation of marginalised communities from the university

Lack of educational opportunity inhibits full participation in society and can lead to cumulative disadvantage, for example through being trapped in low-paid work (Nolan and Whelan 1999; Armano and Murgia 2011). Educational inequality in Ireland and Britain is persistent, some can be mapped to specific geographical areas, some is intergenerational and class based as described below. However, as Dockery, Seymour, and Koshy (2016) point out ascertaining factors influencing access to university education is extremely complex.

The determinants of lack of educational attainment and progression are a combination of personal, economic, social and cultural factors. Financial issues deter disadvantaged groups from entering HE in the first place or make continuing with courses more difficult (McCoy et al. 2009). Lack of or unaffordable childcare is also a significant barrier (Maxwell and Dorrity 2010). There is clear statistical evidence that social class is a significant determinant of education. According to a review by Perry and Francis (2010, 5) 'children's educational attainment is overwhelmingly linked to parental occupation, income, and qualifications'. Those from higher social classes have greater educational attainment and progression. Additionally, research shows large differences in progression to HE depending on where people live. The Irish Higher Education Authority (HEA) reports that 'in Dublin there are differences in participation between postal districts – over 99% of 18–20 year olds in one postal district go on to HE, while in another the rate is as low as 15%' (HEA 2015, 14). Although the Higher Education Funding Council for England (HEFCE) found that 50% of the entrant population to full-time degrees in 2015 had parents/guardians without a HE qualification, just 23% of those students attended a high tariff institution compared to 40% of students who parents/guardians have a HE qualification. There were also significant spatial/area-based differences in participation rates across England (HEFCE 2017).

Discussion on dislocation gains from the use of the concept of Socio-Economic Status (SES) used by Dockery et al. (2016) in which they draw attention to 'strong feedback cycles which operate across generations' (p. 1697). Specifically, they highlight links between parental SES and likely educational outcomes for their children. Higher parental SES 'contribute to informational power' and also to income, prestige, status and civic engagement (p. 1697). Breaking that cycle is critical to enhanced mobility for subsequent generations. What this also indicates is that using postcodes is in itself too simplistic an analysis, even if there are neighbourhood forces that militate against SES progression. It indicates the importance of lifelong learning in breaking intergenerational cycles. Parents, and also grandparents, who return to education create new opportunities for themselves. In doing this they create an intergenerational bridge that mitigates the potential negative impact of their own previous unsatisfactory experiences within the formal educational system on subsequent generations.

While there have been many efforts over many years to widen university participation, including financial supports such as grants and allowances, educational inequality remains persistent. Indeed studies have highlighted 'that equalising formal rights to education, or proportionate patterns of participation, does not equate with equal rates of success or outcomes for disadvantaged groups' (Lynch 1999, 16). In Ireland, the Expert Group on Future Funding for Higher Education (2015) stated that

> neither the rapid expansion in higher education nor the removal of tuition fees have significantly reduced the most glaring inequities in access, namely, the under-representation of the lower socio-economic groups and the small share of mature students. (p. 22)

Similarly, in the UK, the Social Mobility Commission (2017) found that

> Despite universities' success in opening their doors to more working class youngsters than ever before, retention rates and graduate outcomes for disadvantaged students have barely improved over the period… In higher education, it will take more than 80 years before the participation gap between students from disadvantaged and more advantaged areas closes. (p. 4)

The reasons for this continued inequality are multiple and complex, and include the impact of funding cuts, social and cultural barriers and attitudinal factors. In Ireland, the impact of the 2008 crisis and subsequent neo-liberal austerity measures following the collapse of the so-called Celtic Tiger have resulted in cuts to grants schemes (including higher, vocational and trainee grants), changes in eligibility criteria for allowances and grants that have impacted on mature students, increased charges for study at HE through the Student Contribution Fund and cuts to community education funding. Even prior to the onset of these cuts, McCoy et al. (2009, 86) found that 'grant payments typically meet between just one-quarter and one-third of average expenditure levels of disadvantaged students', who are hence under greater levels of financial strain. A further disincentive for people to engage in HE is the lack of supports for part-time study in the Irish system. Part-time students 'are not entitled to receive the basic state grant nor many of the supplementary supports available to their full-time equivalents' (McCoy et al. 2009, 4; OECD 2006). However, in September 2017 the Irish HEA announced the extension of its Student Assistance Fund to certain groups of part-time students covering expenses such as books, rent, heating/lighting bills, food, travel and childcare although it is still too early to assess the impact of this initiative (HEA 2017).

Social and cultural factors also create barriers to education. These could include the feeling that HE is remote and alien to family life (Lynch and O'Riordan 1998), that it does not align with perceptions of masculinity and occupational status in working class areas, it conflicts with caring responsibilities, or could have a psychological dimension such as low self-esteem and limited self-belief related to wider inequalities (Maxwell and Dorrity 2010). Perry and Francis (2010) argue that these factors, combined with economic barriers, lead many working-class people to believe that university is 'not for the likes of us' (p. 8) and propose that education needs to actively include working-class people, 'by supporting their agency to exercise more control over their education' (ibid, p. 18). Such supports must be multifaceted (practical and pastoral) and reflective of a complex range of factors according to Maxwell and Dorrity (2010) in order to sustain students, especially mature students, those with little formal education and those who had previous negative experiences in education. Similarly, McGlynn (2014, 22) argues that quality adult education should include a good matching of courses to the needs of individual learners and provide 'programme supports' and 'flexibility to take into account the life circumstances of the adult participants'. Analyses of widening participation strategies in Wales 'suggest that most effective are programmes such as outreach which provide supported routes to undergraduate degrees' (Stephens 2015, 370).

Like Perry and Francis (2010), Harwood et al. (2013) point to the significance of attitudinal factors, in particular imagining having a university education, and highlight how young people from disadvantaged communities believe that university is not for them. Harwood et al. (2013) explore the perspectives of young people who live in disadvantaged areas in Australia, refugee youths living in Australia and indigenous

Australian aboriginals. They examine the significance of cultural norms and expectations, and how for these young people

> being unable to imagine a university education is intricately bound up with a sense of not belonging to education, a sense that is linked to the experience of poverty and disadvantage. (Harwood et al. 2013, 33)

While the young people in the study have an imagination of the university (e.g. they state that it is a place of big buildings, posh), they lack an imagination of *having or getting* a university education. The young people articulate that university is for smart and rich people and depict themselves and their communities as lazy and not smart (Harwood et al. 2013), which may reflect the internalisation of stigmatisation and low self-esteem. The young people interviewed by Harwood et al. essentially self-identify as not being full members of society, being outside the pale in terms of even imagining the possibility of university education.

How these young people construct their own place in society, plays out in the complexity and interdependence inherent in contemporary society. McCarthy (1990) highlights links between mutual recognition and personal identity which should also extend to collective identity for groups within society that are given designations of exclusion perhaps on the basis of their economic status, their religious beliefs, where they live, their race, their skin colour, gender or any number of other identifiers. McCarthy talks about 'reciprocal vulnerability that calls for guarantees of mutual consideration to preserve both the integrity of individuals and the web of interpersonal relations in which they form and maintain their identities' (1990, x).

How and why ought universities address inequality

Many scholars have written about the role of universities in widening or equalising access to quality HE and breaking cycles of educational inequality, whether class, race, geographical or intergenerationally based (e.g. Wilson-Strydom 2015; Brennan and Naidoo 2008; Kezar, Chambers, and Burkhardt 2005). Harwood et al. (2013) highlight lacunae in how universities relate to those with precarious relationships to education, for example access programmes often pursue links to schools, which can miss those who are not embedded in formal education. They argue that universities have a moral responsibility to both recognise and respond to education inequality and precariousness. Essential to enhancing access for marginalised groups is the building of familiarity with the university as a place in order to normalise and demystify the university environment. As they state, 'the very act of "being" within the campus environment is significant' (Harwood et al. 2013, 36). Universities must listen to 'the other' and connect to people at varying points throughout their experience of education, in different settings and with different programmes. This connection is essential if participation in university education is to be established or maintained (Harwood et al. 2013, 26). Wilson-Strydom (2015) in her work on South Africa argues that while policy and practice to widen participation for those who are excluded from universities is essential, there also needs to be a shift in focus in universities to understand the 'conversion factors that enhance or limit students' capabilities to convert their place at university into successful functioning as a university student' (p.152).

Boyer (1990, 77) proposed an orientation in which 'higher education must focus with special urgency on questions that affect profoundly the destiny of all'. In his model universities would engage, internally as a community of scholars, across and between disciplines, in addressing the big challenges of the day and contributing to and benefitting from a dynamic interaction with wider society. This contribution has been conceptualised in a myriad of ways – as civic, community and democratic engagement (Post et al. 2016; Saltmarsh and Hartley 2011; Biesta 2011) – all of which capture the social responsibility and impact on society of the university sector towards the public good. Such a mission has been embedded through numerous approaches across universities including in participatory and applied research, service learning, access and outreach programmes and advisory services (Doberneck, Glass, and Schweitzer 2010).

Fitzgerald et al. (2016) echo Boyer's (1990) re-evaluation of the role of the professoriate. They advocate that the university should 'make engagement scholarship a central aspect of its work, spanning the spectrum of its disciplinary units, centres, and institutes' (Fitzgerald et al. 2016, 245). They support this contention by identifying universities as social institutions that thus have 'an implicit responsibility to serve the public' (Fitzgerald et al. 2016, 245). They propose that universities become less top-down and more 'demand-driven, creating a culture that reinforces the democratization of knowledge' (Fitzgerald et al. 2016, 247), and adopt co-creative approaches. Universities need to engage in a sophisticated way that recognises individual and collective needs are not only economic or job related. Fitzgerald et al. (2016) analysis is also relevant to the concept of 'reflexive activation' originally developed by Warner et al. (2005). This can be defined as a way to 'balance the educational, social and economic needs of the individual and the wider community' and to include the learner in the decision-making process (Ó Tuama 2016, 108).

Adult education is one of the dynamic ways universities engage with the wider world, but external engagement itself does not necessarily sit comfortably with many universities and can be contentious (Watson et al. 2011). Jongbloed, Enders, and Salerno (2008) talk about universities 'being forced' to re-examine their wider societal mission and the COMMIT project's (2016, 28) analysis of 'external drivers' in European universities seems to endorse this. However, reluctantly or otherwise, universities are embedded in a complex environment. Jongbloed, Enders, and Salerno (2008) summarise this as local, regional, national and international having external functions around social and economic impact. They highlight the liminal fuzzy boundaries between inside and out, which is the very habitus of adult education, in areas like 'teaching, research and knowledge transfer' (Jongbloed, Enders, and Salerno 2008, 304).

Adult education as a community engagement

Adult education does not cover all the bases in terms of the university mission for community engagement. Neither should it be peripheral. From 2013 ACE, the adult education centre at University College Cork, in the Republic of Ireland adopted a mission to 'lead the university's outreach mission through contributing to the networked university concept' (Ó Tuama 2013, 16). Through this mission it is reinvigorating both external engagement with a range of community partnerships and also animating internal partnerships within the university. ACE delivers accredited and non-accredited part-time programmes to approximately 3000 students (primarily over the age of 21) annually ranging from general interest to professional development. These programmes are delivered on-site and online throughout the island of Ireland.

ACE also leads two pilot projects aimed at enhancing access to university in marginalised areas that are dislocated from the university, opening wider educational opportunities, and animating social and economic opportunity through a partnership model with local communities and stakeholder networks. The urban project, Cork Learning Neighbourhoods, fits under the umbrella of the Cork UNESCO Learning City project. University College Cork (UCC) is one of the four founding partners and a strong proponent of the UNESCO Learning City project, in partnership with Cork City Council, Cork Education and Training Board and Cork Institute of Technology (O'Sullivan and Kenny 2016). On behalf of the university, ACE promotes a programme called 'The Free University' in the annual Cork Lifelong Learning Festival which includes learning events on campus and in the community. Learning Neighbourhoods is currently operating in four Cork city neighbourhoods, Ballyphehane, Knocknaheeny, Mayfield and Togher. It aims to include all denizens,[1] agencies and stakeholders to nurture synergies and learning connections at city, national and global levels using an EcCoWell approach (Kearns 2012). Learning Neighbourhoods use a community development approach to build trust, embeddedness and community ownership of the project. People, their skills, knowledge, and identity are the strengths and assets that communities can activate to create futures (McKnight and Kretzmann 1993).

Through consultation and involvement Learning Neighbourhoods aims to build 'authentic reciprocity in partnerships between those working at colleges and universities and those in the wider community' (Hartley and Saltmarsh 2016). The project recognises that working with community and education organisations, 'grass roots networks of learning champions', is essential to developing lifelong learning as they focus 'on building relationships to support people into and through learning' (Sandbrook 2009, 4). It draws on the vision of Learning Cities outlined by Sandbrook (2009) that they should celebrate community and culture, be explicit about encouraging people to recognise their learning and develop a sense of themselves as learners, and actively support the collaboration of networks of providers and other organisations involved in lifelong learning to enable learners pursue their learning pathways.

The pilot rural project, Skellig Centre for Research and Innovation, aims at leveraging the potential of the university through on-site teaching, learning and research to contribute to the overall mission to re-establish the town of Cahersiveen as the agora for the western end of the peninsula of Iveragh. This peninsula has experienced population decline, few career and employment opportunities, reduction of services, feelings of isolation and the outward migration of young people, the university is working in partnership with Kerry County Council and South Kerry Development Partnership and with extensive denizen and stakeholder engagement.

These projects challenge the dislocation from the university highlighted by Harwood et al. (2013). ACE, in a small study of adult learners from areas characterised by deprivation and low SES, has also documented feelings of vulnerability and insecurity in terms of one's identity and sense of belonging to the university (O'Sullivan, Tuama, and Denayer, Forthcoming). Respondents felt that UCC was a foreign place, exclusively for rich and middle class people. They articulated an expectation that they would be told to leave for being the wrong type of person and thus not deserving to be there, and one felt that even the walls were saying 'you do not belong here'. The projects align with McCarthy's (1990) advocacy of mutual consideration to support individual and collective integrity and identity and aim to institutionalise university–community engagement to tackle educational inequality.

Conclusions

Educational exclusion and inequality are the sorts of challenges that are not resolved by short-term policy initiatives nor by any one part of the educational landscape. All of us learn in informal and non-formal contexts, virtually everyone experiences formal learning. The university sector is just one dimension of the formal sector. Aspirations to study at university should be open to as many as possible, but it should never be presented as the ultimate goal. Universities, like all major institutions, have to reinvent themselves to maintain relevance and in the contemporary era one key area of relevance is their role vis-à-vis the wider community and in addressing the grand challenges of today. One of those challenges is in making university education more available and responsive, especially to the needs of those currently excluded as piloted by ACE through a model based on collaborative culture, working in and with the community it serves. In this mission universities need to enhance the links and partnership between HE and disadvantaged communities, drive familiarity with the university and generate a sense of expectation in the community rather than exclusion.

The idea of expectation is to counter the inequalities explored earlier in this article and the sorts of barriers identified by Harwood et al. (2013) amongst others, in order to help build more robust individual and community identities in line with McCarthy (1990) and expand the type of weak ties and cognitive flexibility identified by Granovetter (1983). Together this can build individual and community resilience strategies to help create new imaginaries about full participation in society including access to education, a greater share of economic output, demands for better services and opportunities and recognition as equal citizens and members of society. This can help place greater value on learning as an enabler of individual and community change and reduce cultural barriers to access to university education. It is not the solution to inequality but it has the potential to be a key component in giving individuals and communities new voice, confidence and experiences to address the persistence of educational inequality that directly impacts them intergenerationally.

Note

1. Denizen here refers to all people in a neighbourhood, regardless of their legal or residence status, including citizens and non-citizens, those homeless or in any form of residence including institutional contexts and those who work in, visit and transition through the neighbourhood and others who identify with or have affiliations to the neighbourhood.

Disclosure statement

No potential conflict of interest was reported by the authors.

ORCID

Siobhán O'Sullivan http://orcid.org/0000-0002-1641-0026
Lorna Kenny http://orcid.org/0000-0002-5351-3091

References

Armano, E., and A. Murgia. 2011. "The Precariousness of Young Knowledge Workers: A Subject-Oriented Approach." In *Precariat: Labour, Work and Politics*, edited by M. Johnson. London: Routledge.
Bailey, N., J. Breen, and M. Ward. 2009. *Community Education: More than Just a Course*. Dublin: AONTAS.
Beaven, R., M. May-Gillings, R. Wilson, D. Bosworth, S. Joshi, and S. Nitsch. 2011. "Measuring the Economic Impact of Further Education." BIS Research Paper Number 38.
Biesta, G. J. J. 2011. *Learning Democracy in School and Society: Education, Lifelong Learning, and the Politics of Citizenship*. Rotterdam: Sense Publishers.
Boyer, E. L. 1990. *Scholarship Reconsidered: Priorities of the Professoriate*. Princeton, NJ: Carnegie Foundation for the Advancement of Teaching.
Brennan, J., and R. Naidoo. 2008. "Higher Education and the Achievement (And/Or Prevention) of Equity and Social Justice." *Higher Education* 56 (3): 287–302. doi:10.1007/s10734-008-9127-3.
Clancy, P. 2001. *College Entry in Focus: A Fourth National Survey of Access to Higher Education*. Dublin: Higher Education Authority.
COMMIT 2016. *Embedding the LLL Contribution for Social Engagement into University Structures and Practices (Technical Report)*. Barcelona: Eucen Publications. http://commit.eucen.eu/sites/default/files/COMMIT_Technical_Repport_FINAL.pdf
CSO 2007. *EU Survey on Income and Living Conditions (EU-SILC): Intergenerational Transmission of Poverty*. http://www.cso.ie/en/media/csoie/releasespublications/documents/eusilc/current/intergenpov.pdf
CSO 2012. *Profile 9 What We Know*. Available on: http://www.cso.ie/en/media/csoie/census/documents/census2011profile9/Profile,9,What,we,know,full,doc,for,web.pdf
Doberneck, D. M., C. R. Glass, and J. Schweitzer. 2010. "From Rhetoric to Reality: A Typology of Publically Engaged Scholarship." *Journal of Higher Education Outreach and Engagement* 14 (4): 5–35.
Dockery, A. M., R. Seymour, and P. Koshy. 2016. "Promoting Low Socio-Economic Participation in Higher Education: A Comparison of Area-Based and Individual Measures." *Studies in Higher Education* 41 (9): 1692–1714. doi:10.1080/03075079.2015.1020777.
Expert Group on Future Funding for Higher Education. 2015. "The Role, Value and Scale of Higher Education in Ireland Discussion Paper for Stakeholder Consultation." January. Department of Education and Skills.
Field, J. 2009. "Well-Being and Happiness: Inquiry into the Future of Lifelong Learning." (Thematic Paper No. 4). Leicester, UK: National Institute of Adult Continuing Education.
Fitzgerald, H. E. F., K. Bruns, S. T. Sonka, A. Furco, and L. Swanson. 2016. "The Centrality of Engagement in Higher Education: Reflections and Future Directions." *Journal of Higher Education Outreach and Engagement* 20 (1): 245–253.
Fragosa, A. 2014. "Older Adults as Active Learners in the Community." In *Learning across Generations in Europe*, edited by B. Schmidt-Hertha, S. Jelenc Krašovec, and M. Formosa. Rotterdam: Sense Publishers.
Granovetter, M. 1983. "The Strength of Weak Ties: A Network Theory Revisited." *Sociological Theory*, 1: 201–233.
Hartley, M., and J. Saltmarsh. 2016. "A Brief History of a Movement Civic Engagement and American Higher Education." In *Publicly Engaged Scholars Next-Generation Engagement and the Future of Higher Education*, edited by M. A. Post, E. Ward, N. V. Longo, and J. Saltmarsh. Sterling, VA: Stylus Publishing.

Harwood, V., S. O'Shea, J. Uptin, N. Humphrey, and L. Kervin. 2013. "Precarious Education and the University: Navigating the Silenced Borders of Participation." *International Journal on School Disaffection* 10 (2): 23–42. doi:10.18546/IJSD.10.2.02.

Higher Education Authority 2015. *National Plan for Equity of Access to Higher Education 2015-2019* (ISBN: 1-905135-47-5). http://www.hea.ie/sites/default/files/national_plan_for_equity_of_access_to_higher_education_2015-2019_single_page_version_0.pdf

Higher Education Authority 2017. *Student Assistance Fund*. http://hea.ie/funding-governance-performance/funding/student-finance/student-assistance-fund/

Higher Education Funding Council for England 2017. *Briefing: Additional Equality and Diversity Data*. http://www.hefce.ac.uk/analysis/opthesa/

Jongbloed, B., J. Enders, and C. Salerno. 2008. "Higher Education and Its Communities: Interconnections, Interdependencies at a Research Agenda." *High Education* 56 (3): 303–324. doi:10.1007/s10734-008-9128-2.

Kearns, P. 2012. "Learning Cities as Healthy Green Cities: Building Sustainable Opportunity Cities." *Australian Journal of Adult Learning* 52 (2): 368–391.

Kezar, A., A. C. Chambers, and J. C. Burkhardt, eds. 2005. *Higher Education for the Public Good: Emerging Voices from a National Movement*. San Francisco: John Wiley and Sons.

Lin, N. 1999. "Building a Network Theory of Social Capital." *Connections* 22 (1): 28–51.

Lynch, K. 1999. *Equality in Education*. Dublin: Gill and Macmillan.

Lynch, K., and C. O'Riordan. 1998. "Inequality in Higher Education: A Study of Class Barriers." *British Journal of Sociology of Education* 19 (4): 445–478. doi:10.1080/0142569980190401.

Mahlo, D. 2017. "Teaching Learners with Diverse Needs in the Foundation Phase in Gauteng Province, South Africa." *SAGE Open* 7 (1): 1–9. doi:10.1177/2158244017697162.

Maxwell, N., and C. Dorrity. 2010. "Access to Third Level Education: Challenges for Equality of Opportunity in Post Celtic Tiger Ireland." *Irish Journal of Public Policy* 2 (1).

McCarthy, T. 1990. "Introduction." In *Moral Consciousness and Communicative Action*, edited by J. Habermas, vii–xiii. Cambridge: Polity.

McCoy, S., E. Calvert, E. Smyth, and M. Darmody. 2009. *Study on the Costs of Participation in Higher Education*. Dublin: National Office for Equity of Access to Higher Education, Higher Education Authority.

McGlynn, L. 2014. *Community Education and the Labour Activation Challenge: A Literature Review on Community Education in a Context of Labour Market Activation, Employability and Active Citizenship in Ireland and the EU*. Community Education Facilitators' Association. http://www.cefa.ie/uploads/1/5/8/8/15883224/community_education_and_the_labour_activation_challenge_cefa_2014.pdf

McKnight, J., and J. Kretzmann. 1993. *Building Communities from the inside Out: A Path Towards Finding and Mobilizing a Community's Assets*. Chicago, IL: Acta Pubns.

Nolan, B., and C. T. Whelan. 1999. *Loading the Dice? A Study of Cumulative Disadvantage*. Dublin: Oak Tree Press in association with Combat Poverty Agency.

Ó Tuama, S. 2013. *Delivering UCC's Adult & Continuing Education Mission: 2013-2017*. ACE (Centre for Adult Continuing Education), University College Cork. DOI: 10.13140/RG.2.2.19384.03846

Ó Tuama, S. 2016. "Adult Education and Reflexive Activation: Prioritizing Recognition, Respect, Dignity and Capital Accumulation." *European Journal for Research on the Education and Learning of Adults* 7 (1): 107–118. doi:10.3384/rela.2000-7426.rela0172.

O'Sullivan, S., and L. Kenny. 2016. *Learning Neighbourhoods Pilot Programme*. ACE (Centre for Adult Continuing Education), University College Cork. https://www.ucc.ie/en/media/studyatucc/adulted/LearningNeighbourhoodsPilotReview[5129].pdf

O'Sullivan, S., S. Ó. Tuama, and W. Denayer. Forthcoming. *'Breaking the Barriers': A Reflexive Approach to Adult Education and Lifelong Learning*. Cork: Centre for Adult Continuing Education, University College Cork.

OECD. 2006. *Higher Education in Ireland: Reviews of National Policies in Education*. Paris: OECD.

OECD 2009. *Education at a Glance*. http://www.oecd.org/education/skills-beyond-school/43636332.pdf

OECD 2013. *Education at a Glance*. http://www.oecd.org/edu/eag2013%20(eng)–FINAL%2020%20June%202013.pdf

Perry, E., and B. Francis. 2010. *The Social Class Gap for Educational Achievement: A Review of the Literature*. http://www.thersa.org/__data/assets/pdf_file/0019/367003/RSA-Social-Justice-paper.pdf

Post, M. A., E. Ward, N. V. Longo, and J. Saltmarsh, eds. 2016. *Publicly Engaged Scholars Next-Generation Engagement and the Future of Higher Education*. Sterling, VA: Stylus Publishing.

Putnam, R. D. 1995. "Tuning In, Tuning Out: The Strange Disappearance of Social Capital in America." *Political Science and Politics* 28 (4): 664–683. doi:10.1017/S1049096500058856.

Saltmarsh, J., and M. Hartley. 2011. *"To Serve a Larger Purpose:" Engagement for Democracy and the Transformation of Higher Education*. Philadelphia, PA: Temple University Press.

Sandbrook, I. 2009. "A Learning City Perspective." IFLL Sector Paper 5, National Institute of Adult Continuing Education.

Social Mobility Commission 2017. *Time for Change: An Assessment of Government Policies on Social Mobility 1997-2017*. https://www.gov.uk/government/uploads/system/uploads/attachment_data/file/622214/Time_for_Change_report_-_An_assessement_of_government_policies_on_social_mobility_1997-2017.pdf

Stephens, J. 2015. "Pathway to a Degree – Transformative Education in Action." *Proceedings of SCUTREA 44th Annual Conference*. https://drive.google.com/file/d/0B8CpqlADwoQlU0dyRzdwUTVralU/view

UNESCO. 2015. *Education for All 2000-2015: Achievements and Challenges*. Paris: UNES. http://unesdoc.unesco.org/images/0023/002322/232205e.pdf.

Warner Weil, S., D. Wildemeersch, and T. Jansen. 2005. *Unemployed Youth and Social Exclusion in Europe: Learning for Inclusion?* Oxford: Ashgate.

Watson, D., R. Hollister, S. E. Stroud, and E. Babcock. 2011. *The Engaged University: International Perspectives on Civic Engagement*. New York: Routledge.

Wilson-Strydom, M. 2015. "University Access and Theories of Social Justice: Contributions of the Capabilities Approach." *Higher Education* 69 (1): 143–155. doi:10.1007/s10734-014-9766-5.

REPLY

An ongoing challenge and a chance to diversify university outreach to tackle inequality: a response to O'Sullivan, O'Tuama and Kenny

Ann-Marie Houghton

This is a reply to:

O'Sullivan, Siobhán, O'Tuama, Séamus and Kenny, Lorna. 2017. "Universities as key responders to education inequality." *Global Discourse*. 7 (4): 527–538. http://dx.doi.org/10.1080/23269995.2017.1402250.

Siobhan O'Sullivan, Seamus O'Tuama and Lorna Kenny (2017) explore aspects of inequality all too familiar within higher education and consider ways in which universities are key responders to educational inequality. I found the paper offered many points of connection with my own research in the past as well as current preoccupations. In this reply, I reflect on some past and present connections that relate to factors associated with engaging community groups and the notion of outreach.

Context matters

The nature of our work reflects our working context, the wider policy influences but also our own educational and life stories. For instance, the writers' location within adult continuing education and their obvious commitment to community education and recognition of attendant intergenerational factors is evident. Like them, I believe engagement with community groups needs to be nuanced and responsive to the factors that contribute to inequality, which are not all the same for different communities. Due to their respective stages of development, the authors do not provide many details about their urban project, Cork Learning Neighbourhoods, or the pilot rural project, Skellig Centre for Research and Innovation. This was a pity as it deprived the article of the contextual current evidence to support the approach for which they were advocating. However, the rationale for their approach resonated with similar work by Lancaster's Community Access Programme (CAP) in the 1990s (Preece and Houghton 2000). Based in contrasting communities, our work was located within East Lancashire, where we worked with mainly Muslim women, in Lancashire and Cumbria, where we worked with adults experiencing various physical and sensory impairments, unemployed men in Barrow and parents with no experience of higher education. Our action research enabled us to explore and tackle similar issues to those highlighted by the authors, both project teams engaging in community-based education as part of our respective universities' commitments to regional lifelong learning.

A distinctive feature of the CAP (now known as REAP – Researching Equity Access and Participation) and other projects delivered in English continuing education departments (e.g. Leeds, Leicester, Nottingham, Sussex and Warwick) in the 1990s was the development of culturally and socially relevant access courses. At Lancaster, we developed university-validated frameworks in consultation with the relevant community groups to provide relevant curricula to teach personal development, study, enterprise and basic research skills. We engaged in a mutually beneficial process of what we would describe today as co-creation. Our work reflected our commitment to tackling exclusion and promoting social justice and relied upon university community developer having the skills, cultural and social capital to work across specific community and university contexts.

Another point of continuity in the barriers some learners face is that of gaining access to information advice and guidance (IAG). Based on our research, we identified and explored IAG experiences and expectations of learners who were at, what we described as, a pre, pre-entry stage (Houghton and Oglesby 1996). These learners often lacked the bridging social capital (Granovetter 1983) that O'Sullivan, O'Tuama and Kenny discuss in their paper. What is regrettable is that students from disadvantaged communities continue to *believe that university is not for them*. Sadly, this viewpoint, which was present in our work in the 1990s, is something we continue to encounter in evaluation of current outreach activities working with younger people as well as their parents. Furthermore, it is a view expressed by some current undergraduate students who have overcome some of the attitudinal, social and economic barriers to apply and gain a place at university.

The intergenerational issues raised by O'Sullivan are ones that we explored in-depth during the era of Aimhigher as part of the Families And Higher Education – FAHED – project and Upto Uni a year-long intervention involving parents, teachers and young people and including community-based workshops, a summer residential and campus visit to a contrasting university. These action research projects emphasised the diversity of perspectives of families from different locale and highlighted how parental and wider family attitudes were influenced by previous educational experience as well as the local employment and economic contexts (Houghton 2005).

When reading O'Sullivan, O'Tuama and Kenny's paper, it was interesting to note the similarity of the adult education debates that have grown to accommodate those of lifelong learning, widening participation (WP) and, more recently, social mobility. Whilst the fundamental challenges seem to remain, the focus of attention changes with respect to the identity of the groups of learners that attract funders' attention and, therefore, become a priority. Yes, the funding initiatives colleagues in Cork and elsewhere are seeking to access and use to invest in activities to tackle inequality are different, but the challenges they outline are sadly familiar.

Outreach for what purpose

The second issue I wish to consider is the purpose and nature of outreach and how this does or does not support the suggestion that universities are key responders of education inequality. Although I agree with the authors' general points about factors that perpetuate patterns of participation, it is inevitable that the writers did not explore the complexity of the challenges-facing universities as key responders to inequality. Recent research and evaluation undertaken by the Researching Equity, Access and Participation group at Lancaster have highlighted some of that complexity. For example, we have identified multiple motivations and responses by widening access students to different subject-focused summer schools. The benefits of adopting a collaborative approach to outreach is evidenced in work with the Dukes theatre as part of our Access Agreement, where the university has been able to engage with young women from the Gypsy Roma Travelling community to explore their views of education (see Youtube GRT: Our Voice The Dukes 2016). Changes over time is another feature that adds to the complexity, something I explored when considering the changing issues associated with the transition of disabled students. The more recent evaluation of the transition experiences focused on a group of students on the autistic spectrum that barely participated 10 years previously (Houghton 2017). The outreach and induction activities of these students represent commitment to tackling inequality.

However, REAP's recent evaluation of outreach activities funded as part of our university Access Agreement coincided with a very different project, which also involved outreach, this time with the focus on inspiring the next generation of researchers. The RCUK-School University Partnership Initiative (RCUK-SUPI) project caused me and others to think about the use of the term outreach (further details of this 4-year project involving 12 universities can be found in RCUK 2017). Although SUPI also focused on outreach and had a remit of tackling inequality, its purpose was to increase interest in and supporting progression into research. The emphasis was different and the extent to which this outreach represented a key response to education inequality varied. Over the lifetime of the project as the university began to consider sustainability one specific activity, 'Research in a Box' gained additional access agreement funding designed to increase engagement with WP schools and learners. Some of these boxes also included research targeted at very relevant topics such as 'health inequalities' and 'rethinking disadvantage' (see Lancaster University 2017).

In our evaluation of widening access outreach and SUPI research outreach, we interacted with university staff and teachers in schools who were engaged in marketing and recruitment outreach. It appears that there are multiple groups of staff – community developers, WP practitioners, marketing and recruitment officers, admission tutors, undergraduate and postgraduate student ambassadors, early career researchers and, in our case, researchers involved in evaluation of the outreach activities. Since each group of staff engages in outreach for different reasons there is no guarantee that all activities will automatically tackle educational inequality advocated by the authors. The university is dependent on working in partnership and arguably it is the nature of those partnerships and the way university staff engaged in outreach that will determine whether, and to what extent, universities can be positioned as key responders to education inequality. In thinking about those partnerships, it seems important to consider what we each bring to the challenge of responding to education inequality, so that our work is complementary and not one of further competition, where some win and some lose.

Disclosure statement

No potential conflict of interest was reported by the author.

ORCID

Ann-Marie Houghton http://orcid.org/0000-0003-1289-1878

References

Granovetter, M. 1983. "The Strength of Weak Ties: A Network Theory Revisited." *Sociological Theory* 1: 201–233. doi:10.2307/202051.

Houghton, A. 2005. "Who Needs Outreach to Widen Participation? Families or Higher Education." *Journal of Lifelong Learning and Widening Participation* 7 (3): 5–15.

Houghton, A. 2017. *Getting through the Gate is Only the First Hurdle: Learning from Disabled Students and Staff about Their Experience of Inclusive Teaching and Learning. Adult Education for Inclusion and Diversity, SCUTREA 2017.* University of Edinburgh.

Houghton, A., and K. L. Oglesby. 1996. "Guidance and Learner Support: Developing Threshold Standards." *Adults Learning* 7 (6): 146–147.

Lancaster University. 2017 "Research in a Box." *Lancaster University Website* [Online]. [Accessed November 4 2017]. http://www.lancaster.ac.uk/teachers/rcuk-schools-university-partnerships-initiative/research-in-a-box/.

O'Sullivan, S., S. O'Tuama, and L. Kenny. 2017. "Universities as Key Responders to Educational Inequality." *Global Discourse* 7 (4): 527–538.

Preece, J., and A. Houghton. 2000. *Nurturing Social Capital in Excluded Communities: A Kind of Higher Education.* Aldershot: Ashgate.

RCUK. 2017. "RCUK School-University Partnership Project Website." [online]. [Accessed November 4 2017]. http://www.rcuk.ac.uk/pe/PartnershipsInitiative/.

The Dukes. 2016 *"GRT: Our Voice The Dukes."* Lancaster University Access Agreement. https://www.youtube.com/watch?v=X34G5OzOdl.

REPLY

A reply to O'Sullivan, O'Tuama and Kenny

Tom Fellows

This is a reply to:

O'Sullivan, Siobhán, O'Tuama, Séamus and Kenny, Lorna. 2017. 'Universities as key responders to education inequality.' *Global Discourse*. 7 (4): 527–538. https://doi.org/10.1080/23269995.2017.1400902.

Introduction

Siobhan O'Sullivan, Séamus O'Tuama, and Lorna Kenny (2017) in 'Universities as key responders to educational inequality' offer a novel way to engage communities which struggle to relate to their local universities. The authors rightly remind universities of their status as publicly funded organisations, arguing that this translates into an ethical obligation to engage with local communities and to challenge social mobility and inequality (1–2). The authors draw upon international comparative data which shows that accessing education regardless of age can have positive effects on life chances, collective economic/social prosperity and individual social capital (2–3).

The authors argue that, through initiatives that engage deprived communities, a 'collaborative culture' can be generated which has the potential to 'drive familiarity with the university and generate a sense of expectation in the community rather than exclusion' (O'Sullivan, O'Tuama, and Kenny 2017, 9). Recognising that 'retention rates and graduate outcomes for disadvantaged students have barely improved' (5) over the last few years, the authors offer an innovative suggestion for opening up higher education to those groups that feel 'marginalised' from university life. The authors do this by introducing a case study from the University College Cork (7–9), explaining how adult education promises to give greater 'access to university' for marginalised groups 'through a partnership model with local communities and stakeholder networks' (8) that 'can build individual and community resilience strategies to help create new imaginaries about full participation in society' (9).

Cumulative disadvantage theory (CDT)

Throughout this article, the authors do well to blend theory and practice; drawing upon a nuanced theoretical framework to convey the message that opening up universities to 'disadvantaged' and 'marginalised' groups will offer the potential for challenging 'lifelong' inequality. Specifically, they draw upon a variation of CDT to make their case

(Dannefer 2003), stating that 'lack of educational opportunity inhibits full participation in society and can lead to *cumulative disadvantage*' (O'Sullivan, O'Tuama, and Kenny 2017, 3) which universities are well suited to address.

According to Dannefer (2003, 237) CDT is the 'systematic tendency for interindividual divergence in a given characteristic (e.g. money, health, status) with the passage of time'. CDT is based largely on the idea that societal structures are one of the key sources of inequality because they are 'unfair' and 'benefit … some individuals well beyond the value of their contributions while ignoring or minimizing the equally meritorious contributions of others' (Dannefer 2003, 331–330). Developing the CDT approach further, Ferraro and Shippee (2009) have also suggested that long-term exposure to 'unfair' social processes puts individuals at risk of adverse social and personal outcomes. While CDT (and similar theories) has its strengths, not least for highlighting various institutional barriers to equality, it does have certain structuralist and deterministic overtones. Indeed, there is a sense of inevitability around the notion that exposure to unfavourable social situations leads to inequality throughout life.

This idea that *structural* changes will help tackle lifelong inequality is a key theme in O'Sullivan, O'Tuama and Kenny's (2017) piece. However, the type of university-led community engagement the authors endorse will only make a difference if people choose to engage with universities once the barriers to their participation have been removed. As Ferraro and Shippee (2009, 335) outline, while it is true that 'inequality accumulates over the life course … resource mobilization and human agency play critical roles in how trajectories are shaped'. While the authors address the 'resource mobilisation' (335) side of overcoming lifelong inequality, there is scope for more to be said about the motivations for engaging with, and the response to, university sponsored outreach programmes amongst disadvantaged communities.

Overcoming disadvantage in adulthood: the right approach for universities?

The above comments should not detract from the obvious contribution the authors make in further illuminating the structural barriers disadvantaged groups face in accessing 'lifelong learning' and the benefits that they are excluded from as a result. Nevertheless, the range of approaches available for addressing lifelong disadvantage, and their relative strengths and weaknesses, is not discussed in great depth. As such, the authors' conclusion, that community outreach programmes and adult learning opportunities have 'the potential to be a key component in giving individuals and communities new voice, confidence and experiences to address the persistence of educational inequality that directly impacts them intergenerationally' (O'Sullivan, O'Tuama, and Kenny 2017, 9), lacks the strength it may have had if a more comprehensive examination had been provided.

One particularly prominent issue not considered by the authors is whether culminative disadvantage is best tackled early in life rather than in adulthood, with some contention in the literature as to whether disadvantage is 'reversible' (Ferraro and Kelley-Moore 2003, 4). Indeed, contrary to the central tenet of their article, there is a compelling argument to suggest that exclusion from university for disadvantaged groups is most acute prior to adulthood. Using English state-school education as an example to illustrate this point, inequality begins at an early age for those from economically deprived backgrounds. Disadvantaged status is often narrowly defined by the Department for Education (DfE) as 'pupils eligible for free school meals at any point within the past 6 years (Ever 6 FSM) and pupils looked after by the local authority' (Macleod et al. 2015, 8). As children go through primary and secondary school, the 'gap' between disadvantaged pupils and their non-disadvantaged peers gets steadily wider. According to a recent report, which drew upon data from 2016, for those starting early years education (children under 5 years old), the attainment gap (i.e. what children achieve at a specific point in time) between disadvantaged pupils and their peers was 4.3 months. By age 15/16, pupils in 2014 from an economically disadvantaged background were, on average, 19.3 months behind their non-disadvantaged peers (Andrews, Robinson, and Hutchinson 2017, 13).

This trend means that, by the time students sit their General Certificates of Secondary Education (GCSEs), those from disadvantaged backgrounds are substantially more likely to receive poorer grades than their non-disadvantaged peers. In 2016 (under the 'old' A*-E GSCE system) only 43.1% of disadvantaged students in state-funded schools achieved an A*-C in GCSE English and maths compared to 70.6% of non-disadvantaged pupils (Department for Education 2016, 19). This trend continues throughout a young person's post-16 education. Official 2016/17 DfE statistics showed that disadvantaged pupils were 10% more likely than their non-disadvantaged peers to enter a further education (FE) institution which offered non A-level alternatives. Furthermore, disadvantaged pupils were 8% less likely to be in a 'sustained destination' after school – meaning that they were more likely to change course or drop out of FE study (Department for Education 2017, 10).

The gap in progress and attainment between disadvantaged pupils and their peers means that, by the time young people are considering degree level courses in the UK, disadvantaged pupils are, on the one hand, less likely to have followed traditional academic routes and, on the other, less likely to have achieved grades that permit them admission to top UK universities. Amongst those students receiving top A-level grades, the Russell Group outline on its website (as of November 7, 2017) that 'in 2009, only 232 students who had been on free school meals (FSMs) achieved 3 As at A-level or the equivalent. This was 4.1% of the total number of FSM students taking A-levels, and less than an estimated 0.3% of all those who had received FSMs when aged 15' (http://russellgroup.ac.uk/news/free-school-meals/).

How universities can help break down barriers for disadvantaged young people

Despite evidence to suggest that exclusion from universities occurs prior to adulthood, the authors are still correct to assert that universities can and should play a role in overcoming lifelong inequality and disadvantaged. In terms of motivating disadvantaged individuals to participate in higher education, one area that universities may want to consider revisiting is careers advice in schools. The Technical and Further Education Act (HM Government 2017) will soon give technical education and apprenticeship providers legal 'access [to] registered pupils during the relevant phase of their education'. While a greater emphasis on non-academic careers advice is welcomed, universities also have to make the case for higher education regardless of background. As the authors rightly point out, young people from disadvantaged communities feel 'disengaged' from university life (O'Sullivan, O'Tuama, and Kenny 2017, 5–6) and it is imperative that they understand that technical education and apprenticeships are only two of their options. Indeed, universities can and should help spread the idea that, for all young people, there are a range of high quality academic and non-academic opportunities available. In doing so, universities should also challenge the idea that young people should choose one path in life over another simply because of their background.

Yet, changing attitudes through well rounded careers advice is only half the battle. Even if young people from disadvantaged backgrounds feel motivated to attend university, the data presented above shows that they are statistically less likely to attain the same level of GCSE and A-level grades as their non-disadvantaged peers – impeding their chances of attending the top universities in the country. Therefore, as the authors argue, universities also have an obligation to break down the structural barriers which stop disadvantaged young people from getting on in higher education. This may involve, as Boliver et al. (2017) suggests, admitting disadvantaged young people into university with a worse academic record than their peers. Although Boliver et al. (2017) outline that a lot of work is already being done to consider the contextual barriers facing students' access to university, more still needs to be done. In particular, it is about changing attitudes, not just outside of the university, but also within it – ensuring that all university stakeholders understand that attainment does not always mirror potential, especially for those with less opportunities in early life.

Disclosure statement

The author is an educational professional working for a third-sector organisation. All opinions and views expressed in this article are those of the author and do not necessary reflect those of his employer.

References

Andrews, J., D. Robinson, and J. Hutchinson. 2017. *Closing the Gap? Trends in Educational Attainment and Disadvantage*. Education Policy Institute.
Boliver, V., C. Crawford, M. Powell, and W. Craige. 2017. *Admissions in Context: The Use of Contextual Information by Leading Universities*. London: Sutton Trust.
Dannefer, D. 2003. "Cumulative Advantage/Disadvantage and the Life Course: Cross-Fertilizing Age and Social Science Theory." *The Journals of Gerontology Series B: Psychological Sciences and Social Sciences* 58 (6): S327–S337. doi:10.1093/geronb/58.6.S327.
Department for Education. 2016. *Revised GCSE and Equivalent Results in England: 2015 to 2016*. London: DfE.
Department for Education. 2017. *Destinations of Key Stage 4 and Key Stage 5 Students, England, 2015/16*. London: DfE.
Ferraro, K., and J. Kelley-Moore. 2003. "Cumulative Disadvantage and Health: Long-Term Consequences of Obesity?." *American Sociological Review* 68 (5): 707. doi:10.2307/1519759.
Ferraro, K., and T. Shippee. 2009. "Aging and Cumulative Inequality: How Does Inequality Get under the Skin?." *The Gerontologist* 49 (3): 333–343. doi:10.1093/geront/gnp034.

HM Government. 2017. *Technical and Further Education Act*. London: HM Government.
Macleod, S., C. Sharp, D. Bernardinelli, A. Skipp, and S. Higgins. 2015. *Supporting the Attainment of Disadvantaged Pupils: Articulating Success and Good Practice*. London: DfE.
O'Sullivan, S., S. O'Tuama, and L. Kenny. 2017. "Universities as Key Responders to Education Inequality." *Global Discourse* 7 (4): 527–538.

Affective collaboration in the Westfjords of Iceland

Valdimar J. Halldórsson

ABSTRACT
This article advances the need for participatory, affect-based approaches to research through reflection on two projects: the first, concerning the work of a District Committee, the inhabitants of the district and the Municipal Government in the Westfjords of Iceland; the second, a qualitative research project conducted for Red Cross branches in the same area. Anthropologists and ethnographers have always practised collaboration of some sort. This collaboration was until recently mainly driven by the anthropologist who sought to represent 'native points of view' in 'objective' 'scientific' forms. This unequal hierarchical relationship was severely criticised in the 1970s and 1980s and led to various experiments such as 'Collaborative Anthropology', which shifts the control process out of the hands of the ethnographer into the collective, equal hands of the ethnographer and the community with which they are working. However, collaboration and other social arrangements are based in the intersubjective realm, in which people, things and events affect one another in multifarious ways. This article holds that 'affect' must be granted central consideration when conducting collaborative and other social research.

Introduction

This article is an elaboration of my presentation at Lancaster University's 'Participatory Research: Working and Communicating with Communities' conference held in Newcastle on 7–8 January 2017. The article concerns two projects with which I have been involved in the Ísafjarðarbær Municipality, which is situated in the north-west of Iceland and called 'The Westfjords'.

The first project concerns the work of the District Committee of Súgandafjörður (Hverfisráð Súgandafjarðar), which is one of seven District Committees in the Ísafjarðarbær Municipality. Five persons (including me) were elected in the District Committee of Súgandafjörður and are working voluntarily in the group. The District Committee of Súgandafjörður covers the village, Suðureyri, as well as the fjord, Súgandafjörður, in which the village is situated. During my time in The District Committee of Súgandafjörður (of which I am still a member), I did not participate as a researcher but as a civilian interested in greater direct democracy in Ísafjörður municipality, in which I live. It was not until I was asked to present the work of the District

Committee of Súgandafjörður this year that I started to listen to our meetings (which I had recorded) and to write down and analyse the discussions. The second project was qualitative research which I conducted in 2012 for the Red Cross branches in the area. The main objective of the research was to identify which groups of people were most vulnerable in the north-western part of the Westfjords and suggest means by which the Red Cross could improve their condition. After having some difficulties in finding out what these two very different projects had in common, I decided that the common denominator for them should be seen to be 'collaboration'.

I will begin this article by explaining this term as it is used and understood within the discipline of social anthropology. Then, I will describe the collaboration between the Súgandafjörður District Committee and Ísafjarðarbær municipality government, and between the Súgandafjörður District Committee and the villagers in Suðureyri. Throughout, I also describe my collaboration or, rather, the lack of collaboration, in the research project I conducted for Red Cross branches in the area.

Collaborative research

I became interested in collaborative research during my Red Cross research in 2012, when I encountered the literature on ethnographic collaborative research developed during the last two decades or so. The shifts in cultural anthropology in the 1970s and 1980s have been traced by Choy et al. (2009), who demonstrate the emergence of collaborative research and other experimental projects. Lassiter (2005) *The Chicago Guide to Collaborative Ethnography* is perhaps the clearest articulation of the need for collaboration between academics and communities, tracing the theoretical schools that influenced the concept of collaboration. Campbell and Lassiter (2015) advance the approach further with regard to collaboration in fieldwork situations (participating-observing), interviewing and writing. This North American trend is influenced by an older phenomenon in South America (Rappaport 2005; Rappaport 2008; Keisha-Khan and Rappaport 2013). Rappaport's research focuses more on an organisations than Lassiter's, but her reflection on collaboration with various groups in Colombian society, such as the 'Collaboradores', who 'do not speak *for* a subordinated sector, but are speaking *with* them' (Rappaport 2005, 62), is important. In addition, she discusses the contrasting nature of colonisation and decolonisation of knowledge, the former being dominated by Euro-American thought, creating 'disconnection between universities' needs and communities' needs' (Keisha-Khan and Rappaport 2013, 32). The 'Otro Saberes Initiative' established within LASA (The Latin American Studies Association) in 2004 is a decolonial project that is intended to promote collaborative research between civil society and academy-based intellectuals to explore research topics of interest to both (Hale and Stephen 2013). Carolyn Fluehr-Lobban emphasises ethics in collaborative research in which individuals and groups have 'vested interests in the project through their participation in the research design, execution, publication and outcomes' (Fluehr-Lobban 2008, 175; Fluehr-Lobban 2013, 163). W. B. White talks about the difference between Lassiter's and his colleagues' collaborative approach advanced through the *Journal of Collaborative Anthropologies*, highlighting the contrast between the modern, team-based approach and the post-modern, epistemic approach advanced by George Marcus White regards Lassiter's approach as more hermeneutic, disparate and community-based than the other two, which are primarily targeted at expert and academic audiences (White 2012, 88).

Reading this work stimulated me to think about the value and the relevance of my work as an anthropologist at home and abroad over many years. I did my fieldwork, as part of my studies in Social Anthropology at the University of Aarhus in Denmark, on an organic farm in South India in 1989. Looking back, I must admit that neither the farmer with whom I stayed nor other farmers in South India at that time who were adopting organic methods benefitted greatly from my fieldwork. My field-report sought mainly to explain and understand the farmer's view of nature and his reasons for starting organic farming in the 1970s, which, incidentally, was around the same time as I was introduced to the farming method in Iceland. I was preoccupied with the discussion within the discipline at that time and sought to understand the ways in which the theory of practice and structure fitted with the reality of 'my' Indian farmer and his organic farming. There were several people from the Netherlands in South India during that time who were teaching farmers organic methods, but, unfortunately, I did not contact them because I was too busy seeking to understand 'my' farmer. Otherwise, had I known about collaborative research at that time, I might have started collaborating with the Dutch teachers and 'their' organic farmers in ways that mattered to them.

Nevertheless, the word 'collaboration' is related to a whole lot of other concepts that sometimes overlap, sometimes mean similar things or sometimes relate to each other in similar ways. These concepts include participation, cooperation, involvement, engagement, democratisation and openness, among others.[1] Social anthropologists together with their ethnographic method[2] have always practised collaboration of some sort during their fieldwork in countries around the world. They cannot carry out their craft in the communities in which they work without engaging others, because that work is necessarily focused on the lives of others. Ethnographic fieldwork (i.e. collecting contemporary data on the site) is thus 'saturated with various and multiple ideas, assumptions, expectations, and hopes for collaboration on the part of ethnographers themselves, the collaborators with whom they work and the people and institutions, such as employers and funders, that in most cases make ethnographic work possible' (Campbell and Lassiter 2015, 19). However, this collaboration was, until recently, driven mainly by the needs, wants and wishes of the *ethnographer* rather than the *subject*.[3] My research for the Red Cross branches in the northern part of the Westfjords was also made in this spirit, being oriented around interviews with various people in institutions and NGO organisations in the area working with people who need assistance.

The criticism of collecting, analysing and presenting ethnographic data in this way started to emerge in the 1970s (see Geertz 1973; Asad 1973; Bourdieu 1977) and 1980s (see Clifford 1986; Fabian 1983; Marcuse and Fisher 1986). Critics held that ethnographers monopolised authority in depicting the 'subjects' of study, possessing the capacity to define 'the native point of view', and benefited from hierarchical power relations which left 'subjects' dominated. In contrast to scientific description, it was not possible, within this context, for ethnographers to represent the 'other' objectively. Representation was always grounded in the ethnographer's subjective interpretation of observations, of and accounts provided by, members of the studied society (Clifford 1988, 37; Clifford 1986, 17). The ethnographic field could 'no longer be formulated as innocuous collection of raw, unbiased, or unmediated "data".... Ethnographic description…is an inherently mediated affair that is always surfacing historically, politically, and rhetorically between and among people' (Campbell and Lassiter 2015, 74–75). The unequal power relations between the ethnographer and the 'subject' were seen to be particularly problematic given the colonial and post-colonial contexts within which such work was conducted. Put simply, critics argued that, in such contexts, it was not possible for, generally, white men from colonial countries to engage with subjects of colonialism in non-colonial, non-hierarchical and non-paternalistic forms.[4] This criticism advanced more reflexive, multivocal and co-constructed forms of ethnographic practice that led to various experiments within the discipline in subsequent years. One of these experiments came to be called 'collaborative anthropology' (Low and Merry 2010; White 2012).

The form of collaboration that scholars discuss today within anthropology is different from the one that emerged earlier. In light of critiques of the authority of ethnographers, it is rather questionable today to pursue collaboration based on the control of the ethnographer, because it will only sustain the status quo and normalise this unequal relationship between researcher and subject. Instead, the research should be based on collaboration between equal partners, in which the ethnographer does not have 'subject' or an 'informant' to provide information at the researcher's request, but a consultant or a cooperant, with whom to work together, side by side. Lassiter describes this collaboration well when he says that collaborative ethnography is

> an approach to ethnography that *deliberately* and *explicitly* emphasizes collaboration at every point in the ethnographic process, without veiling it – from project conceptualization, to fieldwork, and, especially, through the writing process. Collaborative ethnography invites commentary from our consultants and seeks to make that commentary overtly part of the ethnographic text as it develops. In turn, this negotiation is reintegrated back into the fieldwork process itself. Importantly, the process yields texts that are co-conceived or co-written with local communities of collaborators and consider multiple audiences outside the confines of academic discourse, including local constituencies. These texts can – and often do – include multiple authors; but not exclusively so. Collaborative ethnography then, is both a theoretical and methodological approach for doing *and* writing ethnography. (Lassiter 2005, 16)

Collaborative research is therefore more than 'traditional' ethnographic research, because it shifts control of the research process out of the hands of the ethnographer and into the collective hands of ethnographer and the community with which they are working on an equal basis, engendering dialogue between and among them, which in turn engenders co-understandings about the similarities and differences between them (Lassiter 2005, 62; Rappaport 2008, 6). Collaborative ethnography emphasises, therefore, finding common ground on which to build shared understandings and mutually directed actions. Both ethnographers and their 'consultants' 'struggle together to co-interpret and even co-theorize experience via the ethnographic text, the process can be multi-directional and multi-transformational … (and) can transcend both ethnographic method and ethnographic product' (Campbell and Lassiter 2015, 6). The collaborative research is then relevant for both the ethnographer and the people with whom they work. It can promote active involvement capable of assisting communities to transform their condition. The research then becomes applied or action-oriented research, and the ethnographer, becomes an advisor and facilitator (Campbell and Lassiter 2010).

As a civilian working voluntarily in the Súgandafjörður District Committee to promote better democracy in Ísafjörður municipality, I neither conducted 'traditional' ethnographic research nor collaborative research with the members of the Committee or other citizens in the area. It was not until after I was asked to give a presentation of our work in the Súgandafjörður District Committee that I started to analyse our meetings and produce the presentation and, subsequently, this article. But I collaborated consciously and unconsciously as a civilian on equal terms with other Committee members and other citizens in the village, although my analysis and the output are mine alone.

The turn to affect

A collaboration between two or more partners for building co-understanding and co-directed actions must be based on recognition of the intersubjective realm of the social. Recently, a new theoretical frame related to the sensory part of the intersubjective realm, called 'affect' theory, has been launched (Clough and Halley 2007). When studies in feelings, sentiments and passions emerged within social anthropology in 1980s, with the writing of Michelle Z. Rosaldo (1980), Lila Abu-Lughod (1986), Fred R. Myers (1986) and Catherine Lutz (Clifford 1988), proponents tried to shift the research focus of these concepts from almost exclusive concern with the psychology of the individual to the social, cultural, historical and political relations of people (Lutz 2017). The concept of affect has recently been added to this body of work and expanded to a variety of disciplines.[5]

The subjects of study within affect studies include experience of emotions such as love, hate, fear, resentment, passions, embodiment or belonging; means of attachment to and detachment from others (people, animals, things and events); contextual pressures that influence the intensity of emotions; the transference of emotions and attachments from person to person and individual differences in affect (Sjöstedt 2016). And yet, there does not seem to exist any 'single, generalizable theory of affect: not yet, and (thankfully) there never will be', as Gregory J. Seigworth and Melissa Gregg write in their *The Affect Theory Reader* (2010a, 3).

Recent interest in affect studies emerged with publication of two essays in 1995: 'The Autonomy of Affect', by the Canadian philosopher, Brian Massumi (2002), and *'Shame in the Cybernetic Fold'* by Eve Sedgwick and Adam Frank (1995) (see Gregg and Seigworth 2010b, 5). These essays, and the subsequent work of these authors, have had a seminal impact on understandings of affect across the humanities (Gregg and Seigworth 2010b,5; Blackman 2010, 182). Massumi is influenced on the work of the French philosophers, Gilles Deleuze and Félix Guattari, who were inspired by Spinoza, Bergson and Hume, among others. Massumi holds that emotion flows, merges, develops and changes. He differentiates in various ways between affect, on the one hand, and other sentiments on the other hand, such as feelings, emotions and passions, saying that affect is a pre-personal, non-conscious and non-intentional experience of intensity, while feelings are personal and biographical, and emotions social.[6]

Conversely, Sedgwick and Frank are influenced mainly by American psychologist Silvan Tomkins, who was inspired by Darwin to investigate the existence of innate, genetically determined basic emotions (Wetherell 2015, 141). Sedgwick and Frank presupposed therefore that emotion, affect and feeling were stable and pure entities. The likes of Wetherell (2015), Leys (2011) and Martin (2013) have criticised Massumi's division of affect and other sentiments thoroughly. They focus on the many complex past and present experienced relationships between sentiments, feelings, emotions, desire, atmospheres, intensity (Deleuze/Guattari and Massumi) and power (Spinoza),[7] as well as other affective influences, which people (and things) have on one another during their daily lives at home, work or, in the instance I discuss, participating voluntarily in a District Committee (Wetherell 2015, 159). In other words, they do not focus on affect per se, nor the state of a feeling in each and every individual, because affects are not static but dynamic between individuals (Mühlhoff and Slaby 2017, 2). Seyfert (2012, 30) suggests therefore that we use 'affect' as a general term that defines relations among all kinds of bodies, of which emotion, feelings, desire, passion, constitute but one particular form. In addition and especially important for the present article is the claim that, whereas 'affect is always an interplay of affecting and being affected' (Mühlhoff and Slaby 2017, 3), this dynamic cannot be reduced only to one individual affecting another – it is an interplay that 'co-depends on all the other participating individuals' and their surroundings (Mühlhoff and Slaby 2017, 3). The unfolding of affect is therefore a co-presence and simultaneity of multiple affects through which we move. It can be found in political rallies, religious gatherings, music concerts, family get-togethers, sports events, mass celebrations and other events and activities. Affect has therefore as much to do with the collective, conscious and unconscious and the body writ large, as it does with an individual's mind, body and emotion. Therefore, affect interactions comprise all kinds of encounters. It is always 'an open process, a process in its becoming' (Deleuze and Guttari 1987/2011 cited in Mühlhoff and Slaby 2017, 3) which also makes it vulnerable and an easy target for manipulation by various powerful persons, firms, corporations and nations (see e.g. Dowling 2012; Richard and Rudnyckyj 2009; Rudnyckyj 2011; Muehlebach 2011; Muehlebach and Shoshan 2012).

Being a condition of both subjection and transformation, can particular social and structural arrangements produce affects that correlate with those arrangements? Can we control whom we affect and how we affect them? Perhaps, up to a certain point. We build various institutions such as homes, schools, religious houses, sport sites, concert halls, shops, malls and markets to control and affect people in certain ways. But a teacher, for example, does not know how their teaching will affect or be received by students in advance. This is due partly to do with the fluctuation, flowing and changing of affect and the fact that we do not confront social structural arrangement as an isolated individual because we are always embedded in social relations, such as family, work, organisations, economics or politics. We are therefore in multiple webs of interdependence where we both exercise our abilities and powers and rely on others for what we are not able to do. In the words of Ian Burkitt, 'one's action is rarely one's own and rarely for one's own sake only, for it is pulled, pushed, harmonised, agitated, coaxed, pleaded … by multiple bonds. In this sense, one could say it is always already co-authored' (Burkitt 2016, 336). Thus, in interactions with others, we are always active and passive, powerful and vulnerable, to varying degrees, acting on others and being acted on by others, formulating plans and intentions in interdependence with people that are deeply dialogical, polyphonic, personal and social (Burkitt 2016, 336). In other words, any social arrangement is a joint movement where it is impossible to determine who is affecting whom (Mühlhoff and Slaby 2017,

3). In addition, as Pedwell points out in referring to Dewey, 'it may only be possible to discern in retrospect which collective actions or interactions made a difference in a given context; what peaked and fizzled and what took shape and endured' (Pedwell 2017, 164–165).

Whether affect is structured or not is therefore 'in part a matter of perspective' according to Slaby, Mühlhoff, and Wüschner (2017, 6). This account is not without consequences, because by focusing on structure, it is more than likely that one becomes preoccupied with questions relating to structure, which is the reason why Mazzarella (In press, 7) suggests that we should rather focus on the encounter, which may be preferable because the participants in the encounter are accounted for more fully than if the researcher focuses on structure of the encounter. In addition, according to Spinoza, affects 'do not only orient mere individual strivings but do so only in and through the encounters and relations with others' (Read 2017, 104). Therefore, it is of paramount importance that research on the encounter is conducted in collaboration and on an equal basis with as many participants of the encounter as possible, to inhibit hierarchical and colonial relationships between the researcher and his 'consultants'. Under such circumstances, affect will provide fertile ground for ethnographic research because it is always related to particular people, places, situations and objects (Skoggard and Waterston 2015; Mazzarella In press; Frykman and Povrzanović Frykman 2016).

Collaboration is one of many social arrangements in society in which affect does take place. The common ground for co-understanding and co-directed actions in collaborative research must involve a certain amount (in form of strength, intensity and energy) of trust towards each other, 'willingness' among participants to collaborate, 'empathy' for each other and a 'common sense' of the goal which they are 'interested' in and 'want' or 'hope' to achieve. In other words, the common ground for collaboration is 'affect'. It does not matter whether the collaboration lies between a researcher and the people they are researching (i.e. hierarchical), between two or more researchers within the same discipline (vertical) or between researchers of various disciplines. All these variously arranged collaborations must deal, to varying degrees, with good/bad, strong/week affects. There is however no guarantee that the collaboration will become successful for the participants.

Here, it is tempting to start analysing various arrangements to ascertain how affect might be controlled (i.e. structured), but that would leave us preoccupied with how structure controls us and how structure is reproduced, while the people with whom we are collaborating will disappear (Mazzarella In press, 7). If, instead, we start analysing the encounter of the collaborators, we become interested with who resonates with whom, and who does not, what sounds promising and what does not, what worries us and what does not, what is threatening to our collaboration and what is not and what are our possibilities and what are not (i.e. how we deal/manage with sameness and differences).

These dynamic interactions and encounters between individuals in collaborative arrangements provoke affects that are important to inspect closer. In the next section, I do this through examination of collaboration of the District Committee of Súgandafjörður with the Municipal Government and other villagers in Suðureyri village.

Collaboration in the Westfjords, Iceland

Iceland is 103,000 km^2 with 337,610 inhabitants and 74 municipalities. Forty one of the municipalities have less than 1000 inhabitants and 6 of them have less than 100 inhabitants. The inhabitants of the Northern part of the Westfjords, called Ísafjörður municipality, are 3639 (Ísafjörður Municipality 2014). They are divided between 5 villages with around 200 inhabitants each, except for the Ísafjörður town which has 2527 inhabitants. People living in the countryside outside of these villages are 187. I will now discuss collaboration between the District Committee of Súgandafjörður and the Ísafjörður Municipal Government, situated in the Northern part of the Westfjords, as well as the collaboration of the District Committee and the villagers of Suðureyri village. Then, I will discuss the collaboration or the lack thereof between me as a researcher and a group of people whom I tried to study for the local branch of Red Cross in this same area.

After the local election in May 2014, a new local government was formed in Ísafjörður Municipality. It was a coalition of three parties, The Left-Green party, The Social Democrats and a liberal party, while the opposition consisted of two right-wing parties, one conservative and the other liberal. The headquarter of Ísafjörður Municipal Government is placed in Ísafjörður Town Hall.

The newly elected Municipal Government decided to establish seven District committees: three in Ísafjörður and one in each of the four other villages, Hnífsdalur, Suðureyri, Flateyri and Þingeyri. These committees are supposed to act as mediators between the people of the Municipality and the Ísafjörður Municipal Government.[8]

The main purpose of the committees is to ascertain the wishes of citizens for their communities and to forge suggestions about how best such wishes can be realised. In addition, the Municipal Government can also ask the seven committees to form an opinion (independently or by asking the people in their villages), on issues that concern the villagers. The Municipal Government can accept or dismiss such opinions, once formed, at its own will. The committees lack therefore formal power and participation is voluntary, with general assemblies, held once per annum.

The district committee of Súgandafjörður

The first general meeting, in which the District Committee of Súgandafjörður was established, was held in the village, Suðureyri, in Súgandafjörður, in autumn 2014. Five people and two substitutes were elected in the Committee. I was one of those five elected members. Suðureyri is a village with 271 inhabitants. The main employers in the village are two fish processing factories, one situated on the western side of the village and the other on the eastern side. The village has a kindergarten (with 24 pupils) and a primary school (with 47 pupils). There are two hotels in the village which are only open during the summer.

The only way to enter the village from the main road (Road 60) is from the east. It is, however, forbidden to drive straight through the village from this direction, because 'The Main Street' (the literal name of the main street) is one way, which can only be driven in the opposite direction – i.e. from west to east. Therefore, if one wishes to drive through the village towards the western part of it, one must turn right when entering the village and turn left towards west at the next street which is parallel to The Main Street.

It has, however, been impossible for large trucks to do this when collecting the fishing products from the factory on the western side because the streets are too narrow. Therefore – and in violation of the law – trucks were forced to drive back and forth on the main street. Over the years, this two-way truck driving has been silently approved by the authorities, until a year ago, when the police 'suddenly' decided that the trucks required a police escort to drive through the village. This escort was paid by the fish factory. The factory made a complaint to the Municipal Government regarding payment. The Government responded by changing the street to a two-way system. However, before they did that, they wanted the newly elected District Committee of Súgandafjörður to discuss this matter and to see if it could find an alternative solution.

Most of the committee members were heavily against the decision of changing The Main Street to a two-way street. They thought that it would be far too dangerous for children living nearby. Instead, the Committee suggested three other solutions which do not require exposition here. A few days later, we read in the local newspaper that the Municipal Government had decided to change the street to a two-way street nonetheless. When the journalist asked the Leader of the Government whether the opinion of The District Committee of Súgandafjörður mattered, he argued in response that it is the elected Municipal Government that has the ruling power in the area and not the District Committees. This decision and the high-handed manner in which it was made by the Municipal Government left the members of the District Committee very angry, frustrated and powerless, creating a relationship of mistrust. It also created mistrust between the villagers and the District Committee. Because of this dispute and other less dramatic incidents, The District Committee of Súgandafjörður suggested a conference for the Municipal Government and all seven District Committees to be held the following autumn (2016) to settle our disputes and to discuss means of proceeding more positively in the future.

Having described a rather unfortunate beginning to our 'collaborative' relationship between The District Committee of Súgandafjörður and Ísafjörður Municipal Government, I now wish to describe the collaborative relationship between The District Committee of Súgandafjörður and the inhabitants of Suðureyri – i.e. the other villagers.

As I mentioned before, the main purpose of the Committee is to ascertain the ways in which the people of Suðureyri wish to make their village a better place to live. In order to identify wishes, the Committee decided to place 'a box of ideas' in the local postoffice in which ideas could be submitted anonymously. After 3 months, only two letters were found in the box. However, many ideas for a better village were expressed in those two letters. As a starting point, we chose two of those ideas to explore. The first idea was to regenerate the old playground for young children in the village – a playground among the oldest in the country. The second idea was to regenerate the surroundings of the primary school and the area in front of the church.

The playground has been neglected by the municipal authorities for several years and is no longer appealing for children or their parents to visit. The District Committee contacted an architectural firm which, after consultation with Members of the Committee and the leaders of the Women's Association in the village, produced ideas for the playground and the school area. These ideas were then introduced to the villagers in a general meeting and posted on a wall in several prominent places in the village. An election was held a week later in which the villagers choose the idea they liked most. However, only four people, besides the District Committee members, participated in the election. As such, it became clear both that the villagers are not particularly keen on coming forward with opinions on how to make the village a better place in the future and that The District Committee of Súgandafjörður is not particularly good at getting them to participate in new initiatives of the Committee. Our collaboration with the villagers is therefore not very successful – yet.[9]

Having described The District Committee of Súgandafjörður, their actions and the context of their actions, I have touched upon contextual or structural problems that might hopefully be changed incrementally in the future. However, even though we might be able to transform these structures and relations into more equitable relations in future, it will not automatically result in greater participation of the villagers in this democratic project. It should also be necessary to establish a feeling or an atmosphere of interest, empathy, positivity, will, hope and trust among the villagers to influence and transform the village in accordance with their vision – if one exists. There was at least one experience among the members of the District Committee that could point in the direction of what we might require to achieve this.

Shortly after we had commenced Committee discussions of the architectural plans for the village, one of us said that she wanted more grass in the playground than the architects had suggested in their drawings. Another member of the Committee answered immediately, 'yes', but that he did not think that it should be around the boat, because it would soon be trodden down and reduced to a mud-hole. Soon, there was a lively discussion between all members of the Committee. Gradually, we reached a common conclusion with regard to the placing of grass, asphalt, stones, sand and other items. All these suggestions were then written down and sent to the architects who made the third drawing for the playground which included our new suggestions. This third plan was elected by the (four) villagers and the Committee Members, with the result that the Municipal Government has a working plan for next summer.

What had happened during that particular meeting was that all the Committee Members had become very interested in the drawings. They felt an ownership of the playground and its drawings and they became enthusiastic about it, felt joy in discussing and creating a new drawing together and became interested and emphatic towards each other and each other's ideas, as well as for the whole creative work involved in this process. The question is, though, how can we create such an empathic, creative, positive and interesting process with other projects in the District Committee in the future?

To advance that discussion further, I will now turn to the other example of collaboration – my attempt to enable the Red Cross branch in the Northern part of Westfjords to identify the most precarious people in the area and to foster ideas for improvement of their situation.

Vulnerability and Red Cross research

The Icelandic Red Cross carries out surveys regularly on a national scale to find out which groups in Icelandic society are most vulnerable in order to develop means of supporting them. Local branches of the Icelandic Red Cross can also carry out surveys to gather information on circumstances in their local communities' if they wish and have the ability to do so.

The last two national surveys were made in 2010 and 2014. The problem with national surveys is that figures and descriptions from local places tend to 'disappear' in the abstract results. In 2012, I therefore contacted the six Red Cross branches in the Northern part of Westfjords and offered to conduct a similar survey in their area to that conducted nationally by the Red Cross on the same topic – the identification of precarious groups and means of improving their circumstances. My local study was qualitative, while the national survey was more quantitative in nature. The headquarters of the Icelandic Red Cross in Reykjavík wanted me to ask similar questions as those they had asked in the national survey in 2010 in order to permit comparison between my research and theirs. In particular, I was asked to interview people in official institutions and non-governmental organisations who assist those who need various kind of assistance because they – according to the Red Cross – are the ones who know best which groups are in need of assistance and what kind of assistance they require. In other words, I was not supposed to interview people who received official assistance, because it would require more time and funding, than just interviewing people in institutions and non-governmental organisations.

Accordingly, I interviewed 30 people in 22 institutions and organisations working in this area. All of them said that the people who needed most assistance were immigrants, people with various disabilities and elderly people who lived alone. This was very similar to the result of the national survey conducted by the headquarters of the Icelandic Red Cross in 2014 with 100 specialists in the social, health and education sectors. The restrictions in engagement left me extremely frustrated, not because the knowledge of doctors, nurses and other service providers is irrelevant. The source of frustration lay in the fact that precluding researchers from engaging with those who are the recipients of support and the subjects of policy is fundamentally inegalitarian and can have serious consequences. In the first place, it is unethical and fails to uphold respect for those who receive official assistance. The research that results is jaundiced and fails fully to take seriously the knowledge of those in a condition of vulnerability who may know best the causes of, and best means of overcoming, their vulnerability. Sometimes, this knowledge is not just qualitatively different, it is also uniquely important within particular contexts that service providers simply may not understand. While this is clearest in colonial or post-colonial encounters, there is good reason to believe that ignorance can persist in situations, such as those in Iceland, in which there is a presumption of understanding on the part of the service providers. This can lead to bad policy that actually exacerbates problems and ends up being more costly, in the long run. More broadly, this all compounds and normalises the hierarchical, dominating and sometimes prejudiced relationship between the service providers and receivers in the health sector and beyond.

However, even though the recipients of official assistance are asked about their needs as well as the providers, both groups are still dependent on the researcher's opinion and interpretation of the data he or she collects. Not only does the researcher interpret the data collected and define the subject people as a group with certain characteristics, they also produce a report which is disseminated to publics. If the subject people are allowed to say anything in the final report, or if they are considered at all, they often take a secondary role – included in an epilogue or a postscript. The research then tends to become irrelevant for the community or the people who are being researched, which most certainly is an ethical matter.

One of the founding ethical principles of liberal society is Kantian respect for persons. This means to acknowledge that man, and in general every rational being, exists as an end in himself, not merely as a means for arbitrary use by this or that will: he must in all his actions, whether they are directed himself or to other rational beings always be viewed at the same time as an end.

For Kant, this ethical tenet rests on the belief that each individual seeks, rationally, to exercise and protect their natural, autonomous facets against the malign, 'unsociableness' of others (Kant 2005, 105). The sorts of research methods discussed thus far fail to respect persons insofar as they treat subjects as means. Much greater care, then, needs to be taken to consider the place of power and the politics of representation and about who has the right to represent whom and for what purposes and about whose discourse will be privileged in texts. So instead of reading

> over the shoulders of those who are being researched ... the researchers have to start to talk about reading and writing '*along*' the researched, through the framework of dialogue in order to escape or shift from the authoritative monologue to one that represents involved, intersubjective exchange between the researcher and the 'informants'. (Lassiter 2005, 4)

As the slogan 'Nothing about us without us' emphatically asserts, research should be conducted *with* people. So,

> what is required from this point of view for the principle of autonomy to be respected is that the people being researched become at least equal partners in the research process. That people have a right to participate on an equal footing with researchers in the pursuit of any research that relates to their lives, making decisions about what is to be investigated and how, what forms of analysis will be used, how the conclusions will be written up, how the findings will be disseminated, and so on. (Hammersley and Traianou 2012, 81)

One of the main purposes of the Red Cross is to ensure respect for persons, upholding the life and health of the most precarious and vulnerable individuals in particular. I think that the collaborative research that I have described here is naturally suited to the purposes of the Red Cross. Research on vulnerability can best promote autonomy and empowerment by placing community members at the active heart of work, identifying issues of importance and determining the methods by which to explore them.

Had I been granted more autonomy over the research, I would also have engaged with people from institutions and non-governmental organisations. However, I would also have asked recipients of the assistance, and members of the community in general, similar questions. Very often there are people who do not fit into the various classifications on which the assistance of the health system is based, and to find the blind spots of the system one has to ask people outside institutions as well as the institutions themselves. In other words, I would have engaged in a form of ethnographic fieldwork. Having identified, collectively, the most vulnerable, the challenge would then be to establish, collectively, their needs and to formulate their demands to institutions. During this process, I, as a researcher with practical and theoretical knowledge, would participate on an equal basis with other parties. I would accept that this is time consuming and that there is no guarantee that the collaboration would achieve its stated aim of promoting the health interests of the most vulnerable. However, the ethical, procedural and practical concerns above mean that there simply is not a preferable alternative.

Conclusion

I have described a collaboration between the District Committee of Súgandafjörður and Ísafjörður Municipal Government in Northern part of Westfjords in Iceland, as well as the collaboration between the District Committee and the inhabitants of Suðureyri village. I have also described very shortly a collaboration between myself as a researcher for a local Red Cross branch and various communities. In the collaboration of the District Committee of Súgandafjörður, I participate and collaborate as a civilian on equal footing to others in the Committee. But I, alone, interpreted and analysed the data and created a narrative in this present article without collaborating with the others. I asked only for their permission to write it. Therefore, this part of the research is a monologue and therefore only partly collaborative. In addition, there is certainly a need for more collaboration with the villagers of Suðureyri, who are a diverse and unequal group of people with various (political) opinions and desires, in order for this democratic project to become successful in the future.[10]

In my research for the Red Cross, a collaboration between me and providers of official assistance in institutions and non-governmental organisations did take place, but at the same time, there was a complete lack of collaboration between me and the recipients of official assistance. The collaboration with the service providers was, however, initiated and controlled by me and the interpretation and analysis of the data I collected was entirely mine. The Red Cross research was therefore similar to the 'traditional' ethnographic research described in the introduction and carries with it the same attendant ethical problems.

One way of overcoming the collaborative gap in those two projects might be to do the research *with* the people who are being researched, through the framework of dialogue that represents involved and intersubjective exchange. However, an involved and intersubjective dialogue is as saturated with conscious and unconscious power relations and positive and negative feelings as any other research methods. We, in the District Committee, became frustrated, powerless, wounded and angry and felt that we were unjustly treated by the Municipal Government when it decided to change the main street in the village to a two-way street. This decision affected strongly the relationship between the Committee and the Government and does so still today. This intense feeling of insult, disempowerment and unjust treatment by the Ísafjörður Municipal Government is something that we do not want to experience often in the future. It destroys the feeling of trust and empathy for people and institutions, makes us angry, hurt and reduces our energy, power and will to collaborate with the Municipality.

However, our work with the landscape architects – in which we discussed enthusiastically their drawings of the playground for the children in Suðureyri village – was an entirely different experience. Here, we felt excitement and joy in our collaboration, creativity, willingness, empathy, eagerness and power, both individually and as a group. It is this kind of feeling which collaboration should aim to achieve and it should be possible to build such an affective arrangement[11] in which positive feelings are enhanced instead of suppressed.

Similarly, if the fundamental roots of collaboration between people is how they affect one another, thereby enhancing or diminishing individual and collective experience and power, then any social research, whether it is collaborative, or 'traditional', must take affect into serious consideration their strong influences on people's daily life.

Notes

1. This has also been called a 'participatory turn' in a number of domains, such as higher education, science and technology, environment, urban regeneration, arts and policy making (see Mahony and Stephansen 2016). These words have also started to become popular in the high-tech industry, the new media (Google and Apple) and hundreds of start-ups, in which almost all are promoted as domains of liberty and autonomy for employees (Kelty 2017).
2. In Greek, '*Ethnos*' means 'people', and '*graphein*' means 'writing' and 'ethnography' therefore means literally 'writing about people' (Boellstorff et al. 2012, 13–14).
3. Collaboration can also involve 'shared management and direction of research project(s) among scholars' (Low and Merry 2010, 209; see also; Konrad 2012), but I am focusing first and foremost on collaboration between the researcher and the subjects of research.
4. Being a 'native' ethnographer, my research for the Red Cross did not include the colonial legacy mentioned here. However, the relationship between me and the people I interviewed was still hierarchical and unequal, because I, alone, did the interviewing, analysed the material that I collected and wrote the final report. That is to say, the research was totally under my control.
5. For example, for influence within feminism, see Pedwell and Whitehead (2012); Liljeström and Paasonen (2010); cultural and communication studies, see Gregg and Seigworth (2010a) and Hemmings (2005); religious studies, see Schaefer (2015); social-psychology, see Wetherell (2012; 2015) and Blackman (2012); phenomenology, see Ahmed (2004); Marxism, see Hardt and Negri (2000), Negri (1999), Lordon (2010); literary studies, see Berlant (2011); cognitive-, neuro- and computer science, see Slaby (2016), Damasio (1994), Barad (2007) and philosophy, see Deleuze and Guttari (1987/2011) and Serilli (2015).
6. In 'Notes on the Translation and Acknowledgments', which is a foreword to his translation of Deleuze's *A Thousand Plateaus*, Massumi writes: 'AFFECT/AFFECTION. Neither word denotes a personal feeling (sentiment in Deleuze and Guattai). *L'affect* (Spinoza's *affectus*) is an ability to affect and be affected. It is a prepersonal intensity corresponding to the passage from one experiential state of the body to another and implying an augmentation or diminution in that body's capacity to act. *L'affection* (Spinoza's *affection*) is each such state considered as an encounter between the affected body and a second, affecting, body' (Deleuze and Guttari 1987/2011, xvii).
7. 'Spinoza's affects … are less determinate states of individuals and properties of objects than passages and transformations, increases and decreases of power' (Read 2017, 107).
8. I was told by one of the people in the Municipal Government that the idea of establishing District Committees in order to enable people in the villages to have influence on the decision-making of their districts/villages was first suggested in 2010. Genealogically, this idea has its roots in the Porto Alegre democratic experiment from the beginning of 1990s where they started to redistribute the city resources in favour of the more vulnerable social groups through participatory democracy. As such, it can be regarded as an act of decolonialisation or a resistance to authoritarian and patrimonial traditions of public policies as well as global capitalism (De Sousa Santos 1998). However, the idea of the District Committees in the Westfjords was introduced by a

member of the right-wing government in Ísafjörður Municipal Government that was in power at that time.
9. The 'Villagers' are, of course, a diverse group of people, both socially and economically. While most of them are Icelandic by origin, some also come from Poland, Thailand and the Philippines.
10. 'Success' means, here, that villagers participate, genuinely and intensively (at least at some points) in the collaborative process.
11. Affective arrangements can, for example, be specific work environments, such as an ordinary office, stock market trading floor, sport site or a particular collaboration – in other words, a kind of 'operational space' for affective interactions (Slaby, Mühlhoff, and Wüschner 2017, 7).

Disclosure statement

No potential conflict of interest was reported by the author.

References

Abu-Lughod, L. 1986. *Veiled Sentiments: Honor and Poetry in a Bedouin Society*. Berkeley: University of California Press.
Ahmed, S. 2004. *The Cultural Politics of Emotion*. Edinburgh: Edinburgh University Press.
Asad, T. ed. 1973. *Anthropology & The Colonial Encounter*. United Kingdom: Ithaca Press
Barad, K. 2007. *Meeting the Universe Halfway: Quantum Physics and the Entanglement of Matter and Meaning*. Durham: Duke University of California Press.
Berlant, L. 2011. *Cruel Optimism*. Durham: Duke University Press.
Blackman, L. 2010. "Embodying Affect: Voice-hearing, Telepathy, Suggestion and Modelling the Non-conscious." *Body & Society* 16 (1).
Blackman, L. 2012. *Immaterial Bodies. Affect, Embodiment, Mediation*. London: SAGE.
Boellstorff, T., B. Nardi, C. Pearce and T. L. Taylor. 2012. *Ethnography and Virtual Worlds: A Handbook of Method*. Princeton: Princeton University Press.
Bourdieu, P. 1977. *Outline of a Theory of Practice*. Cambridge: Cambridge University Press.
Burkitt, I. 2016. "Relational Agency: Relational Sociology, Agency and Interaction." *European Journal of Social Theory* 19 (3): 322–339. doi:10.1177/1368431015591426.
Campbell, E., and L. E. Lassiter. 2010. "What Will We Have Ethnography Do?" *Qualitative Inquiry* 16 (9): 757–767. doi:10.1177/1077800410374444.
Campbell, E., and L. E. Lassiter. 2015. *Doing Ethnography Today: Theories, Methods, Exercises*. Oxford: Wiley Blackwell.
Choy, T. K., L. Faier, M. J. Hathaway, M. Inoue, S. Satsuka, and A. Tsing. 2009. "Matsutake Worlds Research Group: A New Form of Collaboration in Cultural Anthropology'." *American Ethnologist* 36 (2): 380–403. doi:10.1111/j.1548-1425.2009.01141.x.
Clifford, J. 1988. *The Predicament of Culture*. Cambridge, Mass: Harvard University Press.
Clifford, J. 1986. "Introduction: Partial Truths." In *Writing Culture: The Poetics and Politics of Ethnography*, eds. J. Clifford and G. E. Marcuse, 1–26. Berkeley: University of California Press.
Clough, P. T., and J. Halley. 2007. *The Affective Turn: Theorizing the Social*. Durham: Duke University Press.
Damasio, A. 1994. *Descartes' Error: Emotion, Reason, and the Human Brain*. New York: Putman.
De Sousa Santos, B. 1998. "Participatory Budgeting in Porto Alegre: Toward a Redistributive Democracy." *Politics & Society* 26 (4): 461–510. doi:10.1177/0032329298026004003.
Deleuze, G., and F. Guttari. 1987/2011. *A Thousand Plateaus. Capitalism and Schizophrenia*. London: Continuum.
Dowling, E. 2012. "The Waitress: On Affect, Method and (Re)Presentation." *Cultural Studies↔Critical Methodologies* 12 (2): 109–117. doi:10.1177/1532708611435215.

Fabian, J. 1983. *Time and the Other: How Anthropology Makes its Object*. Columbia: Columbia University Press.

Fluehr-Lobban, C. 2008. "Collaborative Anthropology as Twenty-first-Century Ethical Anthropology." *Collaborative Anthropologies* 1: 175–182. doi:10.1353/cla.0.0000.

Fluehr-Lobban, C. 2013. "Ethics and Anthropology." In *Ideas and Practice*. Walnut Creek: AltaMira Press.

Frykman, J., and M. Povrzanović Frykman. 2016. *Sensitive Objects. Affect and Material Culture*. Lund: Nordic Academic Press.

Geertz, C. 1973. *The Interpretation of Cultures. Selected Essays*. New York: Ithaca Press.

Gregg, M., and G. J. Seigworth. 2010a. *The Affect Theory Reader*. Duke University Press.

Gregg, M., and G. J. Seigworth. 2010b. "An Inventory of Shimmers." In *The Affect Theory Reader*, 1–25. Durham & London: Duke University Press.

Hale, C. R., and L. Stephen, eds. 2013. *Otros Saberes: Collaborative Research on Indigenous and Afro-Descendant Cultural Politics*. Santa Fe: School for Advanced Research Press.

Hammersley, M., and A. Traianou. 2012. *Ethics in Qualitative Research: Controversies and Contexts*. London: SAGE.

Hardt, M., and A. Negri. 2000. *Empire*. Cambridge: Harvard University Press.

Hemmings, C. 2005. "Invoking Affect: Cultural Theory and the Ontological Turn." *Cultural Studies* 19 (5): 548–567. doi:10.1080/09502380500365473.

Ísafjörður Municipality. 2014. "Population Statistics." *Ísafjörður Municipality Official Website*, 1 January, Accessed March 17 2017. http://www.isafjordur.is/um_isafjardarbae/isafjardarbaer_i_tolum/

Kant, I. 2005. *Groundwork for the Metaphysic of Morals*. Abingdon: Routledge.

Keisha-Khan, P. Y., and J. Rappaport. 2013. "Making a Case for Collaborative Research with Black and Indigenous Social Movements in Latin America." In *Collaborative Research on Indigenous and Afro-Descendant Cultural Politics*, eds C. R. Hale and L. Stephen, 30–48. Santa Fe: School for Advanced Research Press.

Kelty, C. M. 2017. "Too Much Democracy in All the Wrong Places. Towards a Grammar of Participation." *Current Anthropology* 58 (Supplement 15): S77–S90. doi:10.1086/688705.

Konrad, M. 2012. *Collaborators Collaborating: Counterparts in Anthropological Knowledge and International Research Relations*. New York: Berghahn Books.

Lassiter, L. E. 2005. *The Chicago Guide to Collaborative Ethnography*. Chicago: University of Chicago Press.

Leys, R. 2011. "The Turn to Affect: A Critique." *Critical Inquiry* 37 (3): 434–472. doi:10.1086/659353.

Liljeström, M., and S. Paasonen, ed. 2010. *Working with Affect in Feminist Readings*. London: Routledge.

Lordon, F. 2010. *Willing Slaves of Capital. Spinoza and Marx on Desire*. London: Verso.

Low, S. M., and S. E. Merry. 2010. "Engaged Anthropology: Diversity and Dilemmas." *Current Anthropology* 51 (S2): 203–336. doi:10.1086/653837.

Lutz, C. 2017. "What Matters." *Cultural Anthropology* 32 (2): 181–191. doi:10.14506/ca32.2.

Mahony, N., and H. C. Stephansen. 2016. "The Frontiers of Participatory Public Engagement." *European Journal of Cultural Studies* 19 (6): 583–597. doi:10.1177/1367549416632007.

Marcuse, G. E., and M. J. Fisher. 1986. *Anthropology as Cultural Critique: An Experimental Moment in the Human Sciences*. Chicago: University of Chicago Press.

Martin, E. 2013. "The Potentiality of Ethnography and the Limits of Affect Theory." *Current Anthropology* 54 (S7): S149–58. doi:10.1086/670388.

Massumi, B. 2002. *Parables for the Virtual: Movement, Affect, Sensation*. Durham: Duke University Press.

Mazzarella, W. In press. *The Mana of Mass Society*. Chicago: University of Chicago Press. Accessed March 16 2017. http://www.academia.edu/28743175/A_Certain_Rush_of_Energy_Introduction_to_The_Mana_of_Mass_Society_.pdf.

Muehlebach, A. 2011. "On Affective Labor in Post-Fordist Italy." *Cultural Anthropology* 26 (1): 59–82. doi:10.1111/cuan.2011.26.issue-1.

Muehlebach, A., and N. Shoshan. 2012. "A Special Collection: POST-FORDIST AFFECT. Introduction." *Anthropological Quarterly* 85 (2): 317–344. doi:10.1353/anq.2012.0030.

Mühlhoff, R., and J. Slaby. 2017. *Immersion at Work: Affect and Power in post-Fordist Work Cultures*. Berlin: Freie Universität Berlin. Accessed May 25 2017. https://www.academia.edu/32615026/Immersion_at_work_Affect_and_power_in_post-Fordist_work_cultures.

Myers, F. R. 1986. *Pintupi Country, Pintupi Self: Sentiment, Place, and Politics among Western Desert Aborigines*. Washington, DC: Smithsonian Institution Press.

Negri, A. 1999. "Value and Affect." *Boundary 2* 26 (2): 77–88.

Pedwell, C. 2017. "Mediated Habits: Images, Networked Affect and Social Change." *In Subjectivity* 10 (2): 147–169. doi:10.1057/s41286-017-0025-y.

Pedwell, C., and A. Whitehead. 2012. "Affecting Feminism: Questions of Feeling in Feminist Theory." *Feminist Theory* 13 (2): 115–129. doi:10.1177/1464700112442635.

Rappaport, J. 2005. *Intercultural Utopias: Public Intellectuals, Cultural Experimentation and Ethnic Pluralism in Colombia*. Durham: Duke University Press.

Rappaport, J. 2008. "Beyond Participant Observation: Collaborative Ethnography as Theoretical Innovation." *Collaborative Anthropologies* 1: 1–31. doi:10.1353/cla.0.0014.

Read, J. 2017. *The Affective Economy: Producing and Consuming Affects in Deleuze and Guattari*, Accessed May 25 2017. https://www.academia.edu/33380499/The_Affective_Economy_Producing_and_Consuming_Affects_in_Deleuze_and_Guattari

Richard, A., and D. Rudnyckyj. 2009. "Economies of Affect." *Journal of Royal Anthropological Institute* 15: 57–77. doi:10.1111/j.1467-9655.2008.01530.x.

Rosaldo, M. Z. 1980. *Knowledge and Passion: Ilongot Notions of Self and Social Life*. New York: Cambridge University Press.

Rudnyckyj, D. 2011. "Circulating Tears and Managing Hearts: Governing through Affect in an Indonesian Steel Factory." *Anthropological Theory* 11 (1): 63–87. doi:10.1177/1463499610395444.

Schaefer, D. O. 2015. *Religious Affects*. Durham: Duke University Press.

Serilli, L. M. G. 2015. "Philosophy and Affective Turn." *Parrhesia* 13: 1–13.

Seyfert, R. 2012. "Beyond Personal Feelings and Collective Emotions: Toward a Theory of Social Affect." *Theory, Culture & Society* 29 (6): 27–46. doi:10.1177/0263276412438591.

Sjöstedt, J. 2016. "Introduction." *LIR Journal* 7 (16): 4–10.

Skoggard, I., and A. Waterston. 2015. "Introduction: Toward an Anthropology of Affect and Evocative Ethnography." *Anthropology of Consciousness* 26 (2): 109–120.

Slaby, J. 2016. "Against Empathy and Other Philosophical Beefs", *3:AMMagazine*, October 7. Accessed May 25 2017. http://www.3ammagazine.com/3am/empathy-philosophical-beefs/

Slaby, J., R. Mühlhoff, and P. Wüschner. 2017. "Affective Arrangements." Berlin: Freie Universität Berlin. Accessed March 16 2017. http://janslaby.com/downloads/slaby-muhlhoff-wuschner_affectivearrangements_final.pdf

Wetherell, M. 2012. *Affect and Emotion. A New Social Science Understanding*. London: Sage.

Wetherell, M. 2015. "Trends in the Turn to Affect: A Social Psychological Critique." *Body & Society* 21 (2): 139–166. doi:10.1177/1357034X14539020.

White, W. B. 2012. *From Experimental Moment to Legacy Moment: Collaboration and the Crisis of Representation*. Accessed May 25 2017. https://umontreal.academia.edu/BobWhite

REPLY

Protean possibilities: attending to affect in collaborative research – a reply to Valdimar Halldórsson

Elizabeth Campbell

This is a reply to:

Halldórsson, Valdimar J. 2017. "Affective collaboration in the West Fjords of Iceland." *Global Discourse* 7(4): 548–564. https://doi.org/10.1080/23269995.2017.1355096

For reasons both epistemological and ontological, Valdimar Halldórsson grounds his call for participatory, affect-based research in his own experiences as an ethnographer, applied anthropologist, scholar and engaged citizen. He observes that when social or community research is not constructively engaged with the people it seeks to address or help, it can leave participants – especially on the community side – with bad feelings, and a future unwillingness to participate in social research. He is absolutely right about this; others have been making related observations for quite some time (see, e.g., Brettell 1996). But Halldórsson expands this observation by calling for social researchers to explicitly take up the 'intersubjective realm' out of which all relationships – research, political, commercial, civic, personal and so on – emerge.

That point is compelling, as is his recommendation that research collaborations intentionally craft affective arrangements in ways that cultivate positive feelings and strengthen relationships and communities, thereby strengthening both the quality of the research and the strength of community life. Calling for deeper attention to how all of the varied and shifting agents and elements of collaborations play out, Halldórsson argues that attending to affect offers potentially fruitful ways to both conceptualise and construct participatory research collaborations.

Collaboration

Halldórsson does an admirable job of reviewing the development of collaborative research approaches. I won't go over it again, but I do want to add a bit in terms of the intellectual, practical and activist paradigms that have characterised collaborative research over the last several decades.

Throughout the twentieth century, attempts to justify collaborative research as relevant forms of knowledge production appropriate for institutionally situated researchers (by which I mean those formally affiliated with universities, government agencies, scholarly organisations and so on) appeared rather regularly at the margins of disciplines. Although arguments for collaborative research in the social sciences began to gain ground in the 1970s, they did not gain widespread appreciation. Some of the most powerful objections to collaborative research in those days were that formally trained researchers should not surrender their disciplinary expertise to 'non-experts'; that such a shift in positions could not produce rigorous or objective knowledge; and that, by its very nature, knowledge produced either by or in collaboration with those who were being researched could be neither reliable nor valid.

Those who began to embrace collaborative research approaches in the 1980s and 1990s tended to focus on two different justifications for collaboration: that such researches were more authentically representative and thus more accurate and/or that the approaches themselves were more ethically or morally just. Collaborative research became especially important and relevant in cases that sought to remedy imbalances in the historical record, to redress colonial mis-representations and to foreground previously absent voices, experiences and perspectives. The approaches to collaboration that emerged during that time tended to emphasise agreement and to sometimes privilege the voices of community-situated participants over those in the academy or in other traditional sites of scholarly knowledge production. These approaches became known for their experiments with the 'how to' of researching and writing collaboratively and for their serious attempts to deal (or play) with issues connected to realms of expression and the politics of representation.

As a graduate student in the 1990s, I well remember seminar discussions that passionately upheld the rights of research participants (or 'consultants,' a term we used then that is still often used in fields like folklore or anthropology) to decide what research would do, how it would operate, who would be involved and in what ways – if at all – research findings would be presented or disseminated. During my early years as a fieldworker, I took those earnest discussions to heart, consistently deferring to the wishes and concerns of my consultants. I revisited and revised interpretations with them and shifted voices and points of view based on their positions and perspectives. In a few cases, I returned research materials that participants later decided against sharing and stripped the contributions those materials had made out of the work itself. This is too easy a position to attack now; setting its naiveté aside for the moment, though, I do want to say that say such are much more complex positions than they seem at first glance. Still, in many of its earliest iterations, the ethical imperative of collaborative research was to negotiate interpretations and representations through dialogue; those positions that could not be negotiated were to be surrendered.

It doesn't take flashing yellow arrows to figure out where that would lead. As more and more people – scholars, artists, indigenous rights advocates, environmental activists, citizens, policy makers and others – began engaging collaborative research over broader and broader fields and projects, these acts of deference and privileging became increasingly problematised and difficult. Accounts of collaboration started to raise a whole host of issues, from position to power to process and more. It became clear that simply surrendering or sharing authority did not automatically make research more equitable or accurate. Collaborative researchers came head to head with conflict and difference, which turned their attentions to the complex nature of collaborations, to differently situated participants and to the challenges – and emerging moral imperatives – of working across difference. This was happening even as collaborating with those being researched was becoming a bureaucratic requirement, an issue of law or policy, rather than of ethical preference. And, of course, as more and more researchers and their interlocutors explicitly engaged collaborative research approaches, they came into contact with the discord and disagreement that are as much a part of human relations as accord and harmony.

Over the last decade or so, especially, as research participants across positions have engaged both the possibilities and the challenges of collaborative research, ideas about what it is, how it works and why it matters are in flux again (see, e.g., the journal *Collaborative Anthropologies*). This leads to the important connection Halldórsson points out – that 'collaboration and other social arrangements are based in the intersubjective realm, in which people, things and events affect one another in multifarious ways' – and takes a step further: if collaborations are, in fact, intersubjective and affective, it should be possible to conceptualise and enact our collaborations in ways that make possible the positive change so many of us hope for.

Middletown

Despite the situational, tentative, related and often difficult nature of collaborative work, I remain captivated by it. I have seen collaborative researches, pedagogies and writing change research participants and their relationships in a host of productive and hopeful ways. In the early 2000s, I had the great good fortune of being part of a project called 'The Other Side of Middletown' (TOSM) out of which arose a book by the same title (Lassiter et al., 2004). TOSM was, at times, an extraordinarily challenging endeavour. Seventy-five people of different ages, races, genders, economic levels, educational backgrounds, political persuasions and religious identities participated in that project. We did our work in a variety of places: in an early twentieth-century mansion built by one of the city's wealthiest early industrialists; in a wood frame church where, in 1930, the bodies of lynching victims had been guarded over and protected; in living rooms, in vacant lots and in legislative chambers. We worked, together and alone, in airless archives by day. We walked under old trees at night. We ate at TV trays and banquet tables. We laughed uproariously and fought ferociously. We hoped that some of our emerging romantic attachments would work out and that others would not. We struggled against a backdrop of racist conflict, of professional rivalries, of personal tragedies. We marched and protested.

We embraced an explicit and overriding commitment to writing that book, and living that commitment continuously formed and transformed the relationships between us. Although we did make what we still think is an important contribution to the literature around Middletown, for me, what remains of that encounter is less the knowledge we contributed to Middletown studies than the differences we made in each other's lives.

The place of affect

Halldórsson calls attention to the role (and place and phenomenon) of affect in participatory and collaborative research in ways that are both new and notable. He is especially interested in the affects of collaborative encounters, in what those affective encounters produce and in how they work. This relates, in some ways, to other researchers' calls to take up the role of relationships in collaborative work (cf., Campbell and Lassiter 2015; Haviland 2017; Lassiter 2005). But he is calling here, specifically, for participatory and collaborative researchers to place affect at the centre of those relationships, and thus those collaborations. This offers those who do collaborative work a slightly different take on the connections between collaboration and participatory action research; attending to 'affect' could very well lead to richer understandings of both.

At this point, there seem to be nearly as many different theories and definitions of affect (and affect theory and theory/ies of affect) as there are thinkers who engage it. Halldórsson's cites Gregg and Siegworth's (2011, 3) grateful expression that there is as yet 'no single, generalisable theory of affect', freeing those who wish to explore this nexus of collaboration and affect to focus on that important work. Per Seyfert (2012), Halldórsson proposes that affect be thought of as 'relations among all kinds of bodies' – and here he is talking about bodies beyond those of human agents, for whom emotions, feelings, desires and passions, constitute but one particular form of affect. Skoggard and Waterston (2015, 112) take it further:

> Affect as noun and verb has as much to do with senses and sensibilities of the collective unconscious and conscious and the body writ large – the body politic, the social and the cultural – as it does with an individual's mind, body, and emotion.

Seigworth and Gregg (2011, 1, italics in original) take it further still:

> That is, affect is found in those intensities that pass body to body (human, nonhuman, part-body, and otherwise) in those resonances that circulate about, between, and sometimes stick to bodies and worlds, and in the very passages or variations between these intensities *and* resonances themselves.

Halldórsson's discussion of affect as different from structure is also important. Although it has been common to frame collaborations in terms of structure, he quite rightly suggests that focusing on structure can shift attention away from the people with whom we work and eventually lead to their disappearance. Attending to how people and bodies and events and places and histories (and so on) affect each other (and as this idea rolls around in my mind an idea of ontological dark matter begins to take shape) is an area that is ripe for investigation.

I share Halldórsson's interest in crafting research that leads to productive relationships and stronger communities. I am increasingly convinced that all of us, citizens across positions, need more opportunities to make shared commitments, to build strong connections, and to craft collective solutions to the challenges we currently face.

Affective possibilities

Recently, I had a bit more good fortune, becoming involved in a collaborative research project sponsored by the United Kingdom's 'Imagine: Connecting Communities Through Research' Programme. This particular collaboration is set in Rotherham, a once booming industrial city in Yorkshire that has lately seen more than its share of troubles. A very different kind of collaboratively written book, called *Re-Imagining Contested Communities* (Pahl et al., Forthcoming) arose out of that research. The book aims at multiple audiences: university members, community members and policy makers. Its authors include artists, academics, parents, students, poets, singers and community development workers who juxtapose history, theory, narrative, place, identity and images with memories, poetry, freestyle, hope, rage and dreams. The book's collaborators were motivated by the desire to document the complicated community within which they all lived, and to do so in ways that could actually heal some of the divisions and rifts within that community. The group did not use affect as a conceptual or pragmatic frame for the project or book but, looking back, it was clearly at the collaboration's core. Moreover, embracing the commitment to both the collaboratively produced product and the collaboration out of which that product emerged helped to deepen positive relationships and generate multifaceted understandings among many of the participants.

The still-dominant research approaches born of linear, rational, positivist and post-positivist ideologies that continue to rule over many fields (like my current discipline of Education) can neither describe nor solve the protean problems we face today. What would our work – and our worlds – look like if we took up Halldórsson's call, if we turned our attention to affect and the collaborative encounter? What might we then be able to know and do? These are important questions that all who are engaged in collaborative research should take to heart.

Disclosure statement

No potential conflict of interest was reported by the author.

References

Brettell, C. B., ed. 1996. *When They Read What We Write: The Politics of Ethnography*. Westport: Bergin & Garvey.
Campbell, E., and L. E. Lassiter. 2015. *Doing Ethnography Today*. Chichester: Wiley Blackwell.
Gregg, M., and G. J. Seigworth. 2011. *The Affect Theory Reader*. Durham, NC: Duke University Press.
Haviland, M. 2017. *Side by Side? Community Art and the Challenge of Co-Creativity*. New York: Routledge.
Lassiter, L. E. 2005. *The Chicago Guide to Collaborative Ethnography*. Chicago: University of Chicago Press.
Lassiter, L. E., H. Goodall, E. Campbell, and M. N. Johnson. 2004. *The Other Side of Middletown: Exploring Muncie's African American Community*. Walnut Creek, CA: AltaMira Press.
Pahl, K., Z. Rasool, E. Pente, and Elizabeth Campbell. Forthcoming. *Re-Imagining Contested Communities: Connecting Rotherham Through Research*. Brighton, UK: Policy Press.
Seigworth, G. J., and M. Gregg. 2011. "An Inventory of Shimmers." In *The Affect Theory Reader*, edited by M. Gregg and G. J. Seigworth. Durham, NC: Duke University Press.

Seyfert, R. 2012. "Beyond Personal Feelings and Collective Emotions: Toward a Theory of Social Affect." *Theory, Culture & Society* 29 (6): 27–46. doi:10.1177/0263276412438591.

Skoggard, I., and A. Waterston. 2015. "Introduction: Toward an Anthropology of Affect and Evocative Ethnography." *Anthropology of Consciousness* 26 (2): 109–120. doi:10.1111/anoc.2015.26.issue-2.

Cooperation in adversity: an evolutionary approach

John Lazarus

ABSTRACT
Throughout the organic world cooperation provides mutual benefit but is vulnerable to exploitation from free-riders. Over the last 30 years work in evolutionary biology and game theory has provided understanding of the conditions necessary for the maintenance of cooperation, and advances in gene-culture coevolution theory have extended this understanding to our own species. After a preamble on the evolutionary analysis of behaviour I outline this work. I then consider how cooperation is influenced by environmental adversity and find that in non-human species it is enhanced under these circumstances in a range of taxa. In a sample of human cases the same result is found in a majority, but the opposite effect in some when socioeconomic position is the measure of quality. In anthropological studies of societies living *in extremis*, again the opposite effect is found. I propose a sigmoid shape for the relationship between adversity and fitness (or human well-being) and a consequent inverted-U shaped relationship between adversity and the benefit of cooperation. Most of the data presented on the relationship between adversity and cooperation are consistent with this proposal. I suggest further tests of the proposal and place the study of cooperation in the broader context of prosociality.

1. Introduction

Cooperation offers benefits through the sharing of physical power, resources, skills, knowledge, problem-solving experience, social support and social influence. But cooperation is a fragile condition, vulnerable to exploitation from those who take without contributing. Many disciplines have important contributions to make to its study (Lazarus 2003) and here I apply an evolutionary approach (and for humans a gene-culture coevolutionary approach; see Section 3) to understand what happens to cooperation – throughout the organic world but focusing on our own species – in conditions of adversity. Does it flourish or wither, and why?

Cooperation, as understood in biology and economics, is defined in terms of its consequences for those involved in a social interaction and this is the approach I take here. To be precise an act is cooperative if it results in a benefit to both the actor and the recipient(s) of the act. My metric for evaluating benefit in non-human species is, in principle, Darwinian fitness, although empirically we often have to make do with a proxy for fitness. By Darwinian fitness I mean lifetime reproductive success, the total number of offspring produced. In the human case, where a gene-culture coevolutionary approach is more appropriate, we need to be more cautious in assuming that choices are always adaptive in a Darwinian sense, and I explain this more fully in Section 2.

Defining adversity

An environment is defined as adverse if it has some negative impact on the species concerned. For an evolutionary analysis, and for non-human species, the metric for this impact is fitness. For our own species it is also often the case that fitness is lower in what we deem to be a more adverse environment. However, as I have already said, we cannot assume that all human behaviour is adaptive and it is more parsimonious to claim simply that what I will call 'well-being' is reduced in a more adverse environment, my term being simply a more concise equivalent of 'subjective well-being' which combines measures of cognition (satisfaction) and positive affect (Cummins 2000). I discuss the relationship between well-being and fitness further in Section 2.

Broadly, adversities have abiotic or biotic origins. In the first category are variables such as temperature, aridity and altitude for which a species will have some optimal value at which its fitness (or well-being) is greatest, larger departures from this value bringing greater adversity. Biotic adversity arises from predators, parasites, disease and competitors. Uniquely human adversities, both abiotic and biotic, include pollution, housing, employment, health services, education, poverty, lack of opportunity and the social environment: other people who individually, collectively or institutionally may harm another physically, emotionally, economically or in any other way, either actively or by withholding some good. Adversity may also be felt in terms of relative deprivation (Davis 1959; Wilkinson and Pickett 2010).

Adversity (or harshness as it is also termed) clearly does impact on human well-being and consequently has profound and widespread influences on cognition, behaviour and development beyond its impact on cooperation (Low 1990; Ellis et al. 2009; Frankenhuis, Panchanathan, and Nettle 2016). These influences arise from sources that range from the abiotic environment through the personal to the societal. For example, lower socio-economic status is associated with a 'behavioural constellation of deprivation' that leads to a focus on present-oriented behaviours (Pepper and Nettle 2017). Further, some aspects of adversity, such as extrinsic mortality risks (Nettle 2010; Frankenhuis, Panchanathan, and Nettle 2016; Pepper and Nettle 2017) and economic and political factors (Standing 2011), are outside the individual's control.

Outline

Following a preamble on evolutionary explanation (Section 2) I describe current thinking on the evolutionary origin of cooperation in the human species (Section 3). Then, following an account of how cooperation is influenced by adversity (Section 4) in organisms generally, but focusing on the human species, I offer a contribution to the explanation of these relationships (Section 5). Finally, I extend the discussion briefly to other forms of prosociality (Section 6) and draw conclusions (Section 7).

2. A preamble on the evolutionary analysis of behaviour

Given their very different intellectual histories, social and evolutionary scientists have largely worked independently to understand human behaviour and social structures, and when they have interacted it has been more often in conflict than in productive dialogue. Matters have improved as evolutionary biologists have come to appreciate that any evolved behavioural predisposition must emerge as action through the processes of individual development occurring within a particular cultural environment. And having learned these general lessons from psychology, anthropology and sociology they have gone on to formalize the ways in which organic and cultural evolution interact, as discussed below. But since the rapprochement is not yet complete, it will be useful, I think, to outline the nature of the questions the evolutionary scientist asks about behaviour and the conceptual approach that is brought to bear in searching for answers, before proposing some ideas for understanding cooperation under adversity that have an evolutionary-cultural foundation.

The social scientist seeking a causal understanding of human action is concerned with what the biologist calls *proximate causation*. That is, finding the influences within the environment (including the social and cultural environment), and within the individual, that account for the behaviour of interest influences that the psychologist calls motivational. And, by extension, an understanding is sought for how behaviour varies between individuals and cultures. The evolutionary behavioural analyst asks, in the first place, a different question, one that the biologist calls *ultimate causation*: what were the evolutionary forces (generally forces of natural selection) that have resulted in behaviour appearing in the particular form that it does, in response to particular proximate influences? And the guiding principle in generating hypotheses about ultimate causation is that it is predicted – under the influence of natural selection – to produce *adaptive* behaviour: behaviour that efficiently solves a problem in the organism's life.

But there is a second stage of evolutionary analysis; hypotheses of ultimate causation lead naturally to complementary hypotheses about the environmental cues – the proximate causes – predicted to influence the emergence of behaviour patterns given their proposed adaptive function (Barkow, Cosmides, and Tooby 1992). This is clearly a different source for ideas about proximate causation to those from the social sciences, but one that has a strong foundation in the theory of natural selection.

The generation of hypotheses of proximate causation from natural selection theory has been a particular feature of evolutionary psychology (Tooby and Cosmides 1990) and the evolutionary logic underlying this approach is important for the ideas I present in Section 5 concerning the influence of adversity on cooperation. Using this relationship as an exemplar the argument from evolutionary psychology is that natural selection over our evolutionary history has been responsible for the learned psychological predispositions that we bring to cooperative decision-making in the contemporary world, as well as the proximate causes that turn these predispositions into actions. I would argue that this is a particularly strong premise for our present case since cooperative decisions, environmental adversity and the interaction between the two must have had a great impact on fitness throughout human history. These predispositions govern contemporary behaviour to the extent that 'present conditions resemble past conditions in specific ways made developmentally and functionally important by the design of those adaptations' (Tooby and Cosmides 1990, 375). The approach is perfectly compatible with the evidence that cooperative tendencies vary with the economic and societal structures of different cultures, variation which can sometimes also be understood in adaptive terms (Henrich et al. 2004) as a result of further learned predispositions. Whether any of these predispositions are optimal in terms of fitness enhancement in the changed environments of the modern world remains an open question, is not assumed by the evolutionary psychology approach and is not assumed here. And since the consequences of cooperative decisions for people are my primary focus I will, parsimoniously, refer to 'well-being' (rather than fitness) to describe the relative positive outcomes of cooperating or not cooperating in environments of differing qualities. In the non-human examples the outcome measures are either fitness or, more frequently, proxies for fitness.

An example of how the evolutionary psychology approach seeks to understand evolved proximate causes will be useful here. Lieberman, Tooby, and Cosmides (2003) tested Westermarck's (1921) theory for the proximate causation of incest avoidance, an adaptive phenomenon in that it reduces the damaging effects of inbreeding depression. Westermarck proposed that incest avoidance, and the moral objection to incest, were achieved by the co-residence of siblings from an early age resulting in 'sexual negative imprinting'. Lieberman and coworkers found support for their hypothesis, derived directly from Westermarck's proposal, that duration of co-residence with an opposite-sex sibling would correlate positively with the strength of the moral opposition to sibling incest. The association was independent of degree of relatedness (adopted, step-, half- or full-sib) while relatedness itself, the *functionally* important factor, did not influence the moral attitude to incest. This is understandable in evolutionary terms since a child cannot reliably know its kin relationship to another child it grows up with. Duration of co-residence, however, is a reliable cue since experienced directly, and crucially it correlated significantly with relatedness, the functionally relevant variable. These results illustrate the point that evolved proximate causal factors need not themselves represent the adaptive variable but must map reliably onto it.

Evolutionary biologists and social scientists continue to generate their hypotheses concerning proximate causes from different principles. This is a difficult division to bridge, but on another area of dispute further mutual understanding should be possible. This is the role of genetics in the causation of behaviour and, in particular, the worry by some social scientists that an evolutionary analysis of behaviour assumes genetic determinism, the notion that a particular genetic make-up fully determines a behaviour; given gene X behaviour Y will be shown and will be shown whatever the environment throws at it. While some biologists may have held this view in the past, it is now a straw man. The notion of innateness is discredited; rather behaviour is understood to unfold during life as a continuing interaction between the individual, its genotype and the environment (Mameli and Bateson 2006; Bateson and Mameli 2007), including the cultural environment (Nettle 2009).

It is the complex interplay between the individual, its genotype and the environment just described that is subject to natural selection, behaviour responding flexibly and often adaptively to the environment through processes involving direct experience, social influence and the internalization of norms. Although this means that behaviour is subject to various biases and that we are not blank slates (Pinker 2002), it does not necessitate genetic determinism, just as an enlightened view of the power of the environment to influence behaviour does not merit it with an analogous determinism.

Further, there is no longer a fundamental conflict between the study of culture and of biological evolution as forces for change. In the discipline known as 'gene-culture coevolution' the two are now integrated (Boyd and Richerson 1985; Richerson and Boyd 2005). The logic of the approach is that cultural practices modify the human environment and consequently influence the selection pressures acting on the human genome and directly on the cultural practices themselves, producing feedback loops, both positive and negative. Cultural transmission may be horizontal, vertical or oblique, and natural selection is assumed to act on both genetic and cultural variation in behaviour and cognition, although cultural success may look very different to genetic success. Culture evolves and the methods of evolutionary biology can be used to study its evolution. And gene-culture coevolution theory now has a new importance following recent findings that cultural practices modifying the environment have resulted in changes in gene frequencies (Laland, Odling-Smee, and Myles 2010; Richerson, Boyd, and Henrich 2010). It is therefore no longer possible to dismiss the idea that cultural forces might have changed the human genome by claiming that there has not been sufficient time for natural selection to act. And indeed natural selection continues to act on the human genome (e.g. Byars et al. 2010).

3. How did cooperation evolve in our species?

Understanding the evolutionary origin of cooperation has been a challenge since helping others would not at first sight appear to be favoured by natural selection. The method required to analyse this problem is game theory, developed by mathematicians and economists to predict rational choices when two or more individuals interact and the choices they make influence the payoff for other players. Economic rationality is classically deemed to be self-regarding in that it maximizes some kind of personal payoff (Gintis 2003). However, achieving maximum payoff may not be possible when the consequence of one's choices is under the influence of the choices made by others, as in a social interaction. Instead of reaching the 'best' choice, defined by maximum payoff, therefore, rational players in a game come to settle on the set of choices which means that *no player can do better by choosing to play differently*, such a set of plays being termed a *Nash equilibrium* (Binmore 2007a, 2007b; Colman 1999).

Evolutionary biologists took this economic equilibrium concept in games and applied it to a similar problem, in which natural selection determines the decisions made by the rational player. If at the Nash equilibrium no player can make a more profitable move this is just the outcome to be expected when individual decisions are evolving under the force of natural selection, with fitness as the payoff metric. And, following this logic, the evolutionary equivalent of a Nash equilibrium is termed an *evolutionarily stable strategy*, or *ESS* (Maynard Smith 1982). Both the Nash equilibrium and the ESS are stable equilibrium states and thus, by definition, are what we expect to see in nature. An important difference between the two concepts, however, is that while the Nash equilibrium must take rational play as an *assumption*, a state of affairs on which players cannot improve is *built into* the theory of natural selection and therefore also the ESS concept.

The game theory approach to understanding the conditions for the existence of cooperation can be exemplified by the well-known economic game, the prisoners' dilemma (e.g. Colman 1999). In this game two individuals interact in a scenario in which each actor has a choice of two plays or strategies which, in general terms, can be thought of as cooperating with (C) or defecting on (D) the other player. The original prisoner scenario is unnecessarily complicated and I will illustrate the dilemma with a simpler scenario described by Colman (1999). A Buyer has decided to purchase a diamond from a Seller and a price has been agreed. For some reason the exchange must be made in secret and so the two agree each to leave a bag, the Buyer's containing the agreed price and the Seller's the diamond, at a different place in a wood, after which each will retrieve the other's bag. The problem is, of course, that either party might be tempted to leave an empty bag, thus defecting (D) on the other, rather than cooperating (C) with a full bag. Figure 1 shows the relative payoffs to Buyer and Seller of the four possible outcomes of the exchange. The absolute value of the numbers in the figure is arbitrary; all that matters, and what defines the dilemma, is their ranking, a higher number indicating a more preferred outcome.

If both parties cooperate and fulfil their agreement (a CC outcome), they gain three points, but if both come with an empty bag (DD), they gain only two since they have both failed to close a deal they desired. If one party leaves an empty bag (D) and the other a full one (C), then the defector goes home with both the cash and the diamond (five points), while the other party, the sucker, has neither (0 points).

What is the equilibrium outcome to this game, represented by the best response of each player to the play of the other? The answer, which can be seen in Figure 1, is for both players to defect (DD) since *whatever the other player does it is always more profitable to defect than to cooperate*. The dilemma demonstrated by the game is that this outcome, though a result of rational play, is not the best outcome that can be achieved. Both parties would clearly prefer a CC outcome to a DD outcome, but even if there was some way for them to agree on such an outcome, it would still pay to renege on the agreement.

This game captures the essence of the problem of how to maintain cooperation and the logic can be simply extended to interactions between more than two players. Why should a hunter exert himself fully in the hunt, and why should he share his catch with others in his hunter–gatherer group? Why pull your weight in a team effort or, as a

		Buyer	
		Cooperate (Bag full)	Defect (Bag empty)
Seller	Cooperate (Bag full)	3, 3	0, 5
	Defect (Bag empty)	5, 0	2, 2

Figure 1. Payoff matrix for the prisoners' dilemma. The first payoff in each cell is to the seller.

nation, fulfil promises on reducing greenhouse gas emissions? The temptation to defect is often rational in economic (selfish) terms.

It would therefore seem that an ultimate explanation of the fact that cooperation *is* a feature of human social life cannot rest on the logic of the prisoners' dilemma as I have described it, in which the two parties meet only once. In the real world we often enter into relationships in which we interact repeatedly over days, months or years, and an ultimate explanation must take into account the fact that for most of our evolutionary history we lived in small groups in which all identities were mutually known and people interacted repeatedly throughout their lives (Kelly 2013). In the language of game theory we played iterated (i.e. repeated), not one-shot, games with each other and thus had the opportunity to reward past support, punish past defections or break off a relationship altogether. This complicates enormously the strategies that can be played, compared to the one-shot game I have described, strategies that take into account the history of the relationship. In particular, the fear of retaliation in later encounters encourages cooperation and can be the basis for a cooperative ESS in the repeated prisoners' dilemma, such as the Tit-for-Tat strategy: start by cooperating, then copy partner's last play (Axelrod and Hamilton 1981; see also Nowak and Sigmund 1993; for another cooperative ESS). And, pre-empting these findings, the 'folk theorem', as game theorists call it, concluded that for indefinitely repeated games with little discounting of future payoffs cooperative equilibrium strategies will always exist (Binmore 2005).

So cooperation can result from self-regarding, broadly reciprocal, interactions between pairs of individuals (so called *direct reciprocity*). But understanding how relationships develop in small communities is not just a matter of summing all the dyadic relationships within it. Individuals learn about the cooperativeness of others by interacting with them, observing them directly and talking to third parties (Dunbar 2004). In this way they build up *reputational* knowledge invaluable when responding to offers of interaction with the potential for mutual benefit, or when selecting partners for such interactions themselves (Roberts 1998; Gurven 2004; Craik 2009). Alexander (1987) was the first evolutionary biologist to emphasize the importance of this process for the evolution of cooperation. He coined the term *indirect reciprocity* to describe the biasing of cooperative responses to those known to have been cooperative to others in the past, and there is now experimental evidence that players are more likely to cooperate with other cooperators than with free-riders in small group interactions (e.g. Milinski et al. 2001; Barclay 2004).

The analysis so far shows that self-regarding rationality is compatible with cooperation when individuals interact repeatedly with known partners. However, laboratory and real-world experiments show that people are not fully selfishly rational since participants also cooperate in one-shot prisoners' dilemma games about half the time and contribute in one-shot public goods games, the multi-person equivalent of the prisoners' dilemma in which the rational decision is to give nothing (Camerer 2003). Behaviour in another and much simpler game, the dictator game, is particularly instructive. In this game a dictator simply decides how to split an amount of money between themselves and another player. The rational self-regarding choice is clearly to give nothing away, but giving 10–20% of the fund is common (Camerer 2003). The results from this and other games played in many different societies while showing much variation – understandable in terms of the economic and societal structure of the culture – demonstrate that pure selfishness is rare and suggest the existence of what may be a universal sense of fairness (Henrich et al. 2004).

Such a predisposition for fairness may have been favoured by selection, acting both genetically and culturally (Chudek and Henrich 2011), since it undermines self-regarding rationality and eases the path to the more rewarding cooperative CC (rather than DD) outcome in prisoners' dilemma-type repeated encounters and makes it possible in one-shot encounters too. In a manner that is similar to Roberts's (2005) notion of interdependence, one way of representing the fairness motive is by adding some proportion of the other player's payoff to one's own. If this proportion is great enough (e.g. >0.67 for the payoffs in Figure 1) the Nash equilibrium and ESS become CC even in the one-shot game.

Binmore (2005, Chapter 9) argues that our sense of fairness evolved as a stable social mechanism for sharing resources in the non-hierarchical societies of the earliest hunter–gatherer humans and that we carry this same sense today. If we extrapolate from our knowledge of present-day egalitarian hunter-gatherers, our earliest human ancestors benefited from sharing with their neighbours because of their interdependence (Roberts 2005) – particularly in cooperative hunting and gathering, and food sharing – and consequently had a stake in each other's well-being. In particular, such cooperative practices reduce the risk of periods without food, and free riding on this system is not tolerated (Winterhalder 1986; Kaplan, Hill, and Hurtado 1990; Gurven 2004; Kelly 2013, Chapters 6, 7). (It is probably not a coincidence that the cooperative non-hierarchical structure, collective decision-making, monitoring of resource acquisition by others, graded sanctions for defectors and conflict resolution mechanisms of many hunter–gatherer societies (Kelly 2013) are all features shared with successful common pool resource groups such as coastal fisheries and forestry systems (Ostrom 1990).) An early human social contract characterized by sharing, as a form of enlightened self-interest, may be the origin of the Golden Rule – variations on 'Do as you would be done by' – probably the most universal ethical imperative that we have (Binmore 2005, Chapter 9).

While an early evolutionary origin for our widespread sense of fairness seems likely, scholars differ on how best to explain the fact that we often act fairly in *one-shot* interactions in the real contemporary world (e.g. queuing or returning a lost wallet) and in the lab, when reciprocity is not expected. One explanation is that people think in such situations, consciously or not, *as if* they were repeated non-anonymous games, since the predisposition we bring to such encounters is one that evolved in the small groups of our early evolutionary history described above (e.g. Haselton and Nettle 2006). Gintis et al. (2003) disagree, arguing that early humans would also have engaged in encounters with a low probability of continuing, in which defection would have been the more profitable strategy. However, this doesn't explain the *cooperative* responses that are regularly seen in one-off encounters in both the real world and the laboratory. A further point is that experimental one-shot interactions may be played like repeated games since they inadvertently share cues associated with the reputational indirect reciprocity consequences of being observed by others (Kurzban 2001; Haley and Fessler 2005; Bateson, Nettle, and Roberts 2006).

The behavioural expression of cooperation, or its absence, is inevitably accompanied by emotions including a feeling for the welfare of others, guilt, shame, a personal concern for reputation and a fear of punishment (Milinski et al. 2001; Fehr and Gachter 2002; Barclay 2004; Bowles and Gintis 2011), and develops in the individual under the influence of social norms (e.g. Krupka and Weber 2013; Hugh-Jones and Ooi 2017). It is possible to incorporate these processes into models that combine biological and cultural evolution, as discussed in the previous section, and such a model, simulating internalization of norms transmitted vertically between generations and obliquely by socialization institutions, concludes that cooperation can be maintained when a minority of the population exhibit *strong reciprocity*, cooperating unconditionally and punishing defectors at a personal cost (Gintis 2003). Although the importance of strong reciprocity for the evolution of cooperation is currently a matter of controversy (Guala 2012), the model exemplifies an approach to the problem of understanding *how* individuals and communities reach equilibrium prosocial states. This must occur by some combination of genetic evolution, cultural influence and direct experience, but we are some way from a full understanding of the processes involved and their interaction.

Some discussion of altruism is also necessary here since, although formally distinguished from cooperation, the two prosocial acts share the consequence of benefitting others, differing in that the actor also benefits from a cooperative act but suffers a cost from an altruistic act. It is important to note that focusing narrowly on a single act defined, as above, as altruistic may miss a bigger picture. The single act may be just one of a series of reciprocal altruistic exchanges, so that considered over a longer time period the relationship is seen to be one of cooperation, as in reciprocal food sharing, since both parties benefit. Here the success of cooperation relies on trusting that the other party will reciprocate. In the dictator game described above the single decision involved is 'purely' altruistic if anything is given to the other party, as it commonly is. Acts of cooperation and altruism, in addition to their direct consequences, may accrue delayed benefits due to direct and indirect reciprocity and may be selected for as honest signals of the ability to act in this way in the future (Roberts 1998).

However, a difference between cooperation and altruism important for us here is that acts of pure altruism favoured by selection in the small societies of our early history, due to delayed benefits, may not be personally beneficial in the large anonymous societies of the contemporary world, even though they continue to be selected by gene-culture coevolution due to internalization of norms built on evolved predispositions. The upshot of this, as I will go on to explain, is that *I deal here with the influence of adversity on cooperation only* and not on pure altruism as just described. This is partly because I am concerned with the more straightforward case where costs and benefits are borne in a given individual (the cooperative actor) *in a given environment* in the here and now. In pure altruism immediate benefit is borne only by another party who may inhabit a different (social) environment from the altruistic actor, such as the case of Christians who rescued Jews in Nazi-occupied Poland (Tec 1986) and those who rescued persecuted family members, friends and strangers in Argentina during the military rule of 1976–1983 (Casiro 2006). Any delayed benefits to the self of altruism through direct or indirect reciprocity, if there are any at all, take place in a future environment of an uncertain nature. In addition, even if one wanted to assume that our altruistic tendencies are built on the evolved predispositions mentioned above, it would be very difficult to quantify the contribution of supposed delayed benefits to our altruistic decision-making. For all these reasons altruism is not amenable to the analysis I describe in Section 5. My analysis is suitable for examining cooperation, however, for which I need to consider only direct costs and benefits to the self and not to others (although even here the analysis is not perfect since cooperation may also have delayed benefits for the self).

This account of the origins of human cooperation just scratches the surface of half a century of research on the topic (Ridley 1997; Hammerstein 2003; Gintis et al. 2005; Tomasello 2009; Bowles and Gintis 2011). My aim here has been to outline the kinds of thinking required for an understanding of the origin and maintenance of human cooperation as a prelude to the following discussion of the influence of adversity on cooperative behaviour.

Finally, we should not exaggerate the human tendency to cooperate; like all human traits it is variable and some individuals, in some situations, prefer to freeride on the generosity of others.

4. Adversity and cooperation: data

What follows is by no means an exhaustive or systematic review but I have not been selective. I report all my findings from the literature on the influence of adversity on cooperation.

Non-human cases

There is a widespread tendency in the natural world for organisms to be more cooperative in conditions of adversity and I have not located any evidence to the contrary. The phenomenon has been reviewed by Andras and Lazarus (2005) and many of the following examples are taken from that account:

- In response to environmental stressors, individual bacteria become social and form multi-cellular structures such as biofilms and mushroom bodies (Greenberg 2003) which enhance their resistance to the stressor, such as an antibiotic (Drenkard and Ausubel 2002).
- Social, in contrast to solitary, feeding in the nematode *Caenorhabditis elegans* is triggered by environmental stressors (De Bono et al. 2002).
- Fish school and primate group sizes are larger where predation risk is greater (Seghers 1974; Farr 1975; Hill and Lee 1998). Gregariousness reduces predation risk in various ways (Krause and Ruxton 2002).
- Colonies of the common mole-rat (*Cryptomys hottentotus hottentotus*) are larger in arid areas, which present greater foraging adversity, than in mesic (moderately moist) areas. Movement between colonies is also less frequent in arid areas. Larger and more stable colonies favour resource sharing and the development of cooperative relationships with known individuals (Spinks, Jarvis, and Bennett 2000).
- The phenomenon is also found in plant communities, in which an individual plant, acting respectively competitively or cooperatively, can inhibit or promote the biomass, growth and reproduction of its neighbours. In 11 mountain habitats around the world relationships between neighbours in subalpine plant communities are more competitive, whereas in the corresponding alpine communities, where abiotic stress is higher, cooperative interactions predominate (Callaway et al. 2002).

The human case

For the human case I have sought data from a range of methodologies: real-life case studies and experiments; anthropological work; within- and between-society comparisons; self-report measures; and lab experiments. For reasons that will become clear in Section 5 I divide the data into those in which, like the non-human data, cooperation increases with adversity, followed by those in which the opposite is the case.

Cooperation increases with adversity

While there is a long-standing view in the social sciences that external threats increase group cohesion (Stein 1976), this is not always measured in behavioural terms. However, it seems to be commonplace that people caught up in a natural disaster cooperate in ways they would not consider under more normal circumstances. Members of the Committee on Disaster Studies of the National Academy of Sciences, USA, write that following a natural disaster:

> The net result ... is a dramatic *increase* in social solidarity among the affected populace ... The sharing of a common threat to survival and the common suffering produced by the disaster tend to produce *a breakdown of pre-existing social distinctions* and a great outpouring of love, generosity, and altruism ... persons tend to act toward one another spontaneously, sympathetically, and sentimentally, on the basis of common human needs rather than in terms of predisaster differences in social and economic status. (Fritz and Williams 1957, 48, emphasis added)

This account provides something of a control condition in making a comparison with pre-disaster behaviour.

In the trench warfare of World War I cooperation between British and German infantry was commonplace. Between battles a 'live and let live' reciprocal arrangement developed whereby both sides refrained from firing on the enemy, in spite of the wishes of their commanders. This peaceful arrangement could be signalled, for example, by repeated daily firing at precisely the same position at precisely the same time. Axelrod (1984; drawing on Ashworth 1980) analyses this as an iterated prisoners' dilemma in which, for the infantrymen at least, mutual cooperation was the best outcome.

These real-world case studies show that *some* people behave cooperatively under severe adversity, sometimes at great personal cost, but they do not allow a quantitative comparison with the frequency or degree of cooperative behaviour in less adverse conditions. To provide the kind of data we are seeking here systematic studies are required.

The set of studies probably closest to these real-world cases of external threat are the experiments, carried out mostly in the lab (e.g. Puurtinen and Mappes 2009; Puurtinen, Heap, and Mappes 2015), but also in the real world (Erev, Bornstein, and Galili 1993) in which participants in small groups are found to cooperate more (generally through donations in a public goods game) when competing with other groups. The adversity in these studies is inferred to arise from the competition; it is intrinsic to the task and not a pre-existing condition that participants bring to the experiment, as in the studies that follow. While this is an important distinction, for present purposes it needs to be examined in relation to my analysis in the following section, which is framed in terms of the individual's perception of their adversity. A temporary adverse stimulus that arises immediately before a decision has to be made may have different consequences from that of a long-term adverse condition that one brings to an experiment, such as might arise from low social status or hunger, say. However, there are many psychological studies in which brief priming stimuli are remarkably effective in imitating the influence of long-term conditions, including those of prosociality (Piff et al. 2010; Piff 2014; Nettle et al. 2014). Since brief exposure to competition in an experiment may also have such a priming effect, it seems worthwhile to consider competition experiments as potentially suitable for our analysis here.

Moving on to an anthropological study, in examining the influence of adversity using a random half of the societies in the standard cross-cultural sample, Low (1990) found a significant positive association between extreme cold and the hunting of large game, which is a cooperative enterprise.

Finally, in a US study of social class effects, with class measured by educational attainment and income, lower-class participants offered more points than upper-class participants in a trust game, a cooperative game involving trust that the partner will reciprocate (Piff et al. 2010).

Cooperation decreases with adversity

The results of the following two studies conflict with those of Piff et al. (2010) just described and I will return in the following section to the issue of how these results might be resolved.

In his study of Tyneside neighbourhoods Nettle (Nettle 2015; Nettle, Colléony, and Cockerill 2011; Schroeder, Pepper, and Nettle 2014) has compared 'the informal social relationships and interactions that make up so much of everyday life' (Nettle 2015, 12) of two neighbourhoods in the city of Newcastle upon Tyne, UK. These neighbourhoods, with populations of about 3000 each, are markedly different in adversity as measured by the Index of Multiple Deprivation. The more deprived neighbourhood is at the first percentile of deprivation in England, while the less deprived is at the 79th percentile, and the study was carried out at 'a moment when people in [the former] neighbourhood had endured many years of uncertainty about the future of the whole area' (12). A number of behavioural and self-report measures were made, but the only ones relevant here were two self-report measures; adult respondents in the less-deprived neighbourhood trusted each other more (in two studies) and felt more strongly that people in their neighbourhood looked out for one another. The finding on trust was replicated for children between 9 and 15 years of age across a range of neighbourhoods differing in the level of deprivation. (Trust is not the same as cooperation but it is required if cooperation through repeated altruistic exchanges is to be successful.)

In support of these findings Haushofer (2013) found, in large data sets from the *World Values Survey*, that trust increased significantly with income within countries and with per capita GDP (at purchasing power parity) across countries.

Finally, I come to the tail of the distribution of environmental harshness, where case studies are naturally rare and where experiments are not possible. I describe three cases of societies living in conditions of extreme adversity; societies *in extremis*.

Burch (2006, 272), as described by Kelly (2013, 288n6), found that in Alaskan Iñupiaq Eskimos 'in periods of widespread famine and hunger, the [cooperative] distribution system broke down, families hoarded food, and some tried to steal the stores of others or even to kill the owners'.

In 1969 and 1970 Laughlin (1974, 1978) studied the So, a small society in Northern Uganda: 'The total So ecological/economic picture is grim. It is one of progressive deterioration of alternative resource bases to the point where a period of drought brings extreme and widespread hardship and starvation to the people of So' (Laughlin 1974, 380).

Laughlin quantified 'generalized' reciprocal exchange in the So, 'where the emphasis is upon the act of exchange and not upon immediate return or making a profit' (Laughlin 1974, 381) and compared its expression in two study periods, 'one of extreme hardship [and a second] in relationship to the first a time of plenty' (385). He found more generalized reciprocity in the period of plenty and, although the data are not analysed statistically, the increases compared to the period of extreme hardship are quite large: 48% for feeding guests ('the major medium of generalized reciprocity' [386]), 124% for food transfers and 38% for total (food + non-food) transfers. Generalized reciprocity contrasts with 'negative reciprocity' (i.e. exchange for profit) as a means of resource acquisition and when one type of reciprocity declines it is generally compensated by an increase in the other. This reminds us that in the real world – in contrast to the lab – cooperation is just one means of getting on in the world and is therefore subject, indirectly, to a range of influences, some of which may also be responsive to adversity. Thus in the So, to compensate for the reduction in generalized reciprocity during hardship, the cash value of negative reciprocity increased in that period by 454%.

The So are related to the Ik, who live further north in the mountains of northern Uganda. When studied by Turnbull (1966, 119–136, 1967, [1972] 1974, 1978) from 1964 to 1966, it would seem that the Ik lived in even greater hardship than the So, and their society certainly suffered from a greater absence of cooperativeness. The Ik's former nomadic hunting cycle had been curtailed by the government and this, together with the frequent droughts, led to intermittent famine and eventually the 'disintegration of Ik society' (Turnbull 1978, 53), Turnbull's period of fieldwork coming at 'a critical moment in the process of social change' (Turnbull 1978, 53), though 5 years after Turnbull's study, Joseph Towles, Turnbull's collaborator, found the social system much the same (Turnbull 1975, 355). In Turnbull's account cooperation was limited to house building, which required more than a single builder, and individuals passed their lives in relative isolation. Family and community bonds of care broke down completely, children were weaned at the age of three and then left to forage for themselves, and young and old were left to die if they could not find sufficient food. Although children foraged in gangs, these gangs served only as protection against predators (including adult Ik) and food was not shared.

> [A child] learned that cooperation was rarely beneficial – a temporary expediency at best – and that the unpredictability of circumstances that could make it worthwhile meant that there was no value in establishing permanent bonds with others on grounds of age, sex, or kinship. He learned that systematic sociality itself had no value. (Turnbull 1978, 64)

Turnbull concluded that, given the 'extreme ... circumstances' (Turnbull [1972] 1974, 111) 'the sadly functional nature of the Ik non-social system ... was the only way to survive' (Turnbull 1976, 6).

Turnbull's 1972 book on the Ik, *The Mountain People*, was critically received by some anthropologists, partly for its claimed lack of objectivity (Beidelman 1973; Barth 1974; Wilson et al. 1975; Knight 1976). Two of these eight commentators (Barth and Geddes in Wilson et al. 1975) pointed to inconsistencies in Turnbull's report but none doubted his findings as I describe them above. Heine (1985), who studied the Ik for 2 months in 1983, critiqued many aspects of Turnbull's ethnographic work but again did not dispute the above description of Ik society. The Ik continue to live in northern Uganda today.

5. Understanding the influence of adversity on cooperation

Game theory models have illustrated ways in which environmental adversity selects for cooperation (Andras, Lazarus, and Roberts 2007; Smaldino, Schank, and McElreath 2013). Here I ask more simply, and more generally, *what might the shape of the relationship between adversity and the benefit of cooperation look like*, and *what does that shape allow us to infer about how cooperation will vary with adversity?* These questions were addressed by Andras and Lazarus (2005), with additional mathematical formalities, and I develop the ideas further here. My aim is to see to what extent these proposed relationships might explain the findings described in Section 4. This seems to be a particularly worthwhile exercise given the broad range of contexts and taxonomic groups in which cooperation is enhanced by adversity, while the relationship is reversed *in extremis*. Although I will focus on the human case the conclusions apply to the non-human examples too.

The simple framework to be described is not intended to deny the complexity of environments and of social life but rather to provide an explanation for one feature of that complexity, environmental adversity, while acknowledging that adversity might work on cooperation in additional ways too. Adversity is a ubiquitous variable influencing a wide variety of cooperative interaction types, and it will be achieving its effects alongside a cluster of other influences. My approach does not deny that there are individual differences in what people see as a life of well-being and how that life may be enhanced, or sometimes diminished, by cooperation. As a natural scientist, however, I proceed in the belief that our understanding of how and why people interact with their environment as they do can be advanced by utilizing various methods of behavioural data collection, as well as statistical methods for taking individual differences into account. Finally, I am aware that I have offered only a small sample of human cases and that the pattern of results that emerges does not unequivocally support my analysis. However, studies of these relationships are still in their infancy and a comprehensive understanding is still some way off. In that context the fit between the data and the ideas I present here seems to merit further testing.

It might be thought immediately obvious *why* people seem to cooperate more in adversity, that is, to provide an ultimate, or functional, explanation. People in adversity have a greater 'need', it might be argued, and everything else being equal we would expect that need to be met. Or it might be stated or hypothesized, though without supporting theory or evidence, that cooperation will be greater in a poorer group (Da Costa, de Melo, and Lopes 2014, 455) or that this relationship has an inverted-U shape (Laughlin and Brady 1978). But as cost-benefit analyses such explanations are incomplete, as I will show. In addition, they may not explain the effect of adversity *in extremis* reported above, which *is* given an explanation in the present analysis.

I start with two general assumptions. First, as already stated, that well-being (and, for non-humans, fitness) declines with adversity or, in other words, that it increases with the *quality of the environment*. Second, where cooperation is observed I assume that on average, and including any delayed benefits, it brings greater well-being than its non-cooperation alternative (but not necessarily for all individuals on all occasions, since there will generally be a dynamic which includes some degree of freeriding). This assumption follows from the game theory prediction of how self-interested individuals will behave when the marginal net benefit of cooperation over non-cooperation (call it B) exceeds the threshold value at which cooperation becomes the equilibrium outcome (this kind of analysis was introduced in Section 3 in discussion of the prisoners' dilemma). It follows in turn that cooperation will be more likely to occur where B is greater since a greater value of B is more likely to exceed the threshold relevant to any particular case. And if B increases further, above the threshold value, cooperation is predicted to increase in order to take up this additional benefit, following the same self-interested logic that applied to the switch from non-cooperation to cooperation at the threshold. Such an increase in cooperation can occur by repetition of a cooperative act or by replacing it with a more beneficial alternative, the increase in cooperation being subject to the usual limitations as it comes into conflict with other demands on the individual's time and effort. I consider below the case of how, in fact, B is predicted to change in magnitude with environmental quality.

Though it is important to think in terms of net marginal benefit in defining B, to take account of potential marginal costs involved in cooperation (i.e. costs involved in cooperating that are absent when not cooperating), in some cases there may be no marginal costs. For example: a hunter or gatherer working with others rather than alone, where the benefit is bringing back more resources per capita; a car-sharing scheme where the parties involved get a ride every day for a share of the overall cost; or a sharing of knowledge or expertise where the gain per capita is enhanced when cooperating.

I represent these two assumptions graphically by two increasing functions relating environmental quality (E) to well-being (W), one function for the well-being of a cooperating individual and another for non-cooperation, the former function exceeding the latter for all values of E, for the reasons just argued. The non-cooperation function does not represent a free-rider's well-being but well-being if cooperation does not occur at all. The 'well-being of a cooperating individual' function represents well-being having provided a given cooperative act (at or above the cooperative threshold), and if this act has a marginal cost over non-cooperation, it is assumed to be independent of the quality of the environment.

Next, I add three further assumptions: that the shape of the increasing relationship between environmental quality and well-being is sigmoid, both when individuals do not cooperate and when they do; and that these two sigmoid functions converge at both extremes (Figure 2). The basis for these assumptions is presented in the Appendix. The slope of a sigmoid curve at first increases and then decreases; it is first concave upwards (what I shall call the left segment of the curve) and then concave downwards, also called diminishing returns (the right segment). The pair of sigmoid curves, representing cooperation and non-cooperation, stand for the two conditions as they occur within a particular society or other group under analysis; I am not claiming that there is a common scale across all data sets that might be used to test the predictions. And in testing the predictions it will be important to assure, as far as is feasible, that the groups being compared along the environmental quality axis are indeed comparable on all features except that of some measure(s) of environmental adversity.

The marginal net benefit of cooperating (B), compared to not cooperating, at a given value of environmental quality (E) is therefore the difference in well-being between the cooperation and non-cooperation functions. This is the net benefit of the act over and above the condition of non-cooperation; the benefit gained as a result of the cooperative interaction or enterprise less any marginal cost of the individual's contribution (i.e. cost over and above cost for the case of non-cooperation). It can be readily seen from Figure 2 that *as E increases B at first increases up to an inflection point, E_i, on the environmental quality axis and then declines – an inverted-U relationship*. Although any marginal cost of cooperation has been assumed to be independent of environmental quality, this may not hold if resources for cooperation are required in advance of a cooperative relationship being initiated. In this case those in a higher quality environment may find this initial investment more affordable, which would raise the benefit somewhat in those environments.

Since we would expect the occurrence of cooperation to map directly onto its marginal net benefit, B, this pattern captures the essence of most of the data I have reviewed, if we assume that the *in extremis* cases lie to the left of E_i, which is very

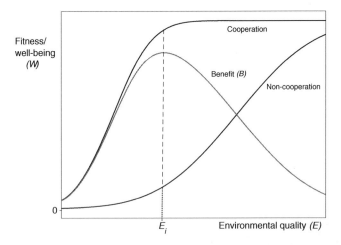

Figure 2. The sigmoid curves are illustrative examples of the proposed relationship between fitness/well-being (W) and environmental quality (E) in conditions of cooperation and non-cooperation. The inverted-U curve shows benefit (B), that is, the difference in fitness/well-being between cooperation and non-cooperation. E_i indicates the inflection point of environmental quality, at which benefit ceases to increase with E and begins to decline as E increases further. The image is the property of the author.

plausible, and all other cases lie to the right of E_i, which is less certain. That is, cooperation declines with adversity *in extremis* but otherwise the opposite is the case. The sigmoid curves could be drawn in many ways; here I have speculatively drawn them so that E_i sits towards the adverse end of the environmental quality continuum. This is not an a priori assumption that I wish to defend; I have done it simply to capture one *post-hoc* interpretation of the data, which is that the reversal of the 'adversity enhances cooperation' effect is rare and that it mostly occurs in extreme adversity (or in the extreme of *relative* deprivation (Davis 1959; Wilkinson and Pickett (2010)) if relative and not absolute deprivation is the influential variable). A consequence of this position for the inflection point is that as environmental quality worsens beyond E_i the cooperation curve must fall steeply to converge with that for non-cooperation, which means that the benefit of cooperation will also fall steeply. A consequence of this is that below E_i the benefit of cooperation is very sensitive to small changes in environmental quality and I will return to the implications of this.

The cases that do not immediately fit into this scheme are Nettle's (2015) Tyneside neighbourhood study and Haushofer's (2013) multi-national study, in both of which cooperation *declines* with adversity. This divergence in results cannot be resolved with any certainty but I offer some observations. First, the deprived neighbourhood in Nettle's study might lie to the left of E_i, which would mean that it fitted into the present scheme. I do not mean to suggest that this community has a life as harsh as that of the So and the Ik. However, its state of relative deprivation – relative to its UK comparators – may be similar; it is in the 1% of the most deprived neighbourhoods in England. In addition, residents of the neighbourhood may share, but to a lesser extent, the problem responsible for the breakdown of Ik society, that of hunger. A recent account of the relationship between hunger, socioeconomic position (SEP) and behaviour reports that, based on US studies,

> a substantial fraction of people from [low-income] households experience an excess of hunger due to their SEP, at least some of the time [and] ... within very affluent populations, individuals of lower SEP eat less satiating diets; do so on more irregular schedules; and a very sizable proportion ... report experiences such as food insufficiency and food insecurity that imply an increased frequency of hunger. (cited in Nettle 2017, 7)

Note also that the area containing the deprived neighbourhood contained an emergency-assistance food bank (Nettle 2015, 19). Nettle's (2015) own analysis of his results bears some similarities to the above arguments, including as it does the proposition that the more deprived neighbourhood is 'closer to the edge' (60) in the sense that the only way to avoid a crisis is to cross this edge in the hope of a happy outcome to a risky venture. And when it comes to a potential cooperative interaction:

> [i]f the people in your neighbourhood are ... close to the edge, then it makes sense that even if you had a lot of interaction with them you might not feel that you had *enough* interaction to say you knew what they were going to do next. (61, emphasis in the original)

Standing (2011, 20) has a similar conception of the precariat which, he suggests:

> lives with anxiety – chronic insecurity associated not only with teetering on the edge, knowing that one mistake or one piece of bad luck could tip the balance between modest dignity and being a bag lady, but also with a fear of losing what they possess even while feeling cheated by not having more.

My second observation is that the average per capita GDP measure used for Haushofer's (2013) between-country comparison may well be unsuitable for the present analysis since a particular average value may be accompanied by very different distributions of values within the nation, and consequently different values for adversity, depending on how adversity maps to per capita GDP from country to country. Third, it is informative to examine Nettle's and Haushofer's trust measures further. These are the only studies reviewed here that employ self-report rather than behavioural measures and, of course, a trusting attitude is relevant in the present context only to the degree that it predicts cooperative behaviour. While Nettle's measure concerned trust of others within the same neighbourhood, Haushofer's question – 'Do you trust people you meet for the very first time?' – was more generic. This 'generic trust' measure is more problematic as evidence here since it is unclear what the *environment* of any imagined cooperation in the mind of the respondent might be: the respondent's own environment, that of an imagined trustee, or something else? (See Nettle (2015, 63) for parallel comments on social environment.)

My suggestion that Nettle's deprived neighbourhood might lie in the left segment of the sigmoid meets a general problem for an explanation that predicts an inverted U-shaped relationship between two variables. As a specific example of this general problem, for the Tyneside neighbourhoods' case to fit my explanation, the wealthier neighbourhood should not lie so far to the right that it is the *less* cooperative of the two. More generally, with few data points it is difficult to support or refute an inverted U-shaped relationship with confidence. With just two data points, a finding of more cooperation under adversity, less cooperation or no difference in cooperation could all be accommodated in the inverted-U relationship between environmental quality and benefit by placing the data points, respectively, on the right arm of the U, the left arm or one on each arm. However, as more data points become available over a wider range of environmental qualities, it is increasingly possible to support or reject the proposed relationship.

In this context it is important to stress that I am not suggesting that a particular pair of sigmoid curves describes all cases (where by 'cases' I mean studies that compare cooperation between two or more levels of adversity) since different cases will involve different populations and will rarely use the same metrics for adversity and cooperation. To the extent that my thesis is correct, each case of the cooperation–adversity relationship will have its own pair of sigmoid curves, the particular shapes of which (and consequently of the benefit curve) are free to vary. Indeed many cases, as in all the examples described here, will cover too narrow a range of adversities (or will compare too few adversity levels) to reveal a sigmoid relationship and instead the relationship will be monotonic. In this monotonic case my account predicts concave upwards functions below E_i, but concave downwards functions above E_i, additional evidence being required to support a case for one or the other position on the environmental quality axis. Finally, although I argue that all cases cannot be placed *quantitatively* within a single two-dimensional adversity–cooperation space, I do want tentatively to propose, on the basis of the studies I have described here, that Figure 2 may represent a broad and qualitative truth about the adversity–cooperation relationship (cooperation being narrowly and behaviourally defined, as I have stressed). That is, that the relationship is negative over much of the range of environmental quality but that in the poorest environments it is reversed and is steeper.

To my knowledge there are no data sets showing an inverted-U relationship between adversity and cooperation but this may be because no study (and particularly no experimental study) has considered a broad enough range of adversities. Another strong prediction of my proposition that needs testing is that the *benefit* of cooperation has an inverted U-shaped relationship with environmental quality.

Although environmental quality takes the role here of an independent variable, this does not mean that it is fixed. A cooperative act might have a sufficiently beneficial outcome to move the actor further to the right along the environmental quality axis. Another point about environmental quality, particularly for the human case, is that the best environments may offer opportunities for individuals to find new ways to cooperate, ways that increase the benefit of cooperation and may also improve environmental quality.

This analysis of response to adversity, in which the environmental state is assumed to be fully known, complements that of Haselton and Nettle (2006), based on signal detection theory, for cases in which judgments are made in conditions of incomplete information.

Populations in extremis

I have found no non-human examples where cooperation is reduced by adversity. Under the present proposals, such an example would represent a population to the left of the inflection point and therefore *in* or close to *extremis*. This lack of data could therefore be explained by such populations having a high risk of dying out, migrating to a more suitable environment, or becoming permanently asocial, unless they were fortunate enough to be saved by environmental change or – particularly for human cases – by an outside agency. The risk of extinction or migration would be particularly acute due to the steep decline in cooperative benefit to the left of E_i. Gintis (2003, 160, emphasis in the original) takes a similar view and points to a cruel irony:

> In the primitive conditions under which human sociality evolved, when a group was threatened with extinction or dispersal, say through war, pestilence, or famine, cooperation was most needed for survival. But since the probability that the group will dissolve increases sharply under such conditions, cooperation based on future reciprocation cannot be maintained. Thus, *precisely when the group is most in need of prosocial behavior, cooperation based on repeated interactions will collapse.*

Turnbull (1976, 6) held that, for the Ik, acting alone brought *greater benefits* than cooperating since, to repeat an earlier quote, 'the sadly functional nature of the Ik non-social system ... was the only way to survive'. In terms of the present formulation this would mean that the cooperation and non-cooperation curves crossed at the adverse extreme.

It is also possible that acting alone may be more beneficial than cooperating under certain circumstances in the very best environments, the cooperation and non-cooperation curves again crossing (John Baker and Siobhán O'Sullivan, personal communications, 8 January 2017).

6. Other forms of prosociality

Cooperative behaviour shares motivational and emotional features, and evolutionary and cultural origins, with related prosocial behaviours, beliefs and attitudes, and the influence of adversity has been studied here too. At the level of individual differences those with more adverse life experience exhibit more empathy, compassion and generosity in charitable giving and aid to a stranger (Lim and DeSteno 2016; Lim 2017). The influence of social class on prosociality is controversial, with recent conflicting findings for a range of measures: utilitarianism, empathy, feelings of entitlement, narcissism, theft, lying, cheating, helpfulness, generosity, trust, trustworthiness, volunteering and charitable donation. Some studies find greater prosociality in higher classes (Korndörfer, Egloff, and Schmukle 2015) but others find the opposite class effect (Côté, House, and Willer 2015), to mention just two of the most recent reports. In understanding these apparently conflicting findings, it will be helpful to develop more tailored predictions for each measure, as attempted here for cooperation. If the inverted-U relationship proposed here between environmental quality and cooperation should hold also for some of these other forms of prosociality, this might resolve some of the (apparent) inconsistencies in the data, since conflicting studies could be situated on opposite sides of the environmental inflection point. As others have noted it is also important to take account of the methodology by which these results have been obtained, from behavioural observations and experiments to self-report, in both the lab and the real world, since they each have their own psychological influences.

7. Conclusions

Putting aside the case of societies *in extremis* for the moment, I have argued that in a more adverse environment a greater benefit is to be gained by cooperating, and consequently that cooperation will be more common in these circumstances. This view is supported by data from a broad range of non-human species and for a range of human contexts. The possible exception for the human case is the influence of SEP, where recent data show an unresolved picture.

The major premise for my conclusions is that fitness or well-being is a sigmoid function of environmental quality and I have suggested ways in which the implications of this premise for patterns of cooperation can be tested.

One can be either despairing or encouraged by this view of life. From the despondent position matters have to get bad before we make the most of our collaborative potential, while others will argue that it's just when life is troublesome that we are able to rise to the occasion by acting together. Putting aside such subjective responses the more objective conclusion is that cooperation seems to be scaled to adversity and responds adaptively to need.

In the very poorest environments, however, prosociality may break down altogether and a tentative conclusion from the arguments and evidence presented here is that quite small changes in adversity might have a large impact on cooperative sociality. Although this might work in either direction (Laughlin 1974, 1978) it requires theory on the dynamics of change to take this idea further. It is uncomfortable to accept, following

Turnbull for the Ik, that individualism in extreme adversity is adaptive; that *in extremis* selfishness is the favoured choice for survival. He may be right, but outside such extreme conditions the unusual human capacity for cooperation is at the heart of our sociality.

Acknowledgements

I am extremely grateful to John Baker whose comments resulted in many improvements and clarifications, including discussion of the comparability of environments when testing the ideas presented here. My thanks also to Tony Bennett, Matthew Johnson and Siobhán O'Sullivan for information and discussion, and to Quoc Vuong for guidance in preparing Figure 2.

Disclosure statement

The author states that there are no potential conflicts of interest.

Appendix: Evidence for the function shapes in Figure 2

This appendix provides evidence for the relationships between environmental quality and fitness or well-being proposed in Figure 2 in three parts: The right (diminishing returns) segment of the sigmoid curves; the left segment; and the convergence of the two curves (cooperation and non-cooperation) at both extremes. The evidence here is not selective but I have not attempted to find evidence for every kind of adversity.

The diminishing returns assumption is made in many behavioural ecological models, for example, for the way in which benefit to an offspring increases with parental investment (Trivers 1974); however, we are seeking empirical support here. Consider the common case of resource acquisition. In healthy animal populations in the wild (i.e. not *in extremis*), the rate of food intake generally increases with food density in a diminishing returns fashion (e.g. Goss-Custard et al. 2006) in accordance with foraging theory, as a consequence of the limiting effect of the time it takes to handle food (Stephens and Krebs 1986, 15). In addition, as an animal becomes satiated, further food intake brings increasingly less benefit no matter how much food the environment holds (as Winterhalder, Lu, and Tucker (1999, 304) also argue). This is why hungry and thirsty pigeons in the lab switch frequently between eating and drinking rather than, say, feeding to satiation before they start drinking (McFarland and Lloyd 1973); a unit reduction in thirst or hunger increases fitness more when the animal is further from its optimal internal state.

For humans, there is evidence of a diminishing marginal utility response of life expectancy to economic variables. This pattern is found across about 140 nations for the measure of national income per person (Wilkinson and Pickett 2010, Chapter 1; but see the main text discussion of Haushofer's 2013, per capita GDP measure) and within a single country, the US, for lifetime earnings (Cristia 2009). In the UK, life expectancy shows diminishing returns to various measures of deprivation, sometimes with a small concave upwards trend for those least deprived (Buck and Maguire 2015). Further, many studies show that subjective well-being, measured as life satisfaction or happiness, has a positive and diminishing marginal utility response to income, income change or wealth, for analyses both between countries, developed and developing (Frey and Stutzer 2002; Howell and Howell 2008), and within countries (Cummins 2000, a review of many studies; Graham and Pettinato 2001; Møller and Saris 2001, calculated from Tables I and II; Frey and Stutzer 2002). The causal relationship is from income to subjective well-being rather than in the opposite direction (Frey and Stutzer 2002; Gere and Schimmack 2017).

In a pioneering study of risk-sensitive foraging the feeding decisions of juncos are described by a sigmoid function. Experimental birds that would suffer a negative energy budget (*in extremis* conditions) if they fed at a predictable source are risk prone and show a concave upwards utility function, whereas those with a positive energy budget (i.e. a high environmental quality) are risk averse and have a diminishing returns utility function (Caraco, Martindale, and Whittam 1980). These results have now been replicated many times in a variety of animal taxa, including two anthropological cases (reviewed by Winterhalder, Lu, and Tucker 1999).

A sigmoid function has also been found significantly to explain the relationship between an individual's quality and their resulting utility, outperforming linear and concave models, for primate sexual success as a function of rank and for social rank (which predicts reproductive success) as a function of hunting yield in Aché hunters (Kuznar 2002). The proximate mechanisms responsible for these relationships is unknown and, although the sigmoid function is offered by Kuznar as an expression of differential risk sensitivity, the mechanisms discussed earlier in this appendix may alternatively, or additionally, be responsible. In other anthropological studies risk-sensitive decision-making fits the predicted sigmoid pattern (Kuznar and Frederick 2003).

A sigmoid function is also suggested by the nature of abiotic factors influencing fitness (or well-being, for the rest of this paragraph), such as temperature, humidity and a great many factors for human populations. For such features (pollutants and suchlike aside), and for a particular species, there is an optimum value that maximizes an individual's fitness, with fitness declining above and below this optimal value: an inverted-U shape. Now, unless the transition through the optimal value is to make a sharp discontinuity, which is biologically implausible, it follows that the function approaches the optimal value, from both sides, in a diminishing returns fashion. Imagine now the environmental quality axis reconceptualized so that fitness reaches a maximum value at the extreme right, representing the optimal value of, say, temperature for the species. In this reconceptualization each point to the left of this optimal value represents a pair of temperatures – one below the optimum and another above it – that have an equal effect on fitness. The axis, therefore, represents adversity whether due to under- or over-shooting of the optimal environmental value and the redrawn function of temperature against adversity will be diminishing returns to the right. If the original inverted-U function is roughly normally distributed, and therefore bell-shaped, the adverse extremes, on the far left of the reconceptualized axis, will be concave upwards and the whole function will then be sigmoid. Son and Lewis (2005) provide a corroborating example relating temperature to survival for three life history stages of an insect. The functions are bell-shaped to the right (high temperature), where survival was extremely low or zero (*in extremis* conditions).

The data on severe food and water deprivation in rats (i.e. *in extremis* conditions, in contrast to natural feeding and drinking schedules (Siegel and Stuckey 1947)) show, as in the left segment of the sigmoid curve, a concave upwards relationship between environmental quality (the inverse of deprivation time) and fitness (the inverse of food or water intake after deprivation, a measure of distance from a homeostatic optimal state) (calculated from Clark 1958; Stellar and Hill 1952, for food and water, respectively). Andras and Lazarus (2005) assumed that the two curves might be convex upwards (diminishing returns) for the whole range of environmental quality but these data show this to be implausible.

Finally, I argue that the two sigmoid curves are unlikely to be parallel (in which case the benefit of cooperation would be a constant for all values of the environment) but are likely to converge at both extremes. For an individual in an extremely high-quality environment it seems likely that additional resources gained through cooperation would add little or nothing to fitness or well-being, either through sharing or by reciprocal altruistic exchanges. However, this may be too simplistic for the human case and I will consider it further in the text.

In the poorest environments, approaching *in extremis* conditions, there are several contexts in which convergence is likely. First, if cooperation consists of the acquisition and sharing of resources, at some point there are simply too few resources for cooperation – by physical help, skill and knowledge sharing, social influence or other means – to increase the resource sufficiently to compensate for the fact that it must be shared. Second, where cooperation consists of a series of altruistic exchanges, the strength of short-term need is sufficiently strong that failing to reciprocate becomes the favoured response. Third, in a life with many pressing needs the *opportunity* to cooperate may be compromised by time constraints (Siobhán O'Sullivan, personal communication, 8 January 2017).

References

Alexander, R. D. 1987. *The Biology of Moral Systems*. New York: Aldine de Gruyter.

Andras, P., J. Lazarus, and G. Roberts. 2007. "Environmental Adversity and Uncertainty Favour Cooperation." *BMC Evolutionary Biology* 7: 240. doi:10.1186/1471-2148-7-240.

Andras, P., and J. Lazarus. 2005. "Cooperation, Risk and the Evolution of Teamwork." In *Teamwork: Multi-Disciplinary Perspectives*, edited by N. Gold, 56–77, Basingstoke: Palgrave, Macmillan.

Ashworth, T. 1980. *Trench Warfare, 1914–1918: The Live and Let Live System*. New York: Holmes & Meier.

Axelrod, R. 1984. *The Evolution of Cooperation*. New York: Basic Books.

Axelrod, R., and W. D. Hamilton. 1981. "The Evolution of Cooperation." *Science* 211: 1390–1396. doi:10.1126/science.7466396.

Barclay, P. 2004. "Trustworthiness and Competitive Altruism can also Solve the "Tragedy of the Commons." *Evolution and Human Behavior* 25 (4): 209–220. doi:10.1016/j.evolhumbehav.2004.04.002.

Barkow, J. H., L. Cosmides, and J. Tooby, eds. 1992. *The Adapted Mind: Evolutionary Psychology and the Generation of Culture*. New York: Oxford University Press.

Barth, F. 1974. "On Responsibility and Humanity: Calling a Colleague to Account (With Reply by Turnbull)." *Current Anthropology* 15 (1): 99–103. doi:10.1086/201443.

Bateson, M., D. Nettle, and G. Roberts. 2006. "Cues of Being Watched Enhance Cooperation in a Real-World Setting." *Biology Letters* 2 (3): 412–414. doi:10.1098/rsbl.2006.05.09.

Bateson, P., and M. Mameli. 2007. "The Innate and the Acquired: Useful Clusters or a Residual Distinction from Folk Biology?." *Developmental Psychobiology* 49: 818–831. doi:10.1002/(ISSN)1098-2302.

Beidelman, T. O. 1973. "Review of 'The Mountain People' by Colin M Turnbull." *Africa* 43: 170–171. doi:10.2307/1159341.

Binmore, K. 2005. *Natural Justice*. New York: Oxford University Press.

Binmore, K. 2007a. *Game Theory: A Very Short Introduction*. Oxford: Oxford University Press.

Binmore, K. 2007b. *Playing for Real: A Text on Game Theory*. New York: Oxford University Press.

Bowles, S., and H. Gintis. 2011. *A Cooperative Species: Human Reciprocity and Its Evolution*. Princeton: Princeton University Press.

Boyd, R., and P. J. Richerson. 1985. *Culture and the Evolutionary Process*. Chicago: University of Chicago Press.

Buck, D., and D. Maguire. 2015. *Inequalities in Life Expectancy: Changes over Time and Implications for Policy*. London: King's Fund.

Burch Jr., E. S. 2006. *Social Life in Northwest Alaska: The Structure of Iñupiaq Eskimo Nations*. Fairbanks: University of Alaska Press.

Byars, S. G., D. Ewbank, D. R. Govindaraju, and S. C. Stearns. 2010. "Natural Selection in a Contemporary Human Population." *Proceedings of the National Academy of Sciences* 107 (suppl 1): 1787–1792. doi:10.1073/pnas.0906199106.

Callaway, R. R. M., R. W. Brooker, P. Choler, Z. Kikvidze, C. J. Lortiek, R. Michalet, L. Paolini, et al. 2002. "Positive Interactions among Alpine Plants Increase with Stress". *Nature* 417: 844–847. 10.1038/nature00812.

Camerer, C. F. 2003. *Behavioral Game Theory*. Princeton: Princeton University Press.

Caraco, T., S. Martindale, and T. S. Whittam. 1980. "An Empirical Demonstration of Risk-Sensitive Foraging Preferences." *Animal Behaviour* 28: 820–830. doi:10.1016/S0003-3472(80)80142-4.

Casiro, J. 2006. "Argentine Rescuers: A Study on the "Banality of Good." *Journal of Genocide Research* 8 (4): 437–454. doi:10.1080/14623520601056281.

Chudek, M., and J. Henrich. 2011. "Culture-Gene Coevolution, Norm-Psychology and the Emergence of Human Prosociality." *Trends in Cognitive Sciences* 15: 218–226. doi:10.1016/j.tics.2011.03.003.

Clark, F. C. 1958. "The Effect of Deprivation and Frequency of Reinforcement on Variable-Interval Responding." *Journal of the Experimental Analysis of Behavior* 1 (3): 221–228. doi:10.1901/jeab.1958.1-221.

Colman, A. M. 1999. *Game Theory and Its Applications in the Social and Biological Sciences.* 2nd ed. London: Routledge.

Côté, S., J. House, and R. Willer. 2015. "High Economic Inequality Leads Higher-Income Individuals to Be Less Generous." *Proceedings of the National Academy of Sciences* 112 (52): 15838–15843. doi:10.1073/pnas.1511536112.

Craik, K. H. 2009. *Reputation: A Network Interpretation.* Oxford: Oxford University Press.

Cristia, J. P. 2009. "Rising Mortality and Life Expectancy Differentials by Lifetime Earnings in the United States." *Journal of Health Economics* 28 (5): 984–995. doi:10.1016/j.jhealeco.2009.06.003.

Cummins, R. A. 2000. "Personal Income and Subjective Well-Being: A Review." *Journal of Happiness Studies* 1 (2): 133–158. doi:10.1023/A:1010079728426.

Da Costa, M. K. B., C. D. de Melo, and P. F. M. Lopes. 2014. "Fisheries Productivity and its Effects on the Consumption of Animal Protein and Food Sharing of Fishers' and Non-Fishers' Families." *Ecology of Food and Nutrition* 53 (4): 453–470. doi:10.1080/03670244.2013.854781.

Davis, J. A. 1959. "A Formal Interpretation of the Theory of Relative Deprivation." *Sociometry* 22 (4): 280–296. doi:10.2307/2786046.

De Bono, M., D. M. Tobin, M. W. Davis, L. Avery, and C. I. Bargmann. 2002. "Social Feeding in *Caenorhabditis Elegans* is Induced by Neurons that Detect Aversive Stimuli." *Nature* 419: 899–903. doi:10.1038/nature01169.

Drenkard, E., and F. M. Ausubel. 2002. "*Psuedomonas* Biofilm Formation and Antibiotic Resistance are Linked to Phenotypic Variation." *Nature* 416: 740–743. doi:10.1038/416740a.

Dunbar, R. I. M. 2004. "Gossip in Evolutionary Perspective." *Review of General Psychology* 8 (2): 100–110. doi:10.1037/1089-2680.8.2.100.

Ellis, B. J., A. J. Figueredo, B. H. Brumbach, and G. L. Schlomer. 2009. "Fundamental Dimensions of Environmental Risk: The Impact of Harsh versus Unpredictable Environments on the Evolution and Development of Life History Strategies." *Human Nature* 20 (2): 204–268. doi:10.1007/s12110-009-9063-7.

Erev, I., G. Bornstein, and R. Galili. 1993. "Constructive Intergroup Competition as a Solution to the Free Rider Problem: A Field Experiment." *Journal of Experimental Social Psychology* 29 (6): 463–478. doi:10.1006/jesp.1993.1021.

Farr, J. A. 1975. "The Role of Predation in the Evolution of Social Behavior of Natural Populations of the Guppy, *Poecilia Reticulata (Pisces: Poeciliidea)*." *Evolution* 29: 151–158. doi:10.1111/j.1558-5646.1975.tb00822.x.

Fehr, E., and S. Gachter. 2002. "Altruistic Punishment in Humans." *Nature* 415 (6868): 137–140. doi:10.1038/415137a.

Frankenhuis, W. E., K. Panchanathan, and D. Nettle. 2016. "Cognition in Harsh and Unpredictable Environments." *Current Opinion in Psychology* 7: 76–80. doi:10.1016/j.copsyc.2015.08.011.

Frey, B. S., and A. Stutzer. 2002. "What Can Economists Learn from Happiness Research?." *Journal of Economic Literature* 40 (2): 402–435. doi:10.1257/jel.40.2.402.

Fritz, C. E., and H. B. Williams. 1957. "The Human Being in Disasters: A Research Perspective." *The Annals of the American Academy of Political and Social Science* 309 (1): 42–51. doi:10.1177/000271625730900107.

Gere, J., and U. Schimmack. 2017. "Benefits of Income: Associations with Life Satisfaction among Earners and Homemakers." *Personality and Individual Differences* 119: 92–95. doi:10.1016/j.paid.2017.07.004.

Gintis, H. 2003. "Solving the Puzzle of Prosociality." *Rationality and Society* 15 (2): 155–187. doi:10.1177/1043463103015002001.

Gintis, H., S. Bowles, R. Boyd, and E. Fehr. 2003. "Explaining Altruistic Behaviour in Humans." *Evolution and Human Behavior* 24 (3): 153–172. doi:10.1016/S1090-5138(02)00157-5.

Gintis, H., S. Bowles, R. Boyd, and E. Fehr, eds. 2005. *Moral Sentiments and Material Interests: The Foundations of Cooperation in Economic Life.* Cambridge, Massachusetts: MIT Press.

Goss-Custard, J. D., A. D. West, M. G. Yates, R. W. G. Caldow, R. A. Stillman, L. Bardsley, and J. Castilla. 2006. "Intake Rates and the Functional Response in Shorebirds (*Charadriiformes*) Eating Macro-Invertebrates." *Biological Reviews* 81: 501–529. doi:10.1017/S1464793106007093.

Graham, C., and S. Pettinato. 2001. "Happiness, Markets, and Democracy: Latin America in Comparative Perspective." *Journal of Happiness Studies* 2 (3): 237–268. doi:10.1023/A:1011860027447.

Greenberg, E. P. 2003. "Tiny Teamwork." *Nature* 424: 134. doi:10.1038/424134a.

Guala, F. 2012. "Reciprocity: Weak or Strong? What Punishment Experiments Do (And Do Not) Demonstrate." *Behavioral and Brain Sciences* 35: 1–59. doi:10.1017/S0140525X11000069.

Gurven, M. 2004. "To Give and to Give Not: The Behavioral Ecology of Human Food Transfers." *Behavioral and Brain Sciences* 27: 543–583. doi:10.1017/S0140525X04000123.

Haley, K. J., and D. M. T. Fessler. 2005. "Nobody's Watching? Subtle Cues Affect Generosity in an Anonymous Economic Game." *Evolution and Human Behavior* 26: 245–256. doi:10.1016/j.evolhumbehav.2005.01.002.

Hammerstein, P., ed. 2003. *Genetic and Cultural Evolution of Cooperation*. Cambridge, Massachusetts: MIT Press in cooperation with Dahlem University Press.

Haselton, M. G., and D. Nettle. 2006. "The Paranoid Optimist: An Integrative Evolutionary Model of Cognitive Biases." *Personality and Social Psychology Review* 10 (1): 47–66. doi:10.1207/s15327957pspr1001_3.

Haushofer, J. 2013. "The Psychology of Poverty: Evidence from 43 Countries." Retrieved on 18 September 2017 from http://www.princeton.edu/~joha/publications/Haushofer_2013.pdf.

Heine, B. 1985. "The Mountain People: Some Notes on the Ik of North-Eastern Uganda." *Africa* 55 (1): 3–16. doi:10.2307/1159836.

Henrich, J., R. Boyd, S. Bowles, C. Camerer, E. Fehr, and H. Gintis, eds. 2004. *Foundations of Human Sociality: Economic Experiments and Ethnographic Evidence from Fifteen Small-Scale Societies*. Oxford: Oxford University Press.

Hill, R. A., and P. C. Lee. 1998. "Predation Risk as an Influence on Group Size in Cercopithecoid Primates: Implications for Social Structure." *Journal of Zoology* 245: 447–456. doi:10.1111/j.1469-7998.1998.tb00119.x.

Howell, R. T., and C. J. Howell. 2008. "The Relation of Economic Status to Subjective Well-Being in Developing Countries: A Meta-Analysis." *Psychological Bulletin* 134 (4): 536–560. doi:10.1037/0033-2909.134.4.536.

Hugh-Jones, D., and J. Ooi. 2017. *Where Do Fairness Preferences Come From? Norm Transmission in a Teen Friendship Network*. University of East Anglia. 2 October 2017. Downloaded from https://sites.google.com/site/davidhughjones.

Kaplan, H., K. Hill, and A. M. Hurtado. 1990. "Risk, Foraging and Food Sharing among the Ache." In *Risk and Uncertainty in Tribal and Peasant Economies*, edited by E. Cashdan, 107–143. San Francisco: Westview Press.

Kelly, R. L. 2013. *The Lifeways of Hunter-Gatherers: The Foraging Spectrum*. 2nd ed. Cambridge: Cambridge University Press.

Knight, J. A. 1976. "On the Ik and Anthropology - Further Note." *Current Anthropology* 17 (4): 777. doi:10.1086/201839.

Korndörfer, M., B. Egloff, and S. C. Schmukle. 2015. "A Large Scale Test of the Effect of Social Class on Prosocial Behavior." *PloS ONE* 10 (7): e0133193. doi:10.1371/journal.pone.0133193.

Krause, J., and G. D. Ruxton. 2002. *Living in Groups*. Oxford: Oxford University Press.

Krupka, E. L., and R. A. Weber. 2013. "Identifying Social Norms Using Coordination Games: Why Does Dictator Game Sharing Vary?." *Journal of the European Economic Association* 11 (3): 495–524. doi:10.1111/jeea.12006.

Kurzban, R. 2001. "The Social Psychophysics of Cooperation: Nonverbal Communication in a Public Goods Game." *Journal of Nonverbal Behavior* 25 (4): 241–259. doi:10.1023/A:1012563421824.

Kuznar, L. A. 2002. "Evolutionary Applications of Risk Sensitivity Models to Socially Stratified Species: Comparison of Sigmoid, Concave, and Linear Functions." *Evolution and Human Behavior* 23 (4): 265–280. doi:10.1016/S1090-5138(01)00105-2.

Kuznar, L. A., and W. G. Frederick. 2003. "Environmental Constraints and Sigmoid Utility: Implications for Value, Risk Sensitivity, and Social Status." *Ecological Economics* 46 (2): 293–306. doi:10.1016/S0921-8009(03)00167-8.

Laland, K. N., J. Odling-Smee, and S. Myles. 2010. "How Culture Shaped the Human Genome: Bringing Genetics and the Human Sciences Together." *Nature Reviews. Genetics* 11 (2): 137–149. doi:10.1038/nrg2734.

Laughlin Jr., C. D. 1974. "Deprivation and Reciprocity." *Man (N.S.)* 9 (3): 380–396. doi:10.2307/2800691.

Laughlin Jr., C. D., and I. A. Brady. 1978. "Introduction: Diaphasis and Change in Human Populations." In *Extinction and Survival in Human Populations*, edited by C. D. Laughlin Jr. and I. A. Brady, 1–48. New York: Columbia University Press.

Laughlin, Jr., C. 1978. "Adaptation and Exchange in So: A Diachronic Study of Deprivation." In *Extinction and Survival in Human Populations*, edited by C. D. Laughlin Jr. and I. A. Brady, 76–94. New York: Columbia University Press.

Lazarus, J. 2003. "Let's Cooperate to Understand Cooperation." *Behavioral and Brain Sciences* 26 (2): 169–170. doi:10.1017/S0140525X03390053.

Lieberman, D., J. Tooby, and L. Cosmides. 2003. "Does Morality Have a Biological Basis? An Empirical Test of the Factors Governing Moral Sentiments Relating to Incest." *Proceedings of the Royal Society B* 270: 819–826. doi:10.1098/rspb.2002.2290.

Lim, D., and D. DeSteno. 2016. "Suffering and Compassion: The Links among Adverse Life Experiences, Empathy, Compassion, and Prosocial Behavior." *Emotion* 16 (2): 175–182. doi:10.1037/emo0000144.

Lim, D. 2017. "The Influence of Suffering, Social Class, and Social Power on Prosociality: An Empirical Review." In *Empathy: An Evidence-Based Interdisciplinary Perspective*, edited by M. Kondo, 81–92. London: Intech.

Low, B. S. 1990. "Human Responses to Environmental Extremeness and Uncertainty: A Cross-Cultural Perspective." In *Risk and Uncertainty in Tribal and Peasant Economies*, edited by E. Cashdan, 229–255. San Francisco: Westview Press.

Mameli, M., and P. Bateson. 2006. "Innateness and the Sciences." *Biology and Philosophy* 21: 155–188. doi:10.1007/s10539-005-5144-0.

Maynard Smith, J. 1982. *Evolution and the Theory of Games*. Cambridge: Cambridge University Press.

McFarland, D. J., and I. H. Lloyd. 1973. "Time-Shared Feeding and Drinking." *The Quarterly Journal of Experimental Psychology* 25 (1): 48–61. doi:10.1080/14640747308400322.

Milinski, M., D. Semmann, T. C. M. Bakker, and H.-J. Krambeck. 2001. "Cooperation through Indirect Reciprocity: Image Scoring or Standing Strategy?" *Proceedings of the Royal Society* 268: 2495–2501. doi:10.1098/rspb.2001.1809.

Møller, V., and W. E. Saris. 2001. "The Relationship between Subjective Well-Being and Domain Satisfactions in South Africa." *Social Indicators Research* 55 (1): 97–114. doi:10.1023/A:1010851412273.

Nettle, D. 2009. "Beyond Nature versus Culture: Cultural Variation as an Evolved Characteristic." *Journal of the Royal Anthropological Institute (N.S.)* 15: 223–240. doi:10.1111/jrai.2009.15.issue-2.

Nettle, D. 2010. "Why are There Social Gradients in Preventative Health Behavior? A Perspective from Behavioral Ecology." *PloS ONE* 5 (10): e13371. doi:10.1371/journal.pone.0013371.

Nettle, D. 2015. *Tyneside Neighbourhoods: Deprivation, Social Life and Social Behaviour in one British City*. Cambridge, UK: Open Book Publishers.

Nettle, D. 2017. "Does Hunger Contribute to Socioeconomic Gradients in Behavior?." *Frontiers in Psychology* 8: 358. doi:10.3389/fpsyg.2017.00358.

Nettle, D., A. Colléony, and M. Cockerill. 2011. "Variation in Cooperative Behaviour within a Single City." *PloS ONE* 6 (10): e26922. doi:10.1371/journal.pone.0026922.

Nettle, D., G. V. Pepper, R. Jobling, and K. B. Schroeder. 2014. "Being There: A Brief Visit to a Neighbourhood Induces the Social Attitudes of that Neighbourhood." *Peer Journal* 2: e236. doi:10.7717/peerj.236.

Nowak, M. A., and K. Sigmund. 1993. "A Strategy of Win-Stay, Lose-Shift that Outperforms Tit-For-Tat in the Prisoner's Dilemma Game." *Nature* 364: 56–58. doi:10.1038/364056a0.

Ostrom, E. 1990. *Governing the Commons: The Evolution of Institutions for Collective Action*. Cambridge: Cambridge University Press.

Pepper, G. V., and D. Nettle. 2017. "The Behavioural Constellation of Deprivation: Causes and Consequences." *Behavioral and Brain Sciences* 1–72. doi:10.1017/S0140525X1600234X.

Piff, P. K. 2014. "Wealth and the Inflated Self: Class, Entitlement, and Narcissism." *Personality and Social Psychology Bulletin* 40 (1): 34–43. doi:10.1177/0146167213501699.

Piff, P. K., M. W. Kraus, S. Côté, B. H. Cheng, and D. Keltner. 2010. "Having Less, Giving More: The Influence of Social Class on Prosocial Behavior." *Journal of Personality and Social Psychology* 99 (5): 771. doi:10.1037/a0020092.

Pinker, S. 2002. *The Blank Slate: The Modern Denial of Human Nature*. London: Allen Lane The Penguin Press.

Puurtinen, M., S. Heap, and T. Mappes. 2015. "The Joint Emergence of Group Competition and Within-Group Cooperation." *Evolution and Human Behavior* 36 (3): 211–217. doi:10.1016/j.evolhumbehav.2014.11.005.

Puurtinen, M., and T. Mappes. 2009. "Between-Group Competition and Human Cooperation." *Proceedings of the Royal Society of London B: Biological Sciences* 276 (1655): 355–360. doi:10.1098/rspb.2008.1060.

Richerson, P. J., R. Boyd, and J. Henrich. 2010. "Gene-Culture Coevolution in the Age of Genomics." *Proceedings of the National Academy of Sciences* 107 (Supplement 2): 8985–8992. doi:10.1073/pnas.0914631107.

Richerson, P. J., and R. Boyd. 2005. *Not by Genes Alone: How Culture Transformed Human Evolution*. Chicago: University of Chicago Press.

Ridley, M. 1997. *The Origins of Virtue*. London: Penguin.

Roberts, G. 1998. "Competitive Altruism: From Reciprocity to the Handicap Principle." *Proceedings of the Royal Society of London B* 265:427–431.

Roberts, G. 2005. "Cooperation through Interdependence." *Animal Behaviour* 70: 901–908. doi:10.1016/j.anbehav.2005.02.006.

Schroeder, K. B., G. V. Pepper, and D. Nettle. 2014. "Local Norms of Cheating and the Cultural Evolution of Crime and Punishment: A Study of Two Urban Neighborhoods." *Peer Journal* 2: e450. doi:10.7717/peerj.450.

Seghers, B. H. 1974. "Schooling Behaviour in the Guppy (*Poecilia reticulata*): An Evolutionary Response to Predation." *Evolution* 28 (3): 486–489.

Siegel, P. S., and H. L. Stuckey. 1947. "The Diurnal Course of Water and Food Intake in the Normal Mature Rat." *Journal of Comparative and Physiological Psychology* 40 (5): 365–370. doi:10.1037/h0062185.

Smaldino, P. E., J. C. Schank, and R. McElreath. 2013. "Increased Costs of Cooperation Help Cooperators in the Long Run." *American Naturalist* 181 (4): 451–463. doi:10.1086/669615.

Son, Y., and E. E. Lewis. 2005. "Modelling Temperature-Dependent Development and Survival of *Otiorhynchus sulcatus* (Coleoptera: Curculionidae)." *Agricultural and Forest Entomology* 7 (3): 201–209. doi:10.1111/j.1461-9555.2005.00260.x.

Spinks, A. C., J. U. M. Jarvis, and N. C. Bennett. 2000. "Comparative Patterns of Philopatry and Dispersal in Two Common Mole-Rat Populations: Implications for the Evolution of Mole-Rat Sociality." *Journal of Animal Ecology* 69: 224–234. doi:10.1046/j.1365-2656.2000.00388.x.

Standing, G. 2011. *The Precariat: The New Dangerous Class*. London: Bloomsbury.

Stein, A. A. 1976. "Conflict and Cohesion: A Review of the Literature." *Journal of Conflict Resolution* 20 (1): 143–172. doi:10.1177/002200277602000106.

Stellar, E., and J. H. Hill. 1952. "The Rat's Rate of Drinking as a Function of Water Deprivation." *Journal of Comparative and Physiological Psychology* 45 (1): 96–102. doi:10.1037/h0062150.

Stephens, D. W., and J. R. Krebs. 1986. *Foraging Theory*. Princeton, New Jersey: Princeton University Press.

Tec, N. 1986. *When Light Pierced the Darkness: Christian Rescue of Jews in Nazi-Occupied Poland*. New York: Oxford University Press.

Tomasello, M. 2009. *Why We Cooperate. Based on the 2008 Tanner Lectures on Human Values at Stanford*. Cambridge, Massachusetts: A Boston Review Book. The MIT Press.

Tooby, J., and L. Cosmides. 1990. "The Past Explains the Present: Emotional Adaptations and the Structure of Ancestral Environments." *Ethology and Sociobiology* 11 (4–5): 375–424. doi:10.1016/0162-3095(90)90017-Z.

Trivers, R. L. 1974. "Parent-Offspring Conflict." *American Zoologist* 14: 249–264. doi:10.1093/icb/14.1.249.

Turnbull, C. M. [1972] 1974. *The Mountain People*. London: Pan Books (Picador).

Turnbull, C. M. 1966. *Tradition and Change in African Tribal Life*. Cleveland: World.

Turnbull, C. M. 1967. "The Ik: Alias the Teuso." *Uganda Journal* 31 (1): 63–71.

Turnbull, C. M. 1975. "Reply." *Current Anthropology* 16 (3): 354–358.

Turnbull, C. M. 1976. "Turnbull Replies." *Rain* 16 (Oct): 4–6. doi:10.2307/3031968.

Turnbull, C. M. 1978. "Rethinking the Ik: A Functional Non-Social System." In *Extinction and Survival in Human Populations*, edited by C. D. Laughlin Jr and I. A. Brady, 49–75. New York: Columbia University Press.

Westermarck, E. A. 1921. *The History of Human Marriage*. 5th ed. London: Macmillan.

Wilkinson, R., and K. Pickett. 2010. *The Spirit Level: Why Equality is Better for Everyone*, 2009. London: Penguin.

Wilson, P. J., G. McCall, W. R. Geddes, A. K. Mark, J. E. Pfeiffer, J. B. Boskey, and C. M. Turnbull. 1975. "More Thoughts on the Ik and Anthropology [And Reply]." *Current Anthropology* 16 (3): 343–358. doi:10.1086/201566.

Winterhalder, B. 1986. "Diet Choice, Risk, and Food Sharing in a Stochastic Environment." *Journal of Anthropological Archaeology* 5 (4): 369–392. doi:10.1016/0278-4165(86)90017-6.

Winterhalder, B., F. Lu, and B. Tucker. 1999. "Risk-Sensitive Adaptive Tactics: Models and Evidence from Subsistence Studies in Biology and Anthropology." *Journal of Archaeological Research* 7 (4): 301–348. doi:10.1007/BF02446047.

REPLY

Cooperation in adversity: a political theorist's response

John Baker

This is a reply to:

Lazarus, John. 2017. "Co-operation in adversity: an evolutionary approach." *Global Discourse* 7 (4): 571–598. https://doi.org/10.1080/23269995.2017.1402426

I found John Lazarus's 'Cooperation in Adversity' (2017) a very interesting read and one that throws up many interesting questions. My response is very much in the spirit of a cross-disciplinary conversation, as the reactions of a political theorist to a natural scientist. I am therefore entirely open to the possibility that the issues I raise reflect a limited understanding.

The central work of Lazarus's paper is to propose a general account of the relationship between adversity, the benefits of cooperation and the propensity to cooperate in the organic world generally, and among human beings in particular. Lazarus proposes that for many species, including humans, the fitness or well-being (see below) of both cooperative and non-cooperative individuals within a given population varies with environmental quality in a sigmoid shape, with fitness or well-being generally rising as the quality of the environment improves, but unevenly. The gap between these two functions defines the net benefit of cooperation compared with non-cooperation. Lazarus argues that the relationship between net benefit and environmental quality has the shape of an inverted-U, that is, it is small under situations of both extreme adversity and high levels of environmental quality, but rises between them. In particular, he argues that we should expect the highest net benefit of cooperation to occur under conditions of relative adversity and that this will be reflected in a higher propensity to cooperate than in either extremely adverse or relatively favourable environments. In this response, I reflect on some of the ways that political theory might complicate this picture.

The proposal made in the paper is summarized in its Figure 2. On that graph, the y-axis represents the benefits of cooperation and non-cooperation, and the net benefit of one over the other. Lazarus notes that in evolutionary biology, benefit is conceptualized as Darwinian fitness (which is, in essence, successful reproduction), but that for application to human social interactions it is more appropriate to formulate the proposal in terms of well-being. Within political theory, however, one of the central premises of contemporary discussions is that people have many different conceptions of well-being. For each potential cooperator, then, the shape of the curves representing well-being that results from some possible form of cooperation or from not cooperating may be significantly different because of their different conceptions of well-being. To take an example from academia, some people seem to relish working as solitary scholars, while others get more satisfaction from working collaboratively with others; some value their teaching, while others value their research. Thus, within a given environment, for example, academics working in the same department, some people may have a strong incentive to cooperate in research, while others have little or no such incentive. I don't think that this poses any problem in principle for Lazarus's central claims, but it does seem to make them more difficult to test empirically.

A similar issue arises for the *x*-axis, representing the quality of the environment. In the non-human cases Lazarus considers, the quality of the environment is (for most purposes) the same for all individuals of the same species. But in the human cases he considers, the quality of the environment can only be defined relative to the particular aims of each individual. Thus, what counts as an adverse environment for the lone scholar who prioritizes research will be different from what counts as adverse for the collaborator who values teaching. People's aims are, of course, shaped by the environment itself. An issue of particular interest to political theorists is the idea of 'adaptive preferences', that is, preferences influenced by what people consider feasible within a given social environment. As a result, members of groups who are badly off in unequal societies typically adapt their preferences to their situation by aiming for outcomes that members of well-off groups may consider undesirable, like secure employment on an assembly line. Again, I don't think that this creates problems in principle for Lazarus's proposal, but it does seem to make testing it more challenging, since comparing the attitudes and behaviour of 'objectively' well-off people with those of objectively badly-off people may not capture the degree to which the individuals in question are located in more or less adverse environments vis-à-vis their actual aims. Perhaps this goes some way towards explaining the apparent anomaly Lazarus discusses about the greater willingness of well-off people to cooperate, because they may inhabit a more 'adverse' environment relative to their aspirations.

What is the environment, anyway? Does it include the cultural and institutional environment or not? It seems to me that the paper relates to this question at two levels. At one level, the analysis provides an explanation for why different human communities have evolved different norms and institutional arrangements of cooperation. The suggestion is that because these norms and institutional arrangements affect the probability of cooperation in circumstances that generate incentives to defect, they are more likely to be strongly cooperative in communities facing more (but not severely) adverse environments, for example, in subordinate social groups. At a different level, norms and institutions are taken to be part of people's environments, and the analysis suggests that individuals are more likely to cooperate in the more adverse of these environments. So, within a given set of norms and institutions, we should expect relatively badly-off (but not severely deprived) individuals to be more disposed to cooperate than relatively well-off individuals.

What political theory inserts into this story is that, to put it in its mildest form, the norms and institutions of any *society* are strongly influenced by the interests of the privileged groups in that society. So although the considerations Lazarus discusses may generate a tendency for subordinate groups to evolve more cooperative norms, practices and behaviour than privileged groups, that tendency may be overridden by living in an environment that has been designed to suit the interests of the privileged. For example, the privileged may make it costly – even potentially lethal – for workers to cooperate through trade unions, whereas they may make it very easy for capitalists to cooperate by forming cartels. Less overtly, it is in the interests of dominant groups to encourage norms of distrust and social division within subordinate groups. These dynamics could provide the basis for quite a different explanation for Lazarus's anomaly, though, again, one that does not undermine the general principles of his approach.

It is interesting in this respect that two of the sources cited in the paper (Haushofer 2013, 8; Wilkinson and Pickett 2009, 52–58) show that trust is higher in more equal societies. It seems implausible, and is contrary to Wilkinson and Pickett's other evidence, to suggest that equality creates a more adverse environment for human well-being. What seems more likely is that equality affects both the preferences of individuals and the norms and institutions of societies in ways that make cooperation more beneficial. In any case, these findings seem to warn against applying Lazarus's account in too simple a manner.

I could not conclude this response without commenting on the suggestion that human beings may possess 'a universal sense of fairness'. The studies on cooperation that the paper reviews suggest that human beings may be predisposed towards fairness, though Lazarus is at pains to point out that this is not necessarily part of our genetic as distinct from our cultural endowment. The fact that, in a wide variety of settings, individuals seem disposed to act 'fairly' rather than in a purely self-interested way seems to provide evidence for this hypothesis. What political theory brings to this discussion is an acute understanding that there are many conceptions of fairness, both between and within societies. It may be a general feature of all of these conceptions that, under certain conditions (particularly those lacking any strong indications that anyone *deserves* anything), individuals are disposed to share rather than hoard resources. But if we don't want to lose the run of ourselves, we should be very clear that this is a long way from believing that there is any one thing called fairness that is universally endorsed.

Acknowledgements

I am grateful to John Lazarus for clarifying a number of issues as I developed this response.

Disclosure statement

No potential conflict of interest was reported by the author.

References

Haushofer, J. 2013. "The Psychology of Poverty: Evidence from 43 Countries." http://www.princeton.edu/~joha/publications/Haushofer_2013.pdf.
Lazarus, J. 2017. "Cooperation in Adversity: An Evolutionary Approach." *Global Discourse* 7 (4): 571–598. doi: 10.1080/23269995.2017.1402426
Wilkinson, R., and K. Pickett. 2009. *The Spirit Level: Why More Equal Societies Almost Always Do Better*. London: Allen Lane.

Index

Note: Page numbers in *italics* refer to figures

absolute precariousness 54, 75–9
Abu-Lughod, L. 106
Access Agreement 95
ACE *see* Adult Continuing Education (ACE)
adaptive behaviour 127
adaptive preferences 154
Adult Continuing Education (ACE) 82, 87–9
adult education: as community engagement 87–9; and lifelong learning 82–3; quality 85
adversity, cooperation in 125–6; behavioural expression of 132; defining 126; evolutionary analysis of behaviour 127–9; evolutionary origin 129–34; human case 135–8; influence of adversity 138–43; inverted-U relationship 142–3; marginal net benefit of 140; non-human cases 134; political theorist's response 153–5; prosociality 144; sigmoid function 144–6
affective labour 12; workers 13
affective collaboration: arrangement 115, 116n11; District Committee of Súgandafjörður 109–11; place of affect 122; possibilities 123; protean possibilities 119–23; Red Cross research 111–14; research 103–6; between two/more partners 106–8; in Westfjords, Iceland 109
affect theory 106, 122
The Affect Theory Reader (Seigworth and Gregg) 106
Agier, M. 57
AHBs *see* approved housing bodies (AHBs)
Alexander, R. D. 131
altruism 133
American Exceptionalism 16
Andras, P. 134, 138, 146
anthropology 6, 9, 10, 55
approved housing bodies (AHBs) 33, 34, 37, 39–40
Arrears Support Unit 35
Ashington, coal mining 8–10

Ashton, coal mining 6–8
Australia: housing precarity in 44–5

Baker, J. 153
Baredi, B. 13
Barrett, D. 2, 75
Beaven, R. 82
Beer, A. 53
Behaviour and Attitudes Traveller Community National Survey 77
Beynon, H. 24
Binmore, K. 132
biotic adversity 126
Boliver, V. 100
borrowings, sustainable 34
'Bowkey Isaac' 9
Boyer, E. L. 81, 87
Bulmer, M. I. A. 5, 18, 19
Burch Jr., E. S. 137
Burrell, G. 1, 5, 23

Campbell, E. 2, 103, 119
CAP *see* Community Access Programme (CAP)
capitalism 11, 12, 20, 24
casualisation 28, 38
CDT *see* cumulative disadvantage theory (CDT)
Celtic Tiger 85
Central Bank of Ireland 34–6
Central Hotel 9
CESCA *see* Cork Equal and Sustainable Communities Alliance (CESCA)
The Chicago Guide to Collaborative Ethnography 103
China, coal production in 17
Choy, T. K. 103
Church, R. A. 23
Clough Marinaro, I. 58, 62
clubland 9
Coal is Our Life (Dennis, Henriques and Slaughter) 6, 9

INDEX

coal mining 1, 5; Ashington 8–10; Ashton 6–8; Chinese coal production 17; Indian coal-mining industry 15, *16*; isolated mass 10–15; pit village globally 15–16; precariousness at work and *12*; Tianfu township 16–18; unsettled settlements 18–20; in USA 16
cognitive capitalism 12, 14, 20
collaboration, affective: District Committee of Súgandafjörður 109–11; place of affect 122; possibilities 123; protean possibilities 119–23; Red Cross research 111–14; research 103–6; between two/more partners 106–8; in Westfjords, Iceland 109
collaborative anthropology 105
collaborative culture 97
collaborative ethnography 105
collaborative research 103–6
collectivism 5, 10, 13
Colman, A. M. 129, 130
colonialism 105; legacy of 115n4
Commission on the Private Rented Residential Sector (2000) 36
communities, marginalised 83–6
Community Access Programme (CAP) 93–4
community-based education 93
community engagement: adult education as 87–9; examples 2
cooperation, in adversity 125–6; behavioural expression of 132; defining 126; evolutionary analysis of behaviour 127–9; evolutionary origin 129–34; human case 135–8; influence of adversity 138–43; inverted-U relationship 142–3; marginal net benefit of 140; non-human cases 134; political theorist's response 153–5; prosociality 144; sigmoid function 144–6
Cork Equal and Sustainable Communities Alliance (CESCA) 79n2
cost-benefit analyses 139
cultural anthropology 103
cultural transmission 129
cumulative disadvantage theory (CDT) 97–8

Darwinian fitness 125–6, 153
denizens 88, 89n1
Dennis, N. 6, 7, 8, 9
Department for Education (DfE) 99
'designer workers' 13
De Swaan, A. 72
DfE *see* Department for Education (DfE)
dilution 28
District Committee of Súgandafjörður 102–3, 106, 108–11, 114
Dockery, A. M. 84
Dupuis, A. 29

economic activity 14, 17
economic rationality 129
education: attainment of 82; community-based 93; further education (FE) institutions 99; higher education (HE) 83–7; *see also* adult education; university, and education inequality
education inequality, university and: addressing 86–7; adult education as community engagement 87–9; lifelong learning 82–3; marginalised communities from 83–6; public good function 81–2
Edwards, P. 1, 23
employment: low- to middle-income sector 36–7; precarity of 53
Enders, J. 87
environmental quality: and fitness 145–6; inflection point of *140*, 141; inverted-U relationship 142–3; and well-being 139–40, 145–6
ESS *see* evolutionarily stable strategy (ESS)
ethnography: data 104–5; research, traditional 105
Evans-Pritchard, E. 6
evolutionarily stable strategy (ESS) 129, 131, 132
evolutionary analysis, of behaviour 127–9
evolutionary biologists 127, 128, 129
exclusionary modality 57
Expert Group on Future Funding for Higher Education (2015) 84

Families And Higher Education (FAHED) 94
farming, organic 104
Fellows, T. 2, 97
Finnerty, J. 1–2, 27, 38
fitness: Darwinian 125–6, 153; environmental quality and 145–6; as payoff metric 129; proxies for 128; sigmoid curves *140*
Fitzgerald, H. E. F. 81, 87
Fluehr-Lobban, C. 103
'folk theorem' 131
Francis, B. 84, 85
Frank, A. 106
free school meals (FSMs) 99
FSMs *see* free school meals (FSMs)
further education (FE) institutions 99

game theory approach, to understanding cooperation 130
GCSEs *see* General Certificates of Secondary Education (GCSEs)
gene-culture coevolution theory 125–6, 129, 133
General Certificates of Secondary Education (GCSEs) 99
Giddens, A. 29
Gintis, H. 132, 143
globalization 25
Gluckman, M. 19
Goffman, E. 13
Graham, M. 79n2
Granovetter, M. 83
Greenop, K. 2, 43

INDEX

Gregg, M. 106, 122
group stigmatisation 71, 72
Gypsy and Traveller sites 50–1, 52; encroachment 65–6; internal conflict 61; liminality and spatial confinement 51, 55–9; mainstreaming 62–3, 66; neglect 60–6; precarious lives 52–5; public space protection 64–5; in United Kingdom 70–3

Hacker, J. 28
Halldórsson, V. J. 2, 102, 119–23
Harrison, T. 9
Harwood, V. 85
Haselton, M. G. 143
Haushofer, J. 136, 141, 142
HEA *see* Higher Education Authority (HEA)
Heine, B. 138
Henriques, F. 6, 7, 9
higher education (HE) 83–7
Higher Education Authority (HEA) 84, 85
Higher Education Funding Council for England (HEFCE) 84
'the Hirst' 8, 9
homelessness 29, 34, 35, 44, 46, 47
Houghton, A.-M. 2, 93
Housing Act (Ireland): 1966 38; 1992 36; 1997 38; 1998 76, 77; 2014 38
Housing Assistance Payment (HAP) 33, 37–8
housing: associations 31–4, 37, 50, 51, 62, 66; culturally appropriate 77; policy 27–9, 33, 40, 43, 79
Housing First programs 46–7
Housing Policy Statement 32
housing precarity: in Australia 44–5; extent of 44; global and historical perspective 45–6; Housing First programs 46–7
Hyman, R. 23

IAG *see* information advice and guidance (IAG)
immaterial labour 12
India: coal-mining industry in 15, *16*
indirect reciprocity 131–3
in extremis conditions 136, 138–46
information advice and guidance (IAG) 94
intersubjective realm 106, 119, 121
investment: in adult education 82–3; directly owned state housing 44; in social housing 32, 39
Ireland, housing system in: AHBs/housing associations 34; HAP 37–8; leasing 37–8; low- to middle-income sector employment 36–7; owner-occupied housing 30–1, 34–5; policy levers and safety nets 35–6; precarity in 27, 28, 34–5; private renting 33; RAS 37–8; repossessions 36; 'snakes' in 28, 34, 47; social housing 31–3, 39; suppliers 30; tenure trends in *30*; and well-being 29–30
Irish Human Rights and Equality Commission (IHREC) 77

The Irish Times 76
Ísafjörður municipality (Iceland) 102, 106, 109–10, 114
isolated mass 1, 10–15, 18, 23–4

Johnson, M. 1, 54
Jones, A. 47
Jongbloed, B. 87
Joseph Rowntree Foundation (JRF) 51–4, 60, 63
Journal of Collaborative Anthropologies 103

Kelly, R. L. 137
Kenny, L. 2, 81, 93–100
Kerr, C. 10, 23, 24

labour 12–13; market regulation 28; movement 11
Lassiter, L. E. 103
The Latin American Studies Association (LASA) 103
Laughlin, C., Jr. 137
Lazarus, J. 2, 125, 134, 138, 146, 153–5
lease 37–8
lifelong learning 82–3, 88
liminal ghetto-like spaces: contested dwelling 55–9; controlling 60; deviance 53; 'meanwhile' use 63–4; neglect and 60–1; strengths of 51
Lin, N. 83
local authority tenancy 37–8, 39
Local Traveller Accommodation Action Committee (LTAAC) 78
Logan, E. 77
long-term mortgage arrears 27, 29, 34–5
Low, B. S. 136
low- to middle-income sector employment 36–7
LTAAC *see* Local Traveller Accommodation Action Committee (LTAAC)
Lutz, C. 106

Maestri, G. 58–9, 66
Mahlo, D. 82
marginalised communities 83–6
MARP *see* Mortgage Arrears Resolution Process (MARP)
Massumi, B. 106
McCarthy, T. 56, 86
McManners, R. 8, 9
mortgages, long-term arrears 27, 29, 34–5
Mortgage Arrears Resolution Process (MARP) 35
The Mountain People (Turnbull) 138
Mulcahy, A. 60, 61
Myers, F. R. 106

Nash equilibrium 129, 132
National Coal Board 5, 6
natural selection theory 127
negative reciprocity 137
'negotiated stopping' approaches 60, 64–5

INDEX

neoliberalism 1, 2, 28
Nettle, D. 141, 143
non-domiciled sector 29
Norris, M. 32
North Seaton Hotel 9
The Nuer (Evans-Pritchard) 6

O'Connell, C. 1–2, 27, 43
O'Dowd, S. 2, 75
O'Mahoney, J. 25
one-shot interactions 132
ontological security 29
O'Sullivan, S. 2, 81, 93–100
The Other Side of Middletown (TOSM) 121
Otro Saberes Initiative 103
O'Tuama, S. 2, 81, 93–100
Outram, Q. 23
owner-occupied housing 29–31, 34–5, 40

Parsell, C. 47
Participatory Research: Working and Communicating with Communities conference 102
'participatory turn' 115n1
Peach, C. 57
perceived precarity/adversity/fear 54
Perry, E. 84, 85
Piff, P. K. 136
pit villages: disadvantages 11; effect on 14; globally 15–16; twenty-first century 14; vanguard of labour movement 11
A Plan for Social Housing 34
Planning and Development (Housing) and Residential Tenancies Act 2016 37
Plater, Alan 6
policy: changes 29; levers 35–6; reformers 40
political theory 153–5
post-Fordism 24
Powell, R. S. 2, 56–8, 58, 59, 70
precarity: housing, in Australia 44–5; employment 53; in Irish housing system 27, 28, 34–5; perceived 54; relative 54, 64; supplier-generated 39–40; see also housing precarity
precarious labour 12
precariousness 1, 11; absolute 54, 75–9; conceptual model for 52–5; of equality 51; in Irish housing system 27, 28, 34–5; perceived precarity/adversity/fear 54; relative precarity/adversity 54; risk and 29; without work 14, *15*; at work and coal mining 12
private mine owners 6
private rented sector 33, 36–7, 38, 53
prosociality 144
proximate causation 127
public good function 81–2
Putnam, R. D. 83

quality, of environment 139, 153, 154

'rampant social insecurity' 28
RAS 37–8
RCUK-School University Partnership Initiative (RCUK-SUPI) project 95
realism 25
Red Cross research 103, 104, 111–14
'reflexive activation' 87
Re-Imagining Contested Communities 123
relative precarity 54, 64
Rent Pressure Zones 37
repossessions 31, 34–8, 40
reputational knowledge 131
Residential Tenancies Act of 2004 36
resource mobilization 98
Richardson, J. 2, 50, 71, 75–9, 76, 78
Roberts, G. 132
Rodrik, D. 25
Rosaldo, M. Z. 106

safety nets 35–6
Salerno, C. 87
Sandbrook, I. 88
Sedgwick, Eve 106
Seigworth, G. J. 106
SEP *see* socioeconomic position (SEP)
SES *see* Socio-Economic Status (SES)
Seyfert, R. 107, 122
Shame in the Cybernetic Fold (Sedgwick and Frank) 106
Shorter, E. 23
short-term capital appreciation 27
short-term income 38
Siegel, A. 10, 23, 24
sigmoid function 139–46, *140*
Skellig Centre for Research and Innovation 88
skill-based technological change 25
Slaughter, C. 6, 7, 9
small-scale mines 17
Smith, D. N. 23
social anthropology 103, 104, 106
social capital 58, 83, 94
social housing: direct and indirect government interventions 31–3, *32*, *33*; investment programme 32; market share of 30; offer 28, 37–8, 39; suppliers 27
Social Housing Strategy 2020 31
Social Mobility Commission (2017) 84
social scientists 128
social security provision 28
social theory 24–5
socioeconomic position (SEP) 141, 144
Socio-Economic Status (SES) 84, 88
The Soul at Work (Biffo) 13
spatial confinement 55–9
Standing, G. 1, 37, 53, 141
stigmatisation 60
strong reciprocity, and cooperation maintenance 133
Student Contribution Fund 85

160

INDEX

subjective well-being 126, 145
supplier-generated precarity 39–40

Technical and Further Education Act 99
tenure neutrality 38
Thorns, D. C. 29
three-level model 23
Tianfu township (China) 16–18
Tilly, C. 23
Tomkins, S. 106
TOSM *see* The Other Side of Middletown (TOSM)
'total social system' 7
township and village coal mines (TVCMs) 17
trade unionism 5
Travellers: accommodation crisis 75–9; *see also* Gypsy and Traveller sites
Traveller Education Services 58
Traveller Visibility Group (TVG) 78, 79n1
Trump, D. 16, 18
Turnbull, C. M. 138, 143
TVCMs *see* township and village coal mines (TVCMs)

ultimate causation 127
university, and education inequality: addressing 86–7; adult education as community engagement 87–9; context matters 93–4; disadvantage in adulthood 98–100; Lancaster 93–4; lifelong learning 82–3; marginalised communities from 83–6; public good function 81–2; purpose and nature of outreach 94–5
University College Cork (UCC) 88
UN Universal Declaration of Human Rights 46

Vesting Day 6
vulnerability, and Red Cross research 111–14

Wacquant, L. 56, 57, 61
Waite, L. 53
Wales, G. 8, 9
Waller, R. J. 23
well-being 128, 139; of cooperating individual 139; education and lifelong learning 82–3; Irish housing system and 29–30; subjective 126
Westfjords (Iceland), affective collaboration in 2, 102–15
White, G. M. 103
widening participation (WP) 94, 95
Wilson-Strydom, M. 86
World Values Survey 136